# FOUNDATIONS OF GROUP COUNSELING

GUIDANCE, COUNSELING,
AND STUDENT PERSONNEL
IN EDUCATION

WALTER F. JOHNSON, *Consulting Editor*

McGRAW-HILL SERIES IN EDUCATION

*The Late* Harold Benjamin    *Consulting Editor-in-Chief*

Arno A. Bellack    *Teachers College, Columbia University*
*Consulting Editor, Curriculum and Methods in Education*

*The Late* Harold Benjamin    *Emeritus Professor of Education*
*George Peabody College for Teachers*
*Consulting Editor, Foundations in Education*

Walter F. Johnson    *Michigan State University*
*Consulting Editor, Guidance, Counseling,
and Student Personnel in Education*

# FOUNDATIONS OF GROUP COUNSELING

C. GRATTON KEMP

*Professor of Education*
*The Ohio State University*

McGRAW-HILL BOOK COMPANY

*New York   St. Louis   San Francisco   Düsseldorf*
*London   Mexico   Panama   Sydney   Toronto*

This book was set in Helvetica by Brown Bros. Linotypers, Inc., and printed on permanent paper and bound by The Maple Press Company. The designer was J. E. O'Connor. The editors were Nat LaMar and Robert Weber. Paul B. Poss supervised the production.

FOUNDATIONS OF GROUP COUNSELING

Library of Congress Catalog Card Number: 72–98051
33945
1 2 3 4 5 6 7 8 9 0    M A M M    7 9 8 7 6 5 4 3 2 1 0

# EDITOR'S INTRODUCTION

From the earliest beginnings of the guidance and counseling movement the value of employing group approaches to help the individual achieve self-discovery, self-direction, and self-realization has been recognized and fostered. Counseling with groups, that is, *group counseling,* while recognized as one of the possible group approaches, has been a controversial issue on both philosophic and semantic grounds. Only relatively recently has it earned a place of acceptance and respectability in the jargon and practice of the profession. Fortunately research and experimentation have produced new data concerning learning processes and developmental needs, along with new insights on group procedures and group behavior which have reestablished the validity and desirability of group approaches to working with people. These approaches are very much in keeping with the changing nature of our society, where urbanization and increasing population density demand that people learn how to interact and interrelate more effectively.

The author of this book has spent a major part of his professional career working with people in group activities of one type or another. In all his endeavors he has been a student of humanity—of man in all the dimensions that make him what he is. He has read widely and deeply in the many disciplines which concern themselves with human behavior and the human condition—philosophy, psychology, sociology, anthropology, literature, religion, history, and the arts. A basic premise of this book is the need for an interdisciplinary approach to a complex process such as group counseling. Too few persons possess the ability to integrate behavioral concepts from such a wide range of disciplines. This book provides ample evidence that Dr. Kemp is one of these persons.

It has been my good fortune to have known and been associated with Dr. Kemp for many years. He has been a productive and effective author whose writings have been dedicated to the idea that the quality of interpersonal relationships is what gives real meaning to life. This book represents his best exposition of this credo for a better life.

*Walter F. Johnson*
*Michigan State University*

# PREFACE

The meaning of life is a function of the quality of our interpersonal relationships. Understanding and new directions result from open, honest, and courageous searching in small groups. This has always been true to some degree. Recently the need for, and usefulness of, this group relationship has come into sharp focus. Persons in all walks of life sense the need for such meaningful relationship, and many look to it as the means of gaining new understanding regarding the significance and purpose of life itself. Hence the interest and increase in the use of what is now known as *group counseling*.

The incentive to engage in intimate small-group relationships arises from the ambiguity, complexity, and uncertainty of modern living. The possibility of the understanding and enrichment of life through such relationships stems from the increasing breadth and depth of significant knowledge and experience. Such knowledge and experience grows apace as organizations from all levels of experience are turning to small groups as the "pearl of great price." The study of, and interest in, small groups as a dynamic means of behavioral change can be viewed as having moved in succession through developmental stages: from a recognition that any significant group experience involves the whole person to the perception that even the most educationally oriented group depends upon feeling and action for results, to the understanding that the nature of any group is not entirely discrete from that of every other.

This stage was followed by an emphasis on interaction as the key to understanding the dynamics of the group. The importance of involvement became increasingly recognized, and the relevance of resistance and conflict in genuine personality change was acknowledged and accepted. A third stage was the developmental understanding that responsibility and caring are integral and necessary to groups who engage in reality testing and who search for meaning in depth.

The present stage has three aspects: the recognition that there is a new kind of truth which comes from within and which may be true only for him who expresses it; a growing acceptance of the meaning of individual differences which at one level suggests that no two persons receive the same help from any group experience; and awareness that congruence in leaders and members is the touchstone in the process of becoming.

The heightening interest in the possibilities of group counseling is reflected in business, professional, national, and family life. Such possibilities can be fully utilized only to the degree that there is an interdisciplinary approach. Group counseling demands that increasing attention be given not only to definitions, skills, and methods but also to its foundation in human nature, to relevant basic principles from many disciplines, and to its potential for human development and sigificant meaning.

The focus of this book is on both dimensions, not only on methodology but also on meaning. There is an emphasis not only on methods, problems, needed skills, and evaluation processes but also on foundational principles drawn from several disciplines which give clarification and understanding to the horizontal dimensions of the process.

The following premises provide a consistent basis for understanding the content: (1) the possibilities of group counseling are based on the potentialities and limitations of man himself; (2) the realization of the possibilities depends upon insights from both science and art as expressed in such disciplines as psychology, sociology, philosophy, religion, literature, history, and art; (3) the concept of individual differences is basic to the provision of the optimal helping relationship; (4) ability to participate and benefit from the group experience is a developmental process; (5) group process enhances the potential for change in the perceptions and self-concepts of the members.

The book is planned for counselors, college students, and teachers who are involved in the constructive development of persons through the group experience. It is hoped that industrial groups, church groups, business groups, and recreational groups will find the discussion of the various aspects of group counseling enlightening and that they will gain ideas and insights which will improve their own understanding and suggest ways to increase their efficiency. Counselors, counselor educators, and counselors-to-be will find explanations of the inherent basicity of groups and the clarification of the functioning of groups and of their own roles as leaders. Ideas and suggestions for research are also presented.

Many persons here and abroad contributed indirectly and directly to the writing of this book. Students in elementary school, high school, and adult groups in church, hospital, business, and recreational settings have shared their ideas and insights. College students, through analysis of the group climate and process, have aided in the task of clarification. The moral support and encouragement of colleagues and friends have contributed more to my life and effort at this time than I could possibly express. I am also indebted to those who have contributed directly, especially to the flexible, judicious, and wise criticism of the editor, Dr. Walter F. Johnson, and to Agnes Lackie Kemp, through whose encouragement and assistance the book was begun and in memory of whom it was completed.

*C. Gratton Kemp*

# CONTENTS

# 1

# THE CURRENT
# SITUATION

*The rate of emerging concepts far exceeds our ability to assess them critically. So it is with group counseling: old issues remain unsettled, while new ones continually make their appearance. An early conclusion may be drawn that this is a disturbing and unsatisfactory condition. However, further reflection may reveal that this is indicative of health and development. Actually it may be best perceived as a natural result of the focus on interpersonal relationships of concepts from many disciplines. Useful as this process may appear, it is threatening to those who view certitude as a prerequisite for further development.*

*These would prefer that definitions be established and issues resolved as a means of providing stability and increasing concentra-*

tion on group counseling per se. Others are more comprehensive in their overview. While they may not welcome ambiguity, they perceive that a flexible developmental and open approach to the problems of group counseling are essential to our needed growth in understanding. Against the background of their own efforts they cultivate the attitude and disciplined inquiry which they hope will eventuate in more dependable directions and concepts.

Chapters 1 and 2 are directed to the latter group, with the aim of stimulating thought regarding live issues and causing the reader to use his productive imagination in his reflection upon his own beliefs and practices.

# 1

## UNRESOLVED ISSUES

### INTRODUCTION

There are many unresolved issues in group counseling. This is to be expected at this stage in its development and should be appreciated since it indicates a necessary tolerance for ambiguity. In fact certainty regarding any of the developments in group counseling could be disastrous. Recognition, analysis, experimentation, and research are necessary. Every attempt should be made to entertain and test a broad spectrum of ideas. If this is done, the probability of arriving at necessary understandings and directions will be much enhanced.

Thus it appears in order to recognize, elucidate, and discuss a number of these issues at the very beginning of this text. This is done not to provide solutions but to clarify some of the problems and ideas which will receive attention. Since group counseling involves the interpersonal relationships of groups of persons, the issues have their roots in those disciplines concerned with human relations. Many viewpoints originate in psychology, philosophy, sociology, education, and religion, to mention a few. No attempt will be made to identify the one or more disciplines involved in each issue. Also it would not be useful to attempt an arrangement in any order of importance, since to some degree all are interdependent. Therefore the selection discussed in this chapter will be arranged in a natural logical order of occurrence.

## BASIC ISSUES

### Categorization

The almost intolerable uncertainty in so many aspects of group counseling has made it exceedingly difficult to resist labeling and categorization. But to work out definitions early in the procedure leads to confusion and possible error. Because of ambiguity we find carefully worked out definitions for group counseling and group psychotherapy. This has an analogy in the period a few years ago when mental illnesses were carefully diagnosed and labeled and many hours spent in defense of these labels. It has been learned that a conceptual framework which could accommodate differences and similarities is more realistic.

Premature categorization hides the fact that sound theoretical support is lacking. In addition, current definitions which treat each form of group process as discrete are limited by a Procrustean bed approach. The distinctions are not as clear, functional, or accurate as the proponents of clear-cut definitions would like to think. For example, in the discussion of the objective content of group process much personal anxiety, exploration of interpersonal relationships indicative of emotional struggle, and evaluation creep in. In group counseling varying emphases both within each session and throughout the total life of the group are placed upon the discussion of topics with an intellectual focus. There is no clear line of separation.

## When Is a Group a Group?

Confusion results from the assumption that there is some mystique about group process. This is the conviction that by placing persons in a small group and proceeding in a certain manner a desirable result is a matter of course.

Frequently the same error is made concerning small groups as is made concerning open-mindedness. We still hear concerning a problem, "Let us take an open-minded approach here." It is just as ridiculous to say, "Let's use small groups to work this out." Not that open-mindedness and small groups are not desirable but rather that a person does not suddenly change. Each of us brings to any experience of interpersonal relationships his attitudes, prejudices, methods of thought and work.

To participate in the development of a group and to assist in the improvement of its functioning demand the attainment of difficult skills and considerable "becoming." A few people in a face-to-face situation may appear to the unsophisticated observer to be a group when actually they have only the outward appearance of one. Simulation is like a fine-looking car which lacks a motor.

The development of a group demands a high degree of interpersonal responsiveness based on a sense of caring and of responsibility. To be most useful to the members each must reach a realization, through his experiences in the group, that he is accepted regardless of what he produces. The presence of these two conditions in the group makes it possible for individual members to communicate genuinely in depth. To cultivate these conditions is difficult, since to varying degrees they are the antithesis of what members experience in the everyday world. May this be one of the reasons for the overwhelming interest in groups?

To believe that a group of people, whether or not they have known one another previously, can come together and immediately or in a short time have a productive group experience is only wishful thinking. Skills must be developed through practice, and feelings and attitudes necessary to meaningful communication become a reality through a process of osmosis. A student in Hawaii expressed the attitudinal progression in this manner in his anonymous self-report: "There is a first stage in which all is a bed of roses. Then a second stage in which you analyze, test, and do a lot of thinking over. You may decide it's not for you. And then if you do decide you are for it, you begin doing all you can to understand and work with it." Others may disagree with this delineation of the process, but all find that the process goes through stages in its development.

### *Perceptions of Group Counseling*

While some are hesitant about its efficacy, most counselors assume that group counseling is possible. The lack of understanding of group process itself has led to several viewpoints regarding the nature of group counseling. It has been called *multiple counseling* on the assumption that it is the counseling of individuals in a group setting. It is viewed by many as a poor second to individual counseling, and its chief value is seen as a possibility of making counseling available to many more who otherwise cannot be helped. Research has focused on the possibilities of group counseling as a means of improvement in academic learning through the discussion of present barriers to concentration and study.

What group counseling means to the practitioner is a function of what he believes about the nature of man and how change in behavior takes place. If he believes in association theory and aggregate group functioning, then change is directly related to his interventions and the number and quality of associations which the members are encouraged to make. Change is chiefly the result of an improved quality of thinking or learning from the associationist point of view.

If, however, the counselor believes in field theory and an organic group functioning, then the possibility of change is directly related to the total involvement of each member in the organismic reasoning. This is the feeling and acting process carried forward by the interaction of the members with his help as a facilitator in clarifying, reflecting, and summarizing.

In fact it is clear that the former's perception of his responsibility and functioning is quite different from the latter's. Also the former chooses to rely on critical analysis, synthesis, and evaluation as the change factor in man, whereas the latter counselor is inclined to place importance not only on "form" but also on "vitality" (feeling, imagination, and will). As well, the former receives his chief ego satisfaction from his ability to understand, direct, and control the group process in a positive manner. The ego satisfaction of the latter derives from his perception of the developing abilities of the members and their attitudinal changes. How the counselor perceives the group and the method he uses are an outcome of the character of his personality, particularly of how he satisfies his own ego demands.

### How Do Group Counseling and Group Therapy Differ?

There is great variation and lack of consensus. Disagreements exist regarding the nature of group therapy. Various schools agree concerning the reality of group therapy but disagree as to what it is. Such disagreements take place among and within schools of thought. Analytic group therapists insist that therapy results from the analysis of transference and resistance. Kubie on the other hand takes the position that group therapy is hardly possible, since it reduces to a minimum or eliminates free association. The analytic group therapist aims to direct the members toward the best solution of the conflicts causing their maladjustments. Minimally he hopes to remove some of the distortions, develop more satisfactory ways of handling anxiety, and assist the development of self-esteem. Maximally he hopes for genuine and pervasive change in attitude and behavior.

Those engaged in group counseling could conceivably express their goals in the same terms. But group counselors are generally conceived by the analytic group therapists to be engaged in thera-peutic work, not in therapy. Therapists recognize, however, that those engaged in group counseling emphasize that the only group forces that have therapeutic potential are those present and active in the particular theory of counseling to which they subscribe.

Although therapeutic change is not considered impossible in group counseling, the analytic group therapists do not expect therapy to result, but rather they believe that although methods in group process improve, individuals change only minimally. Durkin, an analytic group therapist, concludes that in the accomplishment of the development of new leadership and member process "individuals must of course change in some respects: but their problems need not be and in all likelihood cannot thus be resolved. Therapeutic changes take place but not therapy." [1]

[1] Helen E. Durkin, *The Group in Depth,* International Universities Press, Inc., New York, 1964, p. 60.

There is no precise, clear consensus regarding the nature of therapy or conditions under which it takes place. There is agreement, however, that changes in individuals can and do take place in all types of groups. The various theorists agree also that these changes can be therapeutic. The wall of separation revolves around what types of change must result in the individual before therapy may be concluded to have taken place. This issue remains unresolved. Is the therapeutic change designated as descriptive of group counseling outcomes significantly different from therapy as described by the analytic group therapists? If so, does it differ in degree or in kind? A further problem presents itself in the methods used: not all analytic group therapists use interpretation, whereas others engaged in group counseling consider interpretation to be an important leadership function.

### What Should Be the Time Emphasis?

All methods of group counseling recognize the significance of the time perspective. Differences focus on the part played by the past in relation to the present and future. These differences are characterized as the "here and now," the "there and then," and a third which places important emphasis on both the "there and then" and the "here and now," especially on the relationship between them. These points of view have resulted from different assumptions regarding how past actions are related to present behavior. Those who affirm the "here and now" position assume that what needs consideration is what is functioning in the present, that much of the past is irrelevant or no longer functions in present behavior. Those who encourage or permit the group to focus regularly on the past assume that if the past is understood, the individual or group will naturally apply it to the present. Those who encourage discussion of the "here and now," of what is taking place in the group, are critical of groups which do not, since they consider their preoccupation with "there and then" a means of escape from working through their problems. Those who encourage the members to move from the "here and now" and include the "there and then" do so in order to help them establish the connection between past and present action and to recognize the reasons for their present attitudes, feelings, and behavior.

## Should the Counselor Allow Himself to Be Known?

To what degree does the counselor allow himself to be known? Of course to some degree his very presence signifies something to the counselee. The counselee may perceive him as inscrutable, reticent to share any of himself, or on the other hand as friendly, open, and willing to be known. Whether or not the counselor desires it, the counselee's perceptions of him are a functioning reality in what occurs in the counseling sessions. This is the case, of course, regardless of the correctness of these perceptions. Recognizing this, more emphasis has been placed on the importance of the counselor's attitude toward the member. There is wide agreement that the counselor should be accepting of the member as a person, and many even state that for best results the counselor should love the members.

The importance of the counselor's attitude has been reinforced by the development of existential group counseling. The existentialist counselor is more closely aligned with humanism than with science and views the member and himself as seekers of creativity and a living part of the whole of existence.

These trends have led to contrasting viewpoints regarding the degree of mutuality which should exist between the counselor and group members. Group counselors who are not existentially or analytically oriented do not view the expression of their own feelings and fantasies as necessary or even helpful in furthering the process of therapy. They tend to uphold a certain degree of objectivity. In this they are in accord with Buber and Sartre, who also consider that a degree of objectivity is necessary on the part of healing professions. Thus not even all existentialists believe in full mutuality between counselor and counselee. The Jungian school perhaps more than others finds mutuality more acceptable and in agreement with its view that therapy is a mutual undertaking.

A full interchange and experiencing between counselor and members should be entered into only with a clear understanding of its purpose. Otherwise group members may be baffled by this feature of mutuality and equality. Those who favor and use it are not only therapists who feel strong needs to project their inadequacies and failures or successes on the members. The rationale for entering into this relationship is based on the premise that behavioral change is in large measure dependent upon the greater exchange and experiencing among the counselor and the group members. It assumes that the members gain insight into, and acceptance of, their own neurotic patterns as they adjust to the emotions and needs of the counselor.

Some therapists, especially Mowrer, consider mutuality and equality necessary for significant behavioral change. Mowrer believes that the counselor "must be willing and able to share in the confession of sin." [2] This he considers a prerequisite to the counselee's becoming able to know himself fully.

There remain wide differences in the viewpoints and practices of group counselors with reference to the therapeutic possibilities of communicating to the group members their own efforts in trying to become real persons.

### Is Ventilation Enough?

Can therapeutic change take place without the counselee's understanding the antecedent causes of his behavior? Does self-understanding gained from an examination of the present result in positive growth?

Some have concluded that attitudes and behavior which are alive in the present are those which need exploration. If they are not functioning in the "here and now," they are not influential in present becoming. Other training groups discourage discussion of the "there and then," since they consider such exploration as belonging to therapy and outside their province. Durkin describes this position in reflecting upon her experience as a member of a T group. "Differences between therapy and training methods also showed up distinctly. At Bethel there was no exploration of the members' anxiety or its origin and no discussion of other aspects of their lives. Only interpersonal feelings evidenced in the immediate sessions were subject to comment. Moreover, if there was any sign of pathological reaction the leader reassured the member in question and deftly steered toward another subject." [3]

It is clear that some therapists do not consider therapy possible

[2] Hobart Mowrer, *The New Group Therapy*, D. Van Nostrand Company, Inc., Princeton, N.J., 1964, p. 102.
[3] Durkin, *op. cit.*

without the exploration and understanding of antecedent behavior. There is a decided reluctance to consider the possibility that personality change may take place in educational and counseling groups which give only minimal attention to the examination of psychodynamic causes of present attitudes and behavior.

Mowrer emphasizes that the member of Alcoholics Anonymous must "get behind" the drinking problem as such to an older deeper problem that in the first place makes intoxication so appealing. He concludes, "I doubt if anyone ever whips the problem of alcohol or neuroses until he becomes radically open and honest." [4]

Ventilation may encourage understanding in others. A group member on his own initiative may examine his past and gain a new insight. In a self-report a member illustrates this possibility. She writes: "After George said this morning that he didn't talk much in the group because of an incident in his childhood he was trying to understand and overcome, I started thinking. I realized that my reluctance to become engaged to Jim was that I really didn't care for him like that. I realized that I was attracted to him because he is so like my brother I miss so much, who is in Viet Nam." There is the possibility that some members may be prompted and encouraged to examine their lives in depth because of incidents in the "here and now" situation in the group.

Regardless of the point of view of the group counselor he hopes that through some means self-understanding in some depth will result from the group experience. The group procedures that are most useful in bringing this about remain uncertain. It could be that procedures that help one member may not help all members.

### Should Existentialists' Insights Have a Place?

As group members move toward openness, frankness, and honesty, they move from the essentialist to the existentialist position; that is, they move from a discussion of what is to a contemplation of its meaning. They ask the purpose of their activities, the importance of their goals and of life itself, recognizing within them thrusts toward both being and nonbeing. At this juncture the process is making more use of philosophical than of scientific insights.

[4] Mowrer, *op. cit.*

This progression is often unacceptable, since many counselors are adverse to the recognition of any relationship between existentialist philosophy and counseling. This is due in part to the fact that existentialist group counseling is the product of a humanism rather than a science. Also more emphasis is placed on counseling as an art than on the more acceptable, respectable emphasis of counseling as a science.

Some counselors have a different concern. They expect to find in existential group counseling a clear, precise conceptual system and a new technique. They are of course baffled and doomed to disappointment. These counselors find it difficult to discern and accept a new perspective. The existentialists are not interested in the development of a new clearly defined system but instead in the presentation of a new point of view. They are interested in broadening the base of psychotherapy by approaching it from a philosophic point of view.[5]

Sartre indicates two ways in which psychoanalysis and existential analysis differ: (1) Whereas psychoanalysis has decided upon its own irreducibles, existential analysis allows these to make themselves known in a self-evident situation. Existential therapists do not set up in advance definite theses as guides to investigation; instead they are interested in the comprehension of being and the mode of that being in the individual or group members. (2) Whereas psychoanalysts are interested in analysis and interpretation in relation to a scientific system, existentialists are interested in understanding from an ontological viewpoint. This search to understand being and nonbeing permeates the meaning of neurosis, the understanding of man, and the goals of counseling.[6]

Existentialism asks that therapy become fully organismic in viewpoint and practice. To become truly organismic the intangibles, the concern of philosophy, should also more deeply become the concern of psychology and psychiatry. Each discipline would contribute insights to the other in a mutual interchange of theory and practice. Such communication would in time broaden and enrich the counseling of both individuals and groups.

[5] Rollo May et al. (eds.), *Existence: A New Dimension in Psychiatry and Psychology,* Basic Books, Inc., Publishers, New York, 1958.
[6] J. P. Sartre, *Existentialism and Human Emotions,* Philosophical Library, Inc., New York, 1943.

## ISSUES LESS FREQUENTLY CONSIDERED

Less frequently considered basic issues follow. They are concerned with interpersonal relations and behavioral change.

### *What Is the Aim of Group Process?*

Group process has fashioned its aims according to the society at large. Therefore it has emphasized expediency, adjustment, and self-actualization. Most research in the school setting has been concerned with the improvement of grades, better study habits, and patterns of socialization all oriented toward self-understanding and self-actualization. These are understandable and important aims for group process, but are they adequate? Should group counselors be concerned only with the pragmatic, expedient, and immediate needs of the members? Is it not possible that members may gain only or chiefly some self-understanding related to their lack of adjustment to the school or other situation and methods of self-improvement? Is this all that can be accomplished or should be assumed? Should adjustment and self-actualization be accepted as the goal of group process?

Two decades ago the aim of counseling could be described as "self-realization for a social purpose." The writer continues, "In the world today a more acceptable self implies a concern for the welfare of all . . . " but concludes, "This social aspect of counseling has been generally disregarded." [7]

Seldom is the goal of self-actualization challenged. Whereas happiness is no longer accepted as a goal but as a by-product and an incidental outcome of a way of life, the acceptance of self-actualization as a goal has continued to receive uninterrupted emphasis.

Self-actualization as a goal limits the possibilities of group process. If it is accepted as an end in itself, it ignores and contradicts the fact of man's depth potential. Frankl emphasized that "self-actualization is not man's ultimate destination, not even his primary intention." He explains that "self-actualization is, and must remain, an effect, namely, the effect of meaning fulfillment. Only to the extent

[7] Ruth Strang, *Counseling Technics in College and Secondary School,* Harper & Brothers, New York, 1949, p. 15.

to which man fulfills a meaning out there in the world, does he fulfill himself." [8] Maslow, who has written extensively on self-actualization, agrees that the "business of self-actualization can best be carried out via a commitment to an important job." [9]

Goals which are based on adjustment and expediency are superficial. They often cloud the issue for the individual member; that is, they may prevent the individual from remaining open to the experiencing which is going on within himself.[10] Basically members are searching for fulfillment of self. Too often when they ask for bread, we give them a stone. A modern thinker sums it up in these words: "Individuality is something to be built for the sake of something else. It is a structure of potential energies for expenditure in the service of an idea, a cultural endeavor, the betterment of man, an emergent value. . . . An individual self is made only to be lost . . . that is, only to pledge to some enterprise that is in league with a good future, and thereby find itself once more." [11]

### What to Do about Involvement?

There is a general assumption that involvement is necessary if group process is to be meaningful and useful. It is also accepted that total involvement is required for genuine behavioral change. Total involvement as described by Lewin and Grabbe is involvement as it affects the cognitive structure, emotional structure (valences and values), and motoric action.[12]

Differences occur as to the conditions, individual and group, which are conducive to involvement. Are these conditions similar for each group member, or are there wide variations? Is it possible that a certain methodology in group process may helpfully involve some members but not be helpful to others? Do some members require a situation which encourages a direct confrontation of one member

[8] Viktor Frankl, "Self-Transcendence as a Human Phenomenon," *Journal of Humanistic Psychology,* vol. 6, p. 99, 1966.
[9] A. H. Maslow, *Eupsychian Management: A Journal,* Richard D. Irwin, Inc., Homewood, Ill., 1965, p. 136.
[10] Carl R. Rogers, "Toward a Modern Approach to Values: The Valuing Process in the Mature Person," *Journal of Abnormal and Social Psychology,* vol. 68, p. 165, 1964.
[11] Henry A. Murray, "Individuality: The Meaning and Content of Individuality in Contemporary America," *Daedalus,* vol. 87, p. 47, 1958.
[12] Kurt Lewin and Paul Grabbe, "Conduct, Knowledge, and Acceptance of New Values," *The Journal of Social Issues,* vol. 1, pp. 56–64, 1945.

with another on personal issues in order to become involved? Are there members who do not need this kind of confrontation and find it of little help, unnecessary, or even undesirable? May this be so since it is their custom to examine issues in relation to their values? If some members confront life problems in terms of their personal value structures as a matter of course, do they benefit most from a group whose method assumes that if the conditions make it possible, such self-examination will eventuate?

Is it possible that the depth of involvement bears a direct relation to the depth of living of the members? If so, then involvement for members who live according to opportunistic values of expediency and utility and have strong drives for power may differ greatly from involvement for members who endeavor to fulfill meanings other than expediency, utility, and power drives, and can only be in terms of the members' characteristics regardless of its intensity. Methods designed to increase involvement may increase its degree, but there is only a small probability that this will affect the kind of involvement.

To assume that a certain method of group process will be more effective than another in nurturing the necessary degree of involvement for every member is unrealistic. Also the assumption that total involvement will result in a high quality of constructive change for all members requires reexamination.

### What Changes Behavior?

Group counselors are interested in change in behavior. What process they use reflects their beliefs in what is most successful in securing this result. The many processes are indicative of the wide variation in assumptions. It is not that they do not subscribe to the principle of total involvement but rather that they disagree on the method of obtaining it. The descriptions of methods used point to a variety of theoretical assumptions. One or more of these may be in conflict with others. This persists because methods are developed and the theoretical assumptions, if examined, are examined after the fact. Rogers describes the process in these words: "It has spawned various theories to account for its effects." In further describing the theoretical bases of the basic encounter group he writes: "Lewinian and client-centered theories have been most prominent but gestalt theory and various brands of psychoanalysis have all played contributing parts." [13]

When these varieties of theoretical approach are examined, they can be generally separated into those which rely on extrinsic or those which rely on intrinsic motivation, or some combination of these. If the counselor believes that change takes place as a result of outside influences on each member or group, he will use those forms of extrinsic motivation which he perceives as most effective. He is assuming that behavioral change results from drive reduction. It is presumed that drives become energized when certain instigators (such as personal confrontation) produce a generalized state of arousal or excitement.

If the counselor believes behavioral change results from the member's internal consideration of issues in relation to his values, he favors intrinsic motivation. He assumes that the member is motivated by the incongruity between his values and his behavior. He recognizes that too great incongruity may hinder or prevent action and that too little may result in the absence of motivation. Hunt, who places great importance on intrinsic motivation, uses the room thermostat as a means of explanation.

"The setting of the thermostat is the standard, the room temperature the input, and the difference in the reading between the setting (standard) and the room temperature (input) the incongruity that instigates the operation. Thus the incongruity becomes a kind of generic instigator, and congruity between input and standard stops the operation." [14]

Counselors who rely on some form of extrinsic motivation will use external means of involving members. With this as one of the purposes in mind, questions, interpretations, reinforcements, and other methods are used. What results will in part depend upon how the organism is affected, that is, the meaning of interaction of the member. Counselors who rely on intrinsic motivation try to develop conditions of safety and permissiveness which they consider conducive to the member's initiating his examination of the issues at hand. They believe that under the proper conditions the member will

[13] Carl R. Rogers, "The Process of the Basic Encounter Group," unpublished paper, 1967.
[14] J. McV. Hunt, "Intrinsic Motivation and Its Role in Psychological Development," in *Nebraska Symposium on Motivation,* University of Nebraska Press, Lincoln, 1965.

recognize the incongruity or congruity between the principles involved in the issue and his own and will be guided by his perception and conclusions.

Authorities recognize that behavioral change is a complex variable. Two members appear to change identically, but the change may be basically different and for different reasons. Some members change on the basis of expediency. They adapt their behavior to accord with that of significant others. Such change is phenotypical, or "party-line," change. The member, like a chameleon, changes as his authorities change. In reality he lacks a personal center.[15] Such members rely on others for their values and as guides to behavior. They are influenced by significant others.

Other members may consider all points of view, each on its own intrinsic merits, and may be only minimally influenced by significant others. This they find easier to do, of course, in a permissive climate. Whatever decision they reach, the probability is great that it will be put into effect. In fact Lewin concluded that genuine change takes place only when the member is free to do otherwise.[16] Counselors find this paradox hard to accept.

Other factors contributing to behavioral change are such intangibles as imagination, signs, symbols, and love. Philosophers, psychologists, scientists, historians, and others agree that imagination has an important function in behavioral change. Analytic thought and feeling require imagination which brings the future into the present and makes realization possible. An ancient saying was, "He ran away to sea." The truth is that he went to sea many times in his imagination before he set out on the fateful morning. A philosopher of distinction places imagination at the center of change in behavior. "Our inner life is determined by images, produced by practical imagination. Images are the impelling forces in all our actions." [17]

But not all imagination leads to creative action. In much of our teaching and counseling we continue to expect and encourage only what Jung has called a "reproductive imagination." [18] This form of

[15] C. Gratton Kemp, "Influence of Dogmatism on the Training of Counselors," *Journal of Counseling Psychology,* vol. 9, pp. 155–157, 1962.
[16] Lewin and Grabbe, *op. cit.,* pp. 54–64.
[17] Richard Kroner, *The Religious Function of the Imagination,* Yale University Press, New Haven, Conn., 1941, pp. 7–9.
[18] Carl Jung, *Psychological Types,* Harcourt, Brace & World, Inc., New York, 1923, p. 577.

imagination is the sole method used by many in confronting life's issues. It focuses upon the past and the manifest content; it is immediately evident and thoroughly intelligible.

Creative action requires the use of productive imagination. "It does not ignore either the past or manifest content, but transcends them in a manner that permits them to point to other meanings in which they participate—i.e., permits symbolic meanings to arise." [19]

Productive imagination is undoubtedly a creative dynamic in the process of behavioral change. It functions uniquely in the following ways: [20]

> 1. It submits the material of sense perception to our understanding and is an important element in the attempt to understand another from his frame of reference. Kant in his *Critique of Pure Reason* introduces productive imagination into the field of objective knowledge as a necessary link between sensation and understanding.
> 2. It encompasses the group member's goals and represents the concrete life of his convictions. The desired accomplishment of each member and the group is the language of the imagination.
> 3. It unifies sensation and reason and aids in the development of the quality of group interaction which we frequently try to explain by the statement, "The group as a whole is more than the sum of its parts." It enhances the group's quality of cohesiveness, planning, and decision-making. Through imagination each member views the future goal.

Not only do some group members generally change phenotypically, or superficially, and others genotypically, or genuinely, but either may change in terms of signs and/or symbols. The nature of the goals and the changes which may follow are related directly to whether the member uses signs or symbols in his attempts to fulfill meaning in his life. For example, to interpret life in terms of signs is to remove the meaning and significance of depth from our experience. Conceivably, then, freedom would mean the license to do what we can get away with; peace, the absence of conflict; and justice, penalty in proportion to the infraction.

The true symbol has the following characteristics: (1) it points beyond itself to something else; (2) it participates in that to which it points; (3) it opens up levels of reality which are otherwise closed;

[19] Kemp, *op. cit.,* p. 160.
[20] C. Gratton Kemp, *Perspectives on the Group Process,* Houghton Mifflin Company, Boston, 1964, p. 15.

(4) it opens up hidden depths of our being; (5) it cannot be produced intentionally; (6) it dies when it no longer produces a response in the group in which it originally found expression.[21]

Many of us are nominalists at heart, we find it difficult to tolerate the ambiguity that accompanies symbolic thinking. We are unhappy unless we can define the symbol, make it concrete, knowable, and attainable. This action forfeits the possibility of its leading to increasingly creative meaning. The symbol becomes a sign, and our definition of behavioral change is encapsulated in terms of refinement of methods and process. If group counseling is to encourage significant behavioral change in members and leaders, true symbolic thinking must become an integral part of the interaction. Unless this is done, group process is likely to be reduced to each individual's using the experience solely for the advancement of his own purposes.

One disastrous result of the treatment of symbols as signs is the interpretation we make of love in the counseling relationship. We leave nothing for the creative imagination. It is an accomplished relationship among the members. It has no out-beyondness or symbolic dimension. It is assumed that the members comprehend it fully and that they have discovered it in its entirety. As such it *is* a sign; it has lost its meaning and power; it cannot initiate other levels of understanding or point the way to new meanings. It has no referent beyond the members' modes of adjustment.

OTHER ISSUES

Among other issues are those of a different order. These relate themselves to the preparation of leaders of educational groups and group counselors. These issues are interrelated, each bearing its own significance. One issue related to preparation is the proper sequence of courses. Before a conclusion can be reached concerning this issue, other issues present themselves. One is whether the skills required to lead a group or to be an efficient group member develop incidentally or whether they have to be recognized and formally learned with care and understanding.

Is it reasonable to expect that members need experience in a group for a time to understand the nuances, feelings, and responsibili-

[21] Paul Tillich, *Dynamics of Faith,* Harper & Brothers, New York, 1958, pp. 42–43.

ties of what it means to be a member of a group? Need these be experienced in order that members will become more able to understand the difficulties of members in groups with whom they work?

In the development of skills and attitudes feedback on the various levels of members' performance is essential and also participation in the evaluation of their progress. Since these require considerable practice and understanding to be done well, should these experiences be provided in a planned intelligent and intelligible manner?

These considerations strongly suggest the offering of a basic course which would provide the above learning experiences and that such a course be a prerequisite to other courses designed more for increased self-understanding and the working through of personal problems.

In the attempt to plan the learning experiences needed for the preparation of group leaders systematic attention should be given to increasing our information with regard to definite changes and in what order they are experienced by those training for group leadership. A haphazard approach in which each counselor educator offers a kind of course which appeals to him without any short-term or long-term planning is inefficient, inadequate, and narrow in its perspective. An adequate plan must, among other things, give consideration to individual differences. Not all members benefit equally from the same learning experiences.

CONCLUSIONS

Misconceptions, confusions, and conceptual inadequacy designate to some degree the efforts in group processes. These are a function of various situations: One cause is a lack of communication among experimentalists in group processes, particularly between those in group dynamics and group therapy. A second cause is the emphasis given to techniques with only minimal attention to theory. A third is unwillingness to differentiate and examine group therapy and group counseling in its own right and apart from individual counseling. Only recently has attention been turned to the development of group psychology. This has led to a delay in understanding the commonalities and differences among the various theoretical approaches to groups.

Most disastrous is the assumption that something dynamic and constructive can be expected to result when a few persons are brought together in a so-called "small" group. Also disastrous is the belief that a therapeutic result will consistently follow when a few persons sit together and engage in telling one another "what they are like."

Such expectancies are the result of inadequate knowledge and training. In the absence of a sound theoretical foundation there has tended to be an uncritical acceptance of, and value placed upon, many unexamined, uninformed, and inadequate attempts at group process. In an attempt to reduce the ambiguity, categorizations and definitions have been developed which have hindered and suggested as unnecessary the search for more comprehensive and accurate understanding.

Since group counseling has been viewed as the handmaid of individual counseling, it has been assumed that understanding of, and skill in, counseling in a one-to-one relationship equipped one also to work with a group. Only as the dynamics of the group process are gradually becoming known has this erroneous and slightly arrogant assumption begun to disappear. Counselor educators with little or no training in group process will continue unabashedly to use small groups in their supervisory sessions for training enrollees in individual counseling. This is done without an attempt to understand theoretical assumptions regarding learning and behavioral change implicit in this undertaking.

It is also regrettable that some counselor educators and others immediately seize upon some auspicious-sounding title of an experiment in group counseling simply because it "worked," without examination of its basic operational principles and its applicability to their setting, purposes, character, attitudes, and degree of skill. Such action removes one from a professional status to an expediter of techniques.

Group process has frequently been looked upon as a much too simple process. Its complexity in comparison with what takes place in individual counseling has received too casual attention. Its multifaceted, multidirectional dynamics have had to wait till a very recent time for the sophistication which automation can now offer to the study of the interactions in their complexity. Thus research in this area has not been as useful as the practitioner has desired.

Also, much of the research has not focused on group process itself but upon the effects of the process on individuals as a group. The effects studied, such as improvement in academic learning, have centered attention on a few attitudinal outcomes and thereby disconnected, narrowed, or distorted the possible scope and purpose of group process itself. Research concerned with group process has generally been interested in descriptive statistics.

It would be erroneous, however, to give the impression that the present stage of understanding and skill in group process has resulted entirely from the lack of certain research information. It must be conceded that the recognition of the potentialities of group process became more possible when it received psychological support from organismic thinking.

# 2

# NEEDED: A CONCEPTUAL FRAMEWORK

The true nature of group counseling Is obscured by definitions. It is a hybrid of methods, theory, and attitudes of learning on the one hand and of therapy on the other. This overlap and resistance to concreteness and tidiness is its danger and also its potentiality. The danger has at least three aspects: One, we may be pushed by ambiguity into a Procrustean bed approach based solely upon tradition or rigid orthodoxy. This approach would be stultifying and unproductive. Two, the unreflective with misunderstood personal needs may attempt to serve in capacities in which they are not professionally prepared. Three, a confused approach may result in which any practice is rationalized on the basis of creativity and functionalism. Its potential is that the situation may motivate us to recognize our dilemma. We may endeavor to develop a conceptual framework which will clarify the relationship of the different theoretical positions. This attempt would at least increase the possibilities of exploration and understanding, rather than the withdrawal into professional encapsulation.

The attempt to build walls around group process in education, group counseling, and group therapy by the demand for definitions could be disastrous. As related by a state supervisor of guidance and testing, "Counselors attempt group counseling and when it doesn't satisfy their definite and rigid expectancies, throw out everything related to groups." The process must be examined and studied in relation to its perceived usefulness in a particular situation. Then the appropriate relationship of the data of each field to the process may be determined. Such examination and study are needed, since the fields are related by a generic process involved in understanding man as man.

Examination of practices reveals a serious lack of a conceptual framework. Without flexible boundaries real confusion may exist. For example, a group interested in learning more about group dynamics and procedures asked for help from a skilled leader. The leader perceived the situation in almost a "therapy" setting. After a few sessions the members terminated the group. Their frustration and anxiety had reached a breaking point. The leader had seen his function as a nondirective leader in an unstructured situation. He was apparently unaware of the need for content and direction.

Another group expressed an interest in developing greater sensitivity to one another in relation to a cooperative endeavor in which they were involved. They engaged in a session charged with reminiscence, interpersonal strife, and confession. For some it was an expression of their masochism; for others, a time of aggressive projection. The lack of fundamental understanding and commitment to the process made this a questionable experience for all.

A counselor educator asked the school counselor to select a random group of eight students in junior high school to participate in group counseling. At the first meeting the counselor educator gave two quite general purposes for the meetings and then turned the group over to a counselor-in-training. She proceeded nondirectively. The group members were at a loss to know how to respond. They were slightly aggressive with one another. Two of the boys tried to entertain the girls with tales of extravagant behavior. Since the group members had no experience or skills in group process and since the leaders had little insight into, or understanding of, what was taking place, the succeeding periods became increasingly fruitless.

If a group therapist proceeds as if therapy is the purpose when the members perceive the session as one in social education, there will be increasing frustration. Or if the dynamically oriented adult educator functions in a way quite appropriate in an educational setting but does so in a therapy-oriented expectant group, the resulting difficulties may eventuate in wholesale rejection of the process even in the situations in which it has been proved fruitful. It is therefore imperative that a careful appraisal be made of what group process means in relation to the specific kind of situation in which it is to be used. When uncritically and impulsively misapplied, methods which are creative and useful in their own right may be rightly and widely condemned.

The lack of a conceptual framework and confusion resulting from lack of theory mean that we frequently and nonintentionally trust members and leaders in situations in which there exists little possibility for successful outcomes. Some conceptual framework based upon acceptable theory and common sense by which to evaluate different activities and particular emphases is necessary.


## A CONCEPTUAL FRAMEWORK

### *Theoretical*

Artificial divisions based entirely upon tradition or rigid orthodoxy should be avoided. In this field as in others the ability must be developed to use the concept of Dewey that every idea imperils some part of a stable world. One sees everywhere the trend toward experimentation. But experimentation without any theoretical mainland is hardly commendable. When we know reasonably well what we are doing on the basis of some meaningful concepts, our experiments will have more internal authenticity, and the outcomes will be more amenable to evaluation and use.

What, then, is a plausible scheme based on a theoretical foundation and consistent with experience? It is commonly recognized that even a discussion among a few people concerning any subject involves feeling and includes some therapeutic implications. A student discussing with his teacher his progress in algebra is engaged chiefly in talking about algebra but is also to some degree talking about himself, his teacher, the relationship between them, and the world at large. Thus to varying degrees all interpersonal relationships are both content-oriented and emotionally oriented. "All groups have in common some therapeutic aspect, for the very social nature of man makes the group a potential source of his self-esteem and ego gratification." [1]

No subject is wholly an intellectual or an emotional one but more of one and less of the other. Also man uses his cognitive, emotional, and motoric responses integrally as a total organism. Lewin [2] emphasized that genuine change requires that one become totally involved. Again, what the group experience means to the individual is directly dependent upon his perception of the interpersonal relationships. What then becomes significant in distinguishing the degree of thought and emotion is the *focus of attention.* In group counseling and group therapy the focus is the emotional; in educational group process, the focus is the intellectual.

To give each aspect its due significance in the group process is difficult. Frank [3] emphasizes the importance of support, stimulation, and reality testing in therapy, but these are equally necessary in educational group process, especially where a high level of thinking and cooperation is required. Bradford selects the group climate as an important constituent in group learning. He describes the climate conducive to learning as one which "reduces individual defensiveness and anxiety and exposure of one's inadequacy and gives acceptance and emotional support to all students." [4] Such a climate, however, is considered by Hobbs as paramount in group counseling. He writes, "In a situation of growing warmth and acceptance, the members of the group become increasingly able to examine feelings hitherto denied." [5]

[1] Hubert Stanley Coffey, "Socio and Psyche Group Process: Integrative Concepts," *The Journal of Social Issues,* vol. 8, p. 73, spring, 1952.
[2] Kurt Lewin and Paul Grabbe, "Conduct, Knowledge, and Acceptance of New Values," *The Journal of Social Issues,* vol. 1, no. 3, 1945.
[3] Jerome D. Frank, "Group Methods in Psychotherapy," *The Journal of Social Issues,* vol. 8, no. 2, p. 39, 1952.
[4] Leland P. Bradford, "Group Forces Affecting Learning," *Journal of the National Association of Women Deans and Counselors,* vol. 33, p. 116, April, 1960.
[5] Nicholas Hobbs, "Group Psychotherapy in Mental Hygiene," *Teachers College Record,* vol. 50, p. 174, 1948.

The dilemma faced in an attempt to dichotomize educational group process and group counseling has been heightened by the insights of Lewin and others. They saw the imperativeness of incorporation in educational group process an involvement, motivation, and ego fulfillment characteristic of group counseling. The training group in educational group process for teachers, counselors, nurses, medical interns, and others exemplifies an overlap of the intellectual and emotional emphasis. This is so because the objectives of learning in this situation are both content-centered and process-centered. Witness an anonymous self-report of a trainee enrolled in such a group and involved in a discussion on making better decisions: "I enjoyed the discussion on decision making but realized my own inability to make clear-cut decisions. I am so often torn between 'this' and 'that,' and my procrastination often results in the loss of the privilege of making my own decisions. I learned something of what is involved in helping others make decisions, but more than that it forced me to face my own inadequacy and see the need for improvement. Yes, it even gave me an urge to improve."

Thinking and feeling are of course experienced in many kinds of groups. Knowles and Bradford [6] have pleaded for the incorporation in adult education of more of the feeling element through planning and discussion concerned with the group member's needs and aspirations as he perceives them. Hopkins emphasizes the "need experience process" [7] that is the learner's perception of his need as the basis of the developmental educational experience.

It is apparent, then, that in an educational group experience there can be and are brief therapeutic experiences. Likewise in the group-counseling experience there are brief educational or problem-solving experiences. An examination of the dynamics of groups reveals that they rarely exist in pure forms but are a combination of elements. In fact this fusion of, or flow from, focus on thought to focus on emotion can be observed within any session. A content analysis of the material of a sequence of sessions, however, indicates that the group can be characterized as having more of one and less

[6] Malcolm S. Knowles and Leland P. Bradford, "Group Methods in Adult Education," *The Journal of Social Issues,* vol. 8, pp. 11–22, 1952.
[7] L. Thomas Hopkins, *The Emerging Self in School and Home,* Harper & Row, Publishers, Incorporated, New York, 1954.

of the other type of experience. How much more of problem solving and concern with objectives and specific goals is necessary to justify the label of an educational group is rather difficult to establish.

In order to describe adequately and with some accuracy the nature of groups it is useful to use the concept of a continuum and to think of any one group, or group session, or some portion thereof as existing somewhere on the continuum. One end of the continuum might be designated as an educational process group and the other as a counseling process group. Such a conceptual framework is suggested by Coffey.[8] He uses the term *socio group process* to characterize the educational problem-solving group and *psyche group process* to describe the therapy group. In the educational group there is an explicit visualized goal and purpose. There is structure, generally heterogeneous with respect to abilities, interests, and maturity. The educational group may also be heterogeneous with respect to age, status, and vocation. The members of these groups view themselves as being in a learning situation with reference to some content and/or skill achievement. The group is organized to meet for a definite period of time—a number of weeks, a quarter, or a semester.

As we move toward the other end of the continuum, generally characterized as group counseling, differences become increasingly evident. No visible goal is discernible. If one does arise, it quickly evaporates. The structure is loose, informal; if rules do emerge, they are transient. The members view themselves as discussing what they consider important. If they perchance do talk about a topic more relevant to an educational group, their focus is very different. Their satisfaction is not so much dependent upon ideational outcomes or improvement of skills as upon gaining insight into their own motivations and feelings and to some degree into those of others. They are not so much motivated to learn as to understand. Their primary objective, although not made explicit, is the satisfaction of emotional needs of members.

Such a framework will accommodate within its perspective all theoretical formulations including the several modes of psychotherapy. As discussed later, the continuum may be extended to include

[8] Coffey, *op. cit.*

group therapy. Group counseling (therapeutic) moves to psychotherapy (therapy) to the degree that the members are more neurotic and less flexible in their desire and attempts to relate to and handle reality.

Such a conceptual framework may be distressing to those who desire concreteness and explicitness. However, only this type of framework can prevent what Whitehead describes as the *fallacy of concreteness.* The lack of precision in designating groups along a continuum has important usefulness. It avoids rigid categories, helps clarify distinctions, and provides working hypotheses. It may assist us to value more correctly the process in relation to the skills and needs of the group. There is nothing inherently precious about any particular kind of group. In one setting the need for group therapy may be recognized; in another, group counseling; but an educational group experience may be more beneficial in a different setting. To place a value connotation on one kind of group or focus of experience apart from a particular group is unwise.

### Methodological

As stated earlier, the assumption that to participate in and receive benefit from any form of group process requires no preparation or training is illogical and incorrect. Such an erroneous assumption may have evolved from the fact that a small group may engage in satisfying social communication (even this requires evaluation). This implication results from the lack of differentiating between social group behavior and the behavior of social groups.

A second source of difficulty may have been the assumption that since an individual is helped in a one-to-one counseling relationship without previous training, this could be expected to apply in the group situation. This is failure to recognize that in the individual counseling relationship the counselor or therapist may compensate for the lack of skills in the client. Of course even here counselors and clients recognize that better interpersonal relationship is in part a function of the skills they have developed in relation to each other. As the number of interactions increase—as they do in the group situation— such skills as listening, clarification, summarization, asking questions, and providing information must be highly developed. In the beginning students in group process express great difficulty "in keeping up" with the flow of ideas. Through the use of an observer, recorder, and feedback facilities the members become more capable of understanding the process and each his own participation.

At the present time progress in groups is hampered by the ineptitude of the members and lack of at-homeness in the group situation. This is not to say that involvement and readiness to participate must also develop but rather that even these must await the development of skills before needed participation, both verbal and nonverbal, can become a reality. Invariably the ability to listen, clarify, synthesize, summarize which members bring to groups is not adequate for participation in either educational or counseling groups. The development of these skills needs concentration over a fairly long period of time. Attempting to do so without this training is like expecting a beginner to become a great musician without training in finger movements and knowledge of the scales and defending this unlikely procedure by saying that he has attended a number of musical concerts.

The issue is often clouded by the following analysis: Man is a social animal; he has always lived in groups; he spends his time in various kinds of groups. Therefore, he can perform, learn, and change in groups. However, many of his group experiences are in what Hopkins calls "aggregate" [9] situations and quite unproductive. Students who enroll in group process soon find that these kinds of past experiences are of little help to them in developing what is needed to become truly proficient in functioning as a group member or group leader.

Groups have always been with us. But group process as now conceived is recent and necessarily so since it is built upon understandings from many disciplines whose development, if placed in a time perspective, is as recent as today. Growth and change through small groups is now viewed as a way of life. This is to say that these are inherent possibilities in all dynamic interpersonal relationships. This view applies equally well to the home, industry, school, recreation, counseling.

But group process has to be learned, and, like many activities such as swimming, it is learned through experience. We may lecture to the enrollee in swimming about body position, the buoyancy of the

[9] Hopkins, *op. cit.*

water, breathing, but he really does not know any of these until he experiences it. Experiencing makes it a reality.

It follows, then, that training in, and use of, group process should be a normal experience of the elementary school child. In relation to his developmental age he should experience group process through its use by teachers as normal procedures, regardless of the content. His understanding of the group experience and skills as member and leader would develop in relation to other learnings throughout his educational experience. He would learn what it means to work in, for, and with the group. He would experience the meaning of caring and responsibility. He would come to realize the relationship between freedom and responsibility through experiences in using and being permitted as much freedom as he demonstrated he could use responsibly. He would develop such skills as listening, clarification, synthesizing, evaluating, and summarizing. The school counselor would not be involved in group procedures considered as a lesser activity and an adjunct to the school curriculum, but instead he would be using group process in a manner similar to that of other school faculty to teach such extracurricular considerations as moral and ethical values, vocational information, and sociological and psychological understandings. These small groups would vary on the continuum from educational to counseling groups. It is to be expected that less individual and group counseling would be necessary, since students would have learned how to use their abilities in problem solving and have solved many of their problems. Those who needed more assistance would have developed skills necessary and facilitative in working through personality problems through the group process.

Knowledge of, and skills in, group process are considered basic to its use in educational and counseling sessions. The model calls for training and experience in the use of group process to precede training and experience in group counseling. The title *group procedures*, now commonly used, is ambiguous. A logical interpretation might be that this is a course to acquaint counselors-in-training with the various types of procedures such as panel, forum, discussion. The title indicates a lack of understanding of the true nature of group process or implies an erroneous assumption that group process does not require study and/or bears no relationship to group counseling.

It is suggested that the anomalous title of *group guidance* be replaced by the title of *group process.* Group process, in this framework, would be considered a basic experience for all those in professions or trades whose work necessitates working with others in small groups. In institutions of higher learning in which this assumption functions, students enter the course designated group process from a number of disciplines and with a number of professional objectives. This cross-disciplinary interest has, of course, made it necessary to offer such a course continuously. This laboratory course should be a requirement in the preparation of all counselors and student personnel workers. The content of the course now titled *group guidance* would be to some extent included in the course focused on educational and vocational information in which methods of disseminating this information to students in the school would be discussed. A large and increasing number of institutions are now using textbooks dealing only with group process.

Within this proposed prospective the model would take the form of a course in group process for students majoring in various disciplines, including those majoring in counseling and student personnel work. This course would be offered at different levels with progressive goals to permit students to attain the necessary skills and personality development to use this method in their various occupational and other relationships. For majors in counseling this course should be followed by a laboratory course in group counseling, one that is repeatable in order to increase proficiency.

Educational groups, group counseling, and group therapy are, then, differing expressions of group process. All have the same basic foundations. Differences revolve around the purposes and emphasis of each group. Basic to the understanding of any of these expressions of group functioning is an understanding and working knowledge of the concept of the group.

CONCLUSIONS

There are contrasting trends in the struggle to understand the nature, purpose, and functioning of group processes. Some appear to indicate that group process is "natural," that members and even leaders do not need any special knowledge, skills, or insights beyond those necessary for counseling individuals. Others evidently assume that group processes are even now sufficiently understood to be categorized and defined. By such action they may increase their security and suffer less from the frustrations that accompany ambiguity. On the other hand they risk becoming rigid and limiting progress.

Another trend is a patient, open-minded, thoughtful exploration of group process to understand its generic foundation and to recognize and comprehend the commonalities among groups with different purposes. This search has progressed over several decades. Leaders in social work, group work, adult education, psychology, and psychiatry have participated in the search. At first they proceeded independently with little attention to the activity and writing outside their specialty, but later they made increasing efforts to understand what each had to contribute to the total understanding. This led to a rediscovery of early writings, especially those of Freud, in the hope of formulating and developing a group psychology.

These efforts have focused attention on the study of the group and group process as an entity. This has had several results: One resultant insight is the need for, and possibility of, the group experience for the development of open, healthy-minded persons. Another is a growing recognition of the great complexity of interpersonal relationships possible and generally present in the group experience. A third is the supreme importance of the influence of the status of emergent leadership. A greater understanding and appreciation of the therapeutic possibilities inherent in group process has developed as well. There is also a growing conviction that rapprochement among various viewpoints is possible and useful. As early as 1937 Lewin indicated the compatibility of psychoanalytic theory and field theory basic to group dynamics. The same year Brown systematically elaborated principles common to these two theories. These commonalities, now widely accepted, have furthered a rapprochement between group dynamics including counseling and group therapy. The commonalities as elucidated by Brown [10] were essentially as follows: (1) Both theories (field-group dynamics and psychoanalytic) are dynamic, wholistic, and functional. (2) The person is perceived as an organism in an environment; they agree that the individual is a sociopsychobiological organism. (3) They conclude that the organism is a supersummative whole (more than the sum of its parts). (4) They agree that growth and personality development can be understood

[10] J. F. Brown, "Psychoanalysis, Topological Psychology, and Experimental Psychopathology," *Psychoanalytic Quarterly*, vol. 6, pp. 227–237, 1937.

as restructuralization and differentiation out of a global whole. (5) Each invents theoretical constructs in order to achieve a systematized science. (6) Each posits a dynamic force to account for activity and emphasizes the problem of motivation. (7) They agree that motivation is blocked by physical and social factors. (8) They agree that some sources of maturation are unknown. (9) They agree that symptoms have a cause, a significance, and an organized system. (10) Both use the hypotheticodeductive method, which accommodates itself to theoretical constructs such as libido and ego as well as to those such as vector and life space. (11) Each observes behavior and coordinates it into theory in order to integrate the facts.

Rapprochement is still far off, and movement toward it for various reasons has been uneven. Durkin emphasizes that today "differences have been reduced to a mere matter of emphasis. Both groups are now interested in all these phenomena." [11] Leaders in such a rapprochement are striving to recognize and include creative differences.

At present no approach in group counseling or group therapy is more comprehensive than, or superior to, others. Interestingly each seems to be asking what the best approach for the intended purpose is, and if each is based on acceptable theoretical formulations.

The plausible foreseeable outcomes of this trend are that (1) group process will be accepted and respected on its own merits; (2) training in group process, group counseling, and group therapy will become an area of specialty with more adequate and unique emphasis on leadership; (3) group process will be studied, used, and evaluated in ever-increasing numbers and kinds of interpersonal-relationship settings—in fact, the expansion in the use of group process far exceeds the available leadership and the knowledge and experience needed for best results; (4) insights originating in group process experience will be significantly useful in individual counseling and in all one-to-one relationships; (5) as theoretical understandings become validated, education and behavioral change will be positively affected in all educational aspects of life, home, school, office, the plant, the hospital, and also in national and international organizations.

[11] Helen E. Durkin, *The Group in Depth,* International Universities Press, Inc., New York, 1964, p. 65.

# 2

# FOUNDATIONAL CONCEPTS

*It occurs frequently in a developing area that attention focuses on the action and the theoretical basis is established after the fact. It is therefore not a surprise to realize that this in general describes the situation in group counseling. The action came first, and the rationale was often an afterthought.*

*This situation calls for the placing of an increasing importance on the analysis and evaluation of the principles inherent in what we are doing. Do we and can we place our confidence in the foundational concepts on which analysis reveals we presently depend?*

*Chapters 3 and 4 examine the foundational principles of contrasting group-counseling methods. These are analyzed from both a* descriptive and analytic viewpoint. They provide the counselor with the means for study and evaluation of his own method of group counseling. The beginning counselor will be helped in the development of his method in accordance with his convictions concerning behavioral change.

# 3

# THE CONCEPT
# OF THE GROUP

Group life is basic to man's existence. Such titles as *family, tribe, clan, nation, commonwealth, dominion, United States* suggest the breadth and persistence of groups and group life. At all levels of society persons move and have their being in groups. It may be this unquestioned acceptance and familiarity which conceals from us the essence of the group and discourages analysis and discrimination among groups. For instance, we seldom discriminate between social group behavior and the behavior of social groups. In the former each person is relating to others individually or collectively in terms of his own phenomenal field, whereas the latter is concerned with what constitutes a group, how it operates to develop and maintain groupness, and its effect upon the persons who compose it.[1]

[1] L. Thomas Hopkins, *The Emerging Self in School and Home,* Harper & Row, Publishers, Incorporated, New York, 1954, pp. 186–189.

The concept of the group is dynamic. It varies directly with our increased understanding of man and the impingements of the times in which it exists. Its character is a function of all we know and are. Its possibilities are encompassed by the knowledge and understanding which emerge from many disciplines both past and present. A comprehensive concept of the group must include not only understanding acquired through the various scientific pursuits but also that gained through the artistic and philosophic approaches to reality.

Although influences from various disciplines mold both the concept of the group and the functioning of the group itself, each of the main influential sets of developments will be considered independently for the sake of description.


## DEVELOPMENTS

Basic to one's concept of the group is his concept of man. The modern view of man is frequently a blend of several points of view, especially of those formally known as the Biblical and classical viewpoints of man. The pivotal issues are the following: Is man only a superior animal, or is he different in kind as well as in degree? What is the significant aspect of man, "form" or "vitality"? In other words, is his rational capacity his most distinguishing characteristic, or is it his vitality, imagination, feeling, and will? What is to be done regarding spirit? Is it to be recognized, and if its reality is attested, will it be unique or subsumed under either form or vitality?

Those for whom spirit is anathema or too ambiguous and intangible to be seriously considered lack a base for seeing the group in depth, that is, for the recognition and acceptance of its symbolic overtones. Also they hesitate to affirm human freedom except to a limited degree, self-perception and introspection are limited to ways and means, and values exist only as they affect interpersonal relationships. These individuals may be disappointed, since, as Bacon in his day recognized, the "unquietness of the spirit" would "interfere most mischievously in the discovery of causes." [2]

Those who view man as basically rational are by this assumption constrained to be interested in the problem-solving ability and

[2] Francis Bacon, "Novum Organum," trans. by James Spedding, in Benjamin Rand, *Modern Classical Philosophers,* Houghton Mifflin Company, Boston, 1924.

insightful decisions attainable by a group. One who is inclined to place greater emphasis on vitality views the group through the principles of self theory. He perceives improved thinking and planning as a function of better interpersonal relations in which the expression of attitudes and feelings receive a significant emphasis. This position lends itself to an eager acceptance that cooperative inquiry will accomplish the seemingly impossible. In his call for an "organized co-operative inquiry," John Dewey apparently does not recognize that persons do not find it possible to transcend conflicts of interest and achieve the outcomes he attributes to this process.[3] Conclusions go awry when one fails to take account of man's speculative and intuitive insights. Central to man's freedom is his ability to break and remake the antinomies of nature.

Those who have a balanced view, that is, who recognize and accept the integral functioning of form, vitality, and spirit, are inclined to have a more realistic view of the group and are less open to disillusionment or exaggerated enthusiasm. These persons view the group as having great possibilities but recognize that the conditions for developing such possibilities are difficult to achieve. They have a reasonable respect for human freedom and entertain the probability of the functioning of the symbolic in group process.

How a member functions in a group bears a direct relation to his concept of man. If he views man as only a superior animal whose uniqueness is his capacity for critical thought, then he chiefly respects his thinking ability and relates to him on the basis of the quality of his ideas. He is less aware and less interested in other aspects of a member in a group such as how he feels about himself and about the meaning of life, and other symbolic intangibles.

Another person may consider the uniqueness of man to consist of the use he makes of his imagination, feeling, and will. Such a person in a group will concentrate on the feelings and expressions of determination which other members portray. He will of course be interested in their ideas but chiefly as a means of understanding how they feel. In his self-report on the functioning of the group he places much less emphasis on the quality of ideas and more on the feeling climate than does the member primarily interested in ideas.

A third member may believe that either position or both together

[3] John Dewey, *Liberalism and Social Action,* G. P. Putnam's Sons, New York, 1935, p. 51.

fail to encompass all he understands about a person. He may not be able satisfactorily to explain, but he experiences a person as having an intangible pervasive quality in his attitude toward others and in the way he approaches interpersonal relationships. He is willing to accept the notion that there is a creative mystery about a person which he cannot explain in empirical terms. He at times experiences this depth within himself, and he is willing to respect and honor it in others. Such a member in a group has a broad interest; he is interested in another's ideas, his feelings, but also in what life means to him, what he is seeking to say in the depth of his being.

To say that a group member is entirely one or another in his approach toward other members may be somewhat erroneous. To say he is more of one and less of the others in most situations is more likely to be correct. There may be, on the other hand, those who would find themselves unwilling and unable to consider as possible or relevant any depth and intangible quality of personality. Especially may this be so if this quality is described in such terms as "spirit," or "inner choice," or in other philosophic or religious terminology. He may, however, genuinely hold and express these attitudes in his relation to others without recognizing what they are.

### The Group and World Views

The group maximizes its potential through three-way interaction, a willingness on the part of each member to modify his thinking and attitudes, and a readiness to work on a common goal in accord with group purposes. These conditions have become more capable of realization in recent times. Previously and throughout most of the history of mankind the mechanistic conception of the world made impossible an intelligent conception and acceptance of such organic functioning of the group as described above.

The mechanistic view of the world gave support only to aggregate authoritarian groups based on an association theory of learning. Although the mechanistic viewpoint of man has become increasingly less supportable, it has operationally persisted to the present day. It receives its greatest support via the concepts of association learning theory and factor trait theory of personality. In countless classrooms each student is considered a unit. His dynamic and integral relationship to the environment and the functional relationship of thought, feeling, and imagination within him are completely ignored. More-over, teachers and principals consider it their obligation to reward, punish, and move him to new groups as they perceive necessary in terms of information received about him.

Hopkins is critical of the mechanistic authoritarian world con-ception and describes the methods which this view uses as "control compulsion, exploitation, restriction, fear, cold war, hot war, com-promise, peace treaties which do not keep the peace." [4] Rugg de-scribes this philosophy of authority as possessing the following characteristics: (1) the leader has the knowledge, makes the plans, and directs the members of the group, whether they are citizens, employees, students, colleagues, or members of his family; (2) knowledge is gained from a study of the past; and (3) theoretical formulations depend upon reason and faith.[5]

Those who hold this mechanistic authoritarian viewpoint do not believe in the supreme value of the individual. They do not admit that most men have the capacity for self-discipline. In accordance with these assumptions they build and honor authoritarian one-way relationships in politics, business, and educational institutions. This view is the all-pervasive measure of the social order, even the basis of the rearing of children in homes, at school, and on the playground.

This world view was rooted in the thought and writings of Aris-totle. From the fourth century B.C. to the seventeenth century A.D. the intellectual Western world interpreted the natural world and man according to the authority of the past. Established thought patterns were transmitted from age to age in the same form. If at any time original thought or recourse to human experience became visible, there was swift recourse to the safety of authority.

The transition to the organismic world view took place in three stages: The first was the initiation period (from 1600 to the 1840s) of a new naturalism and science via Galileo, Newton, and Descartes and the challenge to the Aristotelian-Thomist authority by Hobbes, Locke, and Berkeley. In the second stage (from 1840 to the 1890s) a new psychology and sociology emerged, turning toward a philosophy of experience. A few leading thinkers were Faraday, Comte, Wundt,

[4] L. Thomas Hopkins, "Democratic Functioning: The Hope of the World," *Teachers College Record,* vol. 49, no. 8, p. 502, 1948.
[5] Harold Rugg, *Foundations for American Education,* World Book Company, Yonkers, N.Y., 1947, p. 36.

Bernard, and Peirce. The third period extended from the 1890s to the 1940s. During this time the organic-field–force–energy concepts were developed and documented in many fields. Many of its great thinkers are familiar names. A few in psychology are John Dewey, John B. Watson, Kurt Lewin; in psychoanalysis, Sigmund Freud, Carl G. Jung, Otto Rank; in the social sciences, Ralph Linton, Ruth Benedict, Arthur Schlesinger; in sociology, Herbert Spencer and Frank Ward. And of course there are many more in these and other disciplines. Through their efforts the transition from mechanism to organism became complete.

However, the mechanistic authoritarian principles are still operational in all forms of interpersonal relations. The change to organic and cooperative relationships has been incredibly slow. This is due in part to two erroneous assumptions: One is that the principles which work for change in the organic and subhuman world can also be applied to the human world of persons. Such a conclusion is possible if one is willing to discredit or ignore both man's capacity for human freedom (to view man as an object to be conditioned) and his capacity for self-transcendence (his potential of viewing himself as subject). Kurt Goldstein, on the basis of his neurological studies, recognized this ability of man to transcend the concrete or the present situation of which he is a part and to think in abstract terms, that is, in terms "of the possible." He and many others consider this capacity of man unique.

The subject-object dilemma has been expressed in many ways by biologists, philosophers, theologians, and artists. Paul Tillich described it as man's "finite freedom." Man is finite in terms of his many limitations but as well has the freedom to relate to these forces. Reinhold Niebuhr takes the position that human experience combines both "nature" and "spirit" and that man functions in both dimensions simultaneously.

The second erroneous assumption is that a social order of democracy requires only the learning of skills. Rugg suggests the clue to our problem in his descriptions of the two views, the mechanistic social order of authority and the organic social order of democracy. He describes the philosophy of the order of authority as follows: "You and I are different. Each is an individual. I am Superior. You are Inferior. So, I shall dictate to you. The greatest thinking has already been done and has been passed on in the Word. I shall interpret the Word of that thinking for you. And I shall rule you." He describes the social order of democracy in these words: "You and I are different, yet we must live together. Each of us is a Person. I am a Supreme . . . but you are a Supreme also. Each has a unique experience and some original power of thought. Together we can distill judgment and decision out of human experience. So we shall rule together." [6]

It is clear that although methods and techniques differ, the more important difference is attitudinal. More than superficial personality change is indicated in the "becoming" required of the person who moves from the first position of mechanistic authoritarianism to the latter or organic democratic functioning. His ego needs are satisfied differently in each setting. In the first setting the group counselor receives his satisfaction from his demonstrated ability to analyze, direct, interpret, motivate. In the second setting he satisfies the same needs to the degree that he perceives the members becoming more adequate and open in their interpersonal relationships.

Nowhere is the current prevalence of the philosophy of authority more apparent and disheartening than in the attitudes of one graduate class of students after another who expect and are only comfortable with authoritarian one-way relationships in which they play a passive role. Students and others so conditioned must radically change before they can participate in, and benefit from, group process.

It is evident that the two world views are in opposition both ideationally and operationally. Those who favor authoritarian relationships believe that the refinement of these relationships will result in a better life for all. Although they may disagree on who should assume the authority, they unite in support of the policy of central authoritarian control. It is apparent that in times of increasing insecurity centralized control becomes more popular. In such times and with those of this persuasion the only acceptable form of group procedure is that of aggregate groups and authoritarian controls.

Those who hold the opposing view consider cooperative human relations based on the organismic concept most useful in solving problems of living among themselves and problems between their own and other societies. "They believe that the cooperative process

[6] Rugg, *op. cit.*

respects individuality, develops intelligence, and promotes creativity. They also believe that it matures personality to the point where thoughtful deliberative human action becomes the accepted pattern in interpersonal relationships." [7]

### The Group and Modern Values

Both types of personalities and groups, whether authoritarian or cooperative, are to some degree and in different ways affected by the cultural values of the society in which they exist. Although the various strands of values are complex and interwoven in their impact on individuals and groups, a few of the most important are here selected for treatment. Attention then will be focused in turn on each of the following: individual competitiveness, technical reason, "the marketplace orientation," horizontal living, pragmatic values, and communication.

INDIVIDUAL COMPETITION  The heritage bequeathed to us by Malthus, Spencer, and Darwin established individual competitiveness as a way of life and survival of the fittest as a norm. This norm was supported by Darwinism as the biological justification. The principles of Darwin were consistent with the thinking and conditions of a new country with an open frontier. But as the open frontier diminished and living became more complex in all aspects, competition came increasingly under question.

Slavson writes of competition as a "mental set." "[It] . . . is derived from the drive to mastery. It has an element of destructiveness, even hostility, and implies that all means to gain one's objectives are permissible. . . . Its goal is most often not a specific end in view, but rather an all-permeating drive. It may even be rationalized into a philosophy and principle of life. As such it is destructive of the one who is afflicted and of those who have to deal and live with him." [8]

It is difficult to choose a topic which leads to more involved discussion and mixed conclusions than that of individual competition. This reveals how this outlook has deeply permeated the tissues of

[7] C. Gratton Kemp, *Perspectives on the Group Process*, Houghton Mifflin Company, Boston, 1964, p. 5.
[8] S. R. Slavson, *Recreation and the Total Personality*, Association Press, New York, 1946, pp. 90–93.

society. Graduate students conditioned in our competitive society find it difficult to become part of a group. Attitudes and skills which have helped them to survive and attain their goals are an impediment and detriment in a cooperative society. This becomes especially apparent in their inability to listen and to follow with understanding the threads of discussion.

Perhaps this ambivalent posture can be expected in a society which does not hesitate to support democratic principles but finds it difficult to incorporate them into its practices. It is discouraging that our educational institutions have shared in the support of educational practices based on the survival of the fittest. That such is the case is apparent in the continuance in varying degrees of the following: (1) the support of a curriculum which eliminates the many and selects the academically minded few, (2) the placing of education on an individual gain basis, (3) the stress on the academic teaching of democracy which becomes vocal but does not engender action, (4) the transmission to children of those aspects of the cultural heritage which glorify the parts while neglecting those which could contribute to the unity of the whole, (5) the use of an authoritarian control system, and (6) the development in children of those qualities and relationships which are considered necessary for survival in a competitive society.

Even in elementary school a teacher who attempts to use democratic procedures especially with groups is viewed by colleagues as a threat to the status quo, and those who would like to reduce competition and conformity via cooperative planning seldom have the courage to do so, since they cannot believe that students will succeed according to their abilities without the competitive motive. This emphasis on individual academic achievement under pressure from parents has greatly increased the nervous tension of high school students and even elementary pupils. As well, it has alienated them from peer friends and from themselves. Observe the number of dropouts and those under the doctor's care.

TECHNICAL REASON   When Spinoza used the word *reason,* he meant something very different from its meaning today. In the seventeenth century the term referred to the whole person, his total attitude toward life, in which the mind united with the emotions and will, unified the person, and gave him a valuing center. Today it is critical thought in the service of a technological society. It is divorced from other aspects of the personality, feeling, imagination, and will. In 1949 Lawrence Kubie strongly criticized this trait approach in education. He emphasized the need for self-knowledge, "a self-knowledge which penetrates below the level of conscious awareness which integrates all levels in the make-up of the human being who is the forgotten man of our educational system." [9]

Will power and technical rationality were applied to the making of machines and ushered in a worldwide emphasis on, and worship of, a technological society. Man lost his valuing center and became part and parcel of the purposes of his age. He found himself molded by the demands of the economy. Life lacked the basis of symbolic and spiritual community. Often he was unable to help or be helped in the fathoming of life. Although he was still physically a part of groups, these were hollow, since communion at purposeful levels with others was almost unknown. Both primary and secondary group life became a mirage. The family became a number of individuals, each living psychically alone and for himself. The sense of responsibility became a forgotten concept. It did not belong in an age of impersonal mass cooperation.

Many individuals felt like atoms, rootless, lonely, and forced by society to be competitive. In their hunger to belong, to relate to others in some meaningful way, they became "joiners" of numerous societies and institutions, and some assumed a sudden interest in the family tree. Groups of all kinds increased in surprising numbers. In some instances they helped to make life and the job endurable. Few groups were or are able to develop meaningful interpersonal relationships.

Technical reason tries to explain the whole in terms of the part. When this principle is applied to groups, it results in placing individuals in groupings on the basis of a single factor or trait. Thus we have the *ability* grouping as recommended in the Conant report on high schools. Such other groupings carrying the labels of *opportunity* classes or *research* courses are quite common. Recently there is also the development of special courses for the "average" student. Thelen, in his studies of such groupings, found that in situations where they were advantageous the teacher modifies his teaching to "fit" the

[9] Lawrence Kubie, "The Psychiatrist Considers Curriculum Development," *Teachers College Record,* vol. 50, p. 242, January, 1949.

group.[10] That is, the teacher uses the organismic concept. He makes the changes which he perceives will make the students more comfortable and more interested. In such a situation the concept of technical reason is expanded and made sufficiently inclusive to accommodate the integrated functioning of the whole person.

THE MARKETPLACE ORIENTATION   A competitive society which idealizes technical and planning reason and is geared to mass production undermines the possibilities of the group experience. This is so because it removes the symbolic basis of community and weakens or eliminates the sense of responsibility. Persons become depersonalized and are viewed and often view themselves as objects. Even the group counselor is caught in this depersonalization. The understanding of persons is not gained only through more and more significant knowledge. It can result in merely impersonal knowledge of actions and reactions viewed within the framework of mechanistic naturalism.

Students at all age levels and workers in all trades and professions quickly perceive that there is a price upon their heads assessed by significant others in terms of their performance. This situation has been referred to by Erich Fromm as the "market-place orientation." In his reference to the skills and qualities of man, he writes: "As with any other commodity it is the market which decides the value of these human qualities, yes, even their very existence. If there is no use for the qualities a person offers, he has none, just as an unsalable commodity is valueless though it might have its use value." [11]

Since one's acceptance is dependent upon the impression he makes on others, real security is illusive, and the difficulties in the development of self-respect and a personal center are immeasurably increased. The result of experiences in this kind of psychological environment is apparent to every group leader. Self-reports invariably describe the apprehension felt by students who commence a group situation. Confronting one another as they do in the customary seating arrangement is anything but a comfortable situation for many. In fact in the case of graduate students the resulting fears and inhibi-

[10] Herbert A. Thelen, *Classroom Grouping for Teachability,* John Wiley & Sons, Inc., New York, p. 118.
[11] Erich Fromm, *Escape from Freedom,* Holt, Rinehart and Winston, Inc., New York, 1941, p. 19.

tions are overcome only with difficulty in the course of a number of sessions.

This apprehension is projected into various kinds of behavior. For some it takes some form of withdrawal; for others it takes various aggressive forms; for still others it means increased conformity. Only as each gradually moves toward the assurance that he is accepted as a person regardless of his attributes or lack of them does he begin to lay aside his defenses and begin to feel comfortable in the group environment. The group counselor who does not take into consideration this sociological conditioning is working within a framework that is narrow and may have difficulty in facilitating the most useful group environment.

It is not surprising that group counselors immersed in authoritarian marketplace relationships throughout their lives find it difficult to accept genuinely and care for the members of the group. Since through reading and lectures it has been impressed upon group counselors that they should be warm, accepting, and loving, they assume that these qualities are implemented by techniques which they use in their professional work. What they may develop unknowingly in such a circumstance is a "condescending, assumed or superficial love," [12] which permits them to simulate these qualities and still retain a "segregated heart," or status superiority, based on the position they have been accorded in the marketplace world.

The psychological impact of the marketplace orientation makes it difficult for both counselors and group members to develop a personal center. The group offers members the opportunity to help one another to gain a deep self-respect, to exercise the "inner choice." Wickes emphasizes that "all decision and choice rests primarily upon our openness to the transforming spirit." [13] Such an experience of inwardness can become a reality only as the counselor is able to help each individual to develop to some degree a personal center.

HORIZONTAL LIVING   The topic chosen and discussed by a group bears a direct relation to the depth of meaning in the lives of the members. If the members as individuals do not probe the meaning

[12] For a full explanation see Sarah Patton Boyle, *The Desegregated Heart,* William Morrow & Company, Inc., New York, 1962.
[13] Frances G. Wickes, *The Inner World of Choice,* Harper & Row, Publishers, Incorporated, New York, 1963, p. 2.

of life in their private reflections, they are unlikely to discuss them within a group. The most serious events can be discussed in a very superficial, or horizontal, manner. In fact they can be discussed only in this manner when people feel inwardly empty. Lacking meaningful communication many remain spiritually isolated and try to cover up their loneliness by talking glibly about the only things remaining for which they have a language, the superficial, horizontal concerns such as the World Series, world tours, and the latest fashions. Thus, although they are often in so-called "small" groups, their deeper emotional experiences may be alluded to but are never discussed. They thus become increasingly alienated from themselves and the sources of meaning.

So many have disregarded so much of life that they have lost the courage for, or interest in, seeing life steadily and seeing it whole. They live only with "the courage to be as a part" and wall themselves off from beauty, tragedy, love. To defend their life they may become aggressive or passive and if seriously threatened may become fanatic in attempts to maintain some security. They have decreased their ability to relate to others in any kind of openness. They are among the last in a permissive group to leave their psychological encapsulation.

Our dashing from one activity to another prevents our deep commitments. We do not permit ourselves to examine in depth the issues of life. Tillich insists that "no one can experience depth without stopping and becoming aware of himself. Only if he has moments in which he does not care about what comes next can he experience the meaning of this moment here and now, and ask himself about the meaning of life." [14]

We are not encouraged to examine life in depth. All about us, radio, TV, and magazines idealize the physical and the sensuous. Furthermore all symbols are understood as signs; love, joy, peace, and beauty are depicted as the result of satisfying the demands of the senses.

The gnawing sense of emptiness is widely accepted as the society of the times. Some endeavor to relieve it by planning for their children and the imposition of their own values. They want them to have what they believe they themselves have missed. They empha-

[14] Paul Tillich, "The Lost Dimension in Religion," in *Adventures of the Mind*, Vintage Books, Inc., New York, 1960, p. 56.

size the attainment of academic achievement, status, position, money and thus inculcate horizontal values. They believe that these ensure the good life or that whatever may be lacking will somehow result through the maturational process. There is little recognition that "interest in the meaning of life and in one's action, in relation to this meaning, must be nourished and developed by the consistent help of those who have this interest themselves and see the need to develop the courage to seek meaning and to live serenely with the results of the search." [15] The group composed of normal young people is an ideal setting for this search. But where do we discover the skilled leadership with sufficiently broad knowledge and understanding to lead them?

Such leaders may be able to extend only knowledge and understanding and not the community necessary to the search for the meaning of life. Many groups, since they develop no consciousness of community, never go beyond the utilitarian or aesthetic. Without this consciousness of community the group is frequently unable to stand the stress created by consideration of issues in depth. What is needed is a personal loyalty. But this can become possible only if the unconscious relations are brought to consciousness. "If these relations are brought to consciousness they must either be affirmed as personal relations or repudiated. In either case the situation is profoundly altered. It is no longer a question of the existence or nonexistence of cooperation but of the acceptance or refusal of community." [16]

The acceptance of community includes the acceptance of responsibility to work for one another's good. It is the relationship which makes possible the safety and encouragement to be open and genuine. It holds the possibility of examination in depth of the issues of life. As it progresses, communion becomes a reality, and love is in the wings waiting to come on stage.

It is only when the utilitarian and the aesthetic are reflected upon in order to realize the qualitative possibilities of personal relationships that we move from the horizontal to the vertical dimension in our group experience. Consciousness of relationship makes the relationship intentional. "The intention expresses itself in the effort

[15] C. Gratton Kemp, *Intangibles in Counseling,* Houghton Mifflin Company, Boston, 1967, p. 124.
[16] John MacMurray, *The Structure of Religious Experience,* Yale University Press, New Haven, Conn., 1936, p. 48.

to realize the relationship in new ways and to find new expressions for it. And these new experiences of relationship become in turn objects of reflection. In this way the meaning and significance of personal relations are gradually disclosed to reflection." [17]

The group's interest in the "here and now" is commended by many writers. However, there can be a strong interest in the "here and now" of the group's experience without intention of community. Without this intention, the "here and now" situations prevent the assimilation of emotionally laden statements and their use to help the individuals to strengthen the community making possible continuing healing and restoration.

PRAGMATISM  Much of the investigation of groups has focused upon those characteristics which make them effective and usable. The utility value is what is considered important. If the outcomes support the objectives of our study, the group is good. It is not that we try so much to understand the group per se but what the group accomplishes. Interest focuses on the causal properties, because these indicate its usefulness for attaining the purpose. The attitude toward the group is analytic and intellectual.

There is another way of considering the group. This is to know and appreciate the group, which means to know and relate to each member of the group as a person. The purpose is to enjoy, appreciate, understand, and become part of a sharing experience. Although objectives and outcomes for the group may also be considered important, equally significant is the depth of the person-to-person relationships. Interest is now focused in the intrinsicalness of the group, and the attitude toward it is contemplative and emotional.

Although the utility attitude and the intrinsic attitude are antithetical, man can and frequently does unite these two attitudes in his approach to the world of objects and to persons. In fact unless he does this in his approach to reality, he narrows his perspective and understanding. The healthy developing person and group are those in which these two attitudes are synthesized.

It could be inferred from the above that reality was waiting for us to decide what attitude we shall take concerning it. This is not altogether so, since we ourselves are part of the field of common experience. For each of us all others are data. The utilitarian attitude

[17] *Ibid.*, p. 50.

misses this perception. Mothers frequently ask, "Did you have a good time at the party?" Another question which should be asked is, "Did others have a good time at the party?" It is not just how we perceive the world but also how the world perceives us. The comprehensive attitude embodies both points of view: not only "Of what value is the group experience to us?" but also "Of what value are we in the group experience?" Early self-reports of group members contain much thought on the former, that is, their perceptions of the group, but little on the latter—of how the members may have perceived them. Such an inclusive position requires a very different attitude of mind. It is an attitude in which we realize that we are partial, temporary, and dependent. It encompasses both an appreciation of the utilitarian and the intrinsic, both what is learned through analysis and evaluation in an empirical framework and what is learned through contemplation using feeling, thought, imagination in the artistic framework.

The empirical emphasis has received much attention. The contemplative artistic emphasis has received very little attention. Thus the understanding of the group suffers from lack of depth. Its potential is rarely viewed in other than pragmatic terms. Any student of groups is grateful for this painstaking empirical approach. It has added greatly to our understanding of the dynamics of the group process and of man himself. One of these clear presentations is that of Shepherd in his writing on small groups.[18] Useful as this empirical approach may be, it must be recognized as partial and limited. It is the utilitarian approach. Groups themselves as well as industries and institutions which use them do not thrive because of their empirical accomplishments so much as they do because the true group provides the symbolic relationships through which meaning for the members evolves.

To understand the emphasis on the utilitarian aspects of the group it is necessary to accept the influence of pragmatism. Much of the present interpretation of the group may be a direct result of the application of the pragmatic principle. Peirce first enunciated the principle in America in 1878.[19] He took the position that to develop

[18] Clovis R. Shepherd, *Small Groups: Some Sociological Perspectives,* Chandler Publishing Company, San Francisco, 1964.
[19] William James, "What Pragmatism Means," in *Pragmatism and American Culture.* D. C. Heath and Company, Boston, 1950, p. 13.

the meaning of a thought we need to determine only what conduct it is qualified to produce. Utility in terms of workability became the yardstick for the measurement of ideas and beliefs.

Pragmatism is first a method and second a generic theory. It has added great impetus to scientific advancement, but it lacks a dimension which aids in the study of human relations at the level of meaning and character. When persons are considered more than objects, pragmatism lacks both method and criteria as a means toward further understanding. Within its limitations the use of the pragmatic method has contributed much to the knowledge of groups and group process. This is, however, only a part of the potential of groups for human growth. With the I-It relationship of pragmatism we must, to realize the full circle of understanding, include the I-Thou relationship of contemplative art and philosophy.

COMMUNICATION   Adeptness in the use of words does not ensure ability to communicate. Although our training in vocabulary is an important emphasis, there is a tendency to confuse an interchange of language with communication. In fact our facility with words may decrease our effectiveness in the communication of meaning.

Many have become so skilled in using words that they use them to obscure the meaning. Often when we fear that a clear, concise, forthright statement of our thoughts might encourage rejection, we try to approach the matter with superfluous adjectives and adverbs to induce vagueness. Our intention is merely to suggest our meaning, hoping to avoid verbal or nonverbal abuse.

When group discussion moves toward the examination of values and personal beliefs, certain members are inclined to withdraw, while others, more verbal and perhaps less able to tolerate the ambiguity, use an intellectual presentation with a wealth of words to avoid any examination in depth by either themselves or other members. They readily rationalize and conclude that they were the ones who were willing to examine the problem while others had nothing to contribute. Frequently they try to cloak their own threatened attitudes by criticizing with many complex phrases the system, the regulation, the leadership, the objectives, or some other target perceived as safely remote.

The group leader and members together can discuss this verbose intellectualism, examining it from all aspects. It is a common experience for members to become able and willing to speak more concisely and to the point as the group progresses and acceptance and trust becomes a reality. The decrease in verbalization for its own sake can be aided if recognized for what it is in the evaluation period.

Another deterrent to communication is our inability to be congruent. This is centered in our unwillingness to allow ourselves to know how we actually feel and to express these feelings honestly. When the speaker is knowingly or purposely incongruent, the listener, in either case, is uncertain whether or not he understands him. He wonders what the feelings of the speaker are and tends to be cautious and more closed with such a person. On the other hand, the more fully the listener understands and feels he can place trust in what he hears, the more inclined he is in turn to express himself openly to the other. Rogers sums it up in these words: "The greater the congruence of experience, awareness and communication on the part of one individual, the more the ensuing relationship will involve: a tendency toward reciprocal communication with a quality of increasing congruence." [20]

Regardless of the reason for the incongruence the speaker senses that if he truly tries to be congruent, he accepts risk of change. If he tries to know himself and express his conclusions honestly, the other members, as far as each has the ability, try to be honest and open. All perceive intuitively in advance that the situation is becoming dynamic. As the communication of meaning increases and improves, the risk of having to change one's attitudes increases proportionately.

In any group a number of the members fear change. Those who inwardly feel threatened and who live only with "the courage to be as a part" are most uncomfortable when the other members endeavor to be congruent. And these most probably need more help. The manner in which this becomes a reality varies with the theoretical position of the leader, who plays an important part in establishing and maintaining the group climate. The leader may base his hopes on the theory that if frustration of members is heightened by lack of structure, even the threatened will respond by striking out. Other leaders assume that a climate of safety and acceptance is most conducive in helping the threatened to become congruent.

[20] Carl R. Rogers, *On Becoming a Person,* The Riverside Press, Cambridge, Mass., 1961, p. 344.

Certain group leaders place little value on nonverbal communication. Others consider verbal expression and communication synonymous. Evaluation of both assumptions is necessary. For communication which deepens the lives of those engaged in trying to communicate one condition is paramount: that those communicating must perceive one another as persons. The members must hear and speak to one another as subjects. When one vents his hostility on another for the purpose of humiliating or is quite courteous and seemingly interested to hide his hostility, the other is treated as an object, a thing, and communication is impossible. Communication is built not only on genuineness but requires also that each has a sense of responsible caring in his approach to the other. "Communication becomes meaningful and effective only when carried on between people who truly care what they hear and say to others." [21] It is in this meaningful relationship that we come to know ourselves. Furthermore, in our affirmation by others our own being is affirmed. We are interdependent in the quest for the self.

The communication which helps us to know ourselves and one another has meaning which cannot be fully described by reference to what is rational, objective, and concrete. We are referring to something which is not fully known; there is a meaning conveyed beyond the rational mind; the conscious and unconscious are equally involved; there is an awareness of different levels of psychosomatic being; we are in the area of the symbolic. Whenever the members seek genuine values and authentic selfhood, and engage in a living encounter, symbols come alive and further the search, and communication becomes communion.

The experience of the symbolic is more than the result of critical thought. Karl Jaspers puts it in philosophical terms as follows: "One of man's supreme achievements is the genuine communication from person to person, when from out of their historical situation in their search for the ultimate meaning of existence, the transcendent breaks into thought, revealing to each the authenticity of his Selfhood and their common ground in the Encompassing." [22]

The most productive group discussion is not necessarily a wholly conceptual experience but remains so unless the members

[21] Earl A. Loomis, *The Self in Pilgrimage,* Harper & Brothers, New York, 1960, p. 63.
[22] Karl Jaspers, *Truth and Symbol,* Twayne Publishers, London, 1959, p. 17.

progress beyond manipulation from without toward what may be a transforming experience within.

Beginning groups hesitate to discuss anything which suggests symbolism. They are apprehensive and tend to regress to familiar ways. They prefer to remain in the land which they know, for concretes are clear, manageable, and understandable. Without the symbol which, as Martin Buber states, is a covenant "between the Absolute and the concrete," [23] we cannot reach the depth of meaning for which we yearn in our human relationships. It is not that we do not sense this, for we sprinkle the description of the group experience with an abundance of symbols, such as freedom, sense of belonging, love, sense of responsibility, and personal center. In our attempts to explain them we often treat them as signs, and in so doing we reduce them to horizontal experiences.

However, as we do this, we are conscious that the group experience is more. We are aware of a reality in the group that commands our respect and arouses our contemplative admiration. Our senses provide the clues, but our awareness "transcends this experience by embracing the vision of a reality beyond the impression of our senses, a vision which speaks for itself in guiding us to an ever deeper understanding of reality."[24] It is possible with effort to accept and be open to the insight that "there is more here than meets the eye."

Our horizontal living, our marketplace orientation, pragmatic thinking, emphasis on the tangible, and other subtle, pressing influences have caused us to evade consideration of the symbolic. In fact we have been so concerned with the ever-present sensuous needs that in the area of symbolism we are virtually on the edge of bankruptcy. Our turn toward insolvency was noted by Susanne Langer in the 1940s. She wrote: "In modern civilization there are two great threats to mental security, the new mode of living which has made the old nature symbols alien to our minds, and the new mode of working which makes activity meaningless, unacceptable to the hungry imagination. . . . All symbols are gone and thousands of average lives offer no new materials to a creative imagination." [25]

[23] Maurice S. Friedman and Martin Buber, *The Life of Dialogue,* Harper & Brothers, New York, 1960, p. 320.
[24] Michael Polanyi, *Personal Knowledge,* The University of Chicago Press, Chicago, 1958, p. 85.
[25] Susanne Langer, *Philosophy in a New Key,* Harvard University Press, Cambridge, Mass., 1942, chap. 1.

Without symbolism the group becomes an array of thinking objects who discuss ways and means and develop only the ability of greater expertness in pragmatic, horizontal values. Even communication is difficult, since the members do not and perhaps cannot completely disregard the symbolic. The only approach for some groups appears to be the use of many symbols, which are then treated as signs. Each member assumes the others understand what he means and that each symbol, now a sign, has the same meaning for everyone. In this manner we are able to ignore symbols and, if apprehension arises, to consider the difficulties only semantic.

When symbolic meanings are ignored or treated only as signs, group counseling is forced to become counseling for adjustment. Signs suffice when adjustment to the world of signs only is desired. However, without the probing use of the symbolic, existential meanings are unlikely to be found, and personality changes are unlikely to take place. It is possible to consider the what, when, and how of the present and future, using only signs, but when the search moves to the why, we find ourselves almost inevitably in the world of the symbolic.

A group discusses freedom and responsibility. They explore the regulations and codes of ethics pertaining to members in professions, law, medicine, and psychological counseling. They provide examples of situations in which much freedom was exercised by individuals within such frameworks. They recognize that individuals differ widely in their use of this existing freedom. Some know of those who complained of the little freedom they had but were not using the freedom others had found existed. Then they turn to the question of why these individuals behave differently from those who use the existent freedom. At this stage symbolic expressions are introduced. One member says that an individual must have a personal center if he is going to use the freedom in a situation. He is challenged to explain what he means by a personal center. He and the other members are plunged into trying to understand. Several responses are made, and they recognize that although the meaning cannot be completely fathomed, the discussion nevertheless has pointed to meanings that they feel are significant. At the close several remain for further discussion. One member asks, "How do you go about getting a personal center? I know I haven't one."

It may be more comfortable to rule out and disparage any reference to the symbolic in the group and the group process—comfortable because it is then possible to define and explain the group and group counseling. A goal is set up which is fairly attainable; there is no "out beyond" experience. By so doing, however, we limit drastically the usefulness of the group; it is denied its generative power. It is only a tool or a technique for the accomplishment of something. The possibilities for the growth and development of the individual exist in those very symbols spoken so glibly and unwittingly treated as signs. In relation of symbolic thought per se to the practical and ethical decisions of life lies the most significant freedom of the group experience. To reduce this to signs is to diminish the possible uniqueness of the group.

Unless the symbolic roots of the group are nourished, it will become a closed system. As a closed system it becomes another technique for the accomplishment of ways and means in a status-ridden, sensuous, and materialistic world.

SUMMARY

The concept of the group has been examined from two foci: from the empirical, analytic, utilitarian, horizontal, and sign level and from the contemplative, artistic, aesthetic, vertical, and symbolic level. It is emphasized that either focus alone leads to a partial, incomplete, and less than adequate conception of the group.

The first-mentioned focus is much the more common. This approach agrees well with our world of technical reason and empirical research. It is pragmatic in that the usefulness of the group is determined by its measured, utilitarian results. The concern is primarily learning what techniques will make the group more productive and only incidentally the effect of those methods on the members. Existential meanings are on the periphery, seldom recognized, and infrequently voiced. It is assumed that empirical research on group process can or will in time explain completely the meaning of the group.

The great scientific achievements, the pragmatic approach to all things, the emphasis on materialism, and the growing irrelevancy of religion and humanism have made any other conception of the group difficult, if not naïve. It may be that the vanity of our minds and shallowness of our understanding make it difficult to consider other possibilities.

The second focus requires a different approach for its understanding. It is not in opposition to the first but appreciates its usefulness. However, it examines the meaning of the group from a different perspective. It takes its premise from the assumption that there are dimensions of the group which cannot be fully known. It is also assumed that the more significant understandings and possibilities for meanings emerge from the depth dimension in communication. Communion is possible in interpersonal relations on the symbolic level.

One can be cooperative, analytical, and constructive in his group functioning and remain on a horizontal level. Although the self-centered member is comfortable in the world of signs, he is threatened in the world of symbols. The occurrence of symbolic thinking in the group requires such a member to be more open to his own and others' experiences than he is capable or desirous of being.

Whereas in the first focus the intention and expectation is to reduce ambiguity, in the second it is to accept and entertain ambiguity as a basic constituent of relationship. In this manner contemplation of the meaning of being, in many relationships, can be entered into as a purposeful activity of the group. To the degree that members can accept this lack of certainty and can convey to one another their attempts to understand, a new acceptance and security develop in which new insights can emerge.

Present concepts of the group run the risk, in particular settings, of becoming merely descriptions of interpersonal relations. Such descriptions consider the leader and member roles, the quality of thinking, and the productive conclusions attained. The massive impact of such influences as pragmatism, horizontal values, and impersonal relationships has moved to the periphery or dismissed any consideration of the potential of the small group in the examination of existential meanings. Such influence modifies the goal of group counseling to one of adjustment and planning rather than a confrontation of the meaning of behavior and its relation to the meaning of life.

To assume that the essence of the group can be fully known through empirical study is to miss its possibilities for meeting the deep needs of alienated and frustrated individuals which only the contemplative, artistic approach of symbolic meanings makes possible. When the possibility that all things can be fully known is relinquished, men are able against this background to profess that they are wise.

## CONCLUSIONS

The group is inherently a part of our civilization. The interpretation placed upon the group is in part a function of the interpreter's concept of the nature of man. The purpose and process are in large measure determined by what is considered significant about man's nature and functioning. Possible objectives for a group are also subject to the emphasis placed on current values. These values determine to a large degree whether the group will be concerned only with pragmatic, horizontal values or will also be open to the examination of existential meanings.

The objectives and the process are also directly related to the theories of social behavior and behavioral change. Thus, presently, democratic group functioning is in the ascendancy, and the organismic concept of behavior and intrinsic motivation are taking their place downstage. With increasing emphasis on the contributions of existentialist thought more attention is now being given to the symbolic possibilities of the group as a means of exploring significant meanings.

In the pursuance of the depth possibilities and contributions of the group the significance of trust, caring, and responsibility receives attention. Such an orientation and focus brings into sharp relief the fact that other members are perceived as objects and that we in turn are perceived as objects, and indeed frequently perceive ourselves as objects. This recognition is dismaying and confronts us with the fact that unless we are able to and do relate to one another as subjects (persons), all our words of caring, trust, and responsibility are really empty.

# 4

## CONCEPTS OF
## THE PROCESS

## INTRODUCTION

Since the forms taken by group process are on a continuum, no form
is uniquely different from another. However, despite the overlap in
objectives and function it is necessary for descriptive purposes to
attach labels and consider the commonalities and differences of
each. In this manner it is hoped that concepts of the process in its
different forms may become more meaningful.

Three broad descriptive labels have been chosen: educational
groups, group counseling, and group therapy. A description will be
given for each of these: first descriptions of the goals and process;
second, descriptions of the internal dynamics of each; and, finally,
comparisons between individual and group counseling and among
the three types of groups.

GOALS AND PROCESS

### *Educational Groups*

These groups have visualizable and specific goals. In the public school, goals (as determined cooperatively) are usually the knowledge of content, development of skills, and increased self-understanding. The last two are perceived as conducive to optimum learning experiences. At present only a minority of situations in elementary and high school exists in which true organic group functioning prevails. In higher education (since students have not experienced group functioning as herein described) the goals are similar. These, determined cooperatively, are invariably acquaintance with the literature on group process, development of skills, and increased self-understanding. In all situations critical thinking is focused maximally on ideas and minimally on emotional problems. It is oriented to the "there and then" as a means of understanding the "here and now" of the process. In educational groups there is the achievement of skills, and occasionally there is self-understanding and understanding of others.

Through recognizing and experiencing the nature of an organic group, the members deepen the permissiveness and acceptance demonstrated by the leader. Each member comes to understand and accept the fact that his membership is not dependent upon what he produces. He realizes that he is not in a competitive situation but is a member and person in his own right. The members also discover that their ideas are considered genuine expressions and significant. As they develop increasing responsibility for the process and for assisting one another, the leader moves to the periphery, and his ideas are considered and discussed as those of any other. As he loses the traditional image of director, supervisor, teacher, manager, or professor, depending on the situation, the member's feeling of adequacy develops, and participation becomes easier and more spontaneous.

Three-way interaction develops concurrently. The members learn and experience the various ways in which they can contribute to the process. They learn the necessity of listening and become increasingly able to listen on all three levels. They develop the skills of membership and leadership by involvement in each of these. They learn also to supply information, use illustrations, ask questions, clarify, reflect, synthesize, and summarize. Evaluation and goal setting are continuous. Each session is concluded with an evaluation period. Through the use of an observer and recorder insight is increased as the experience is examined by the leader, observer, recorder, and group members. This evaluation is an important and effective means in the clarification of concepts and the development of attitudes and skills necessary to the understanding of, and performance in, group process.

Group process is basic to all interpersonal relationships. It should be a required course for teachers, administrators, counselors, dietitians, medical interns, politicians, and many others. Each of these in his leadership relationships would use it and assist others to use it, and together they would improve their performance, efficiency, self-understanding, and understanding of others and develop a sense of responsibility toward others. Understanding of, and progress in, group process is enhanced to a significant degree in relation to the participants' knowledge and training in psychology, education, sociology, philosophy, and related disciplines.

### Group Counseling

The goals in group counseling are not verbalized or visualizable but are generally understood to be the satisfaction of emotional needs. Critical thinking is focused on the emotional content of interpersonal and intrapersonal relationships and frequently concentrated on the "here and now," that is, what is occurring in the group at the time.

Problem solving is only incidentally related to ideational situations. Instead it is focused on understanding of emotions and the resolving of emotional conflicts. There is occasional decision making in relation to self-understanding and understanding of others. Listening takes place on all levels and is especially significant as interpreter of the emotional state and as an aid to understanding.

There is considerable emotional involvement directly related to the satisfaction of needs. Three-way interaction prevails with emphasis put on the group-to-member and member-to-member responses. Interactions are those of clarifications, reflections, summarizations, syntheses, and nonverbal supportive gestures. Questioning is minimal and generally member-to-member.

### Group Therapy

As compared with educational groups there are no perceptible goals. The members have a greater awareness of the need to change as compared with those in other groups, and their defense mechanisms are more fixed.

Critical thinking is directly related to stages of therapy, commencing with learning by association, moving through learning by sensitivity and identification, and finally reaching learning by insight. The focus is the "here and now," but often in realtion to the "there and then."

Problem solving is only incidentally related to ideational situations and is informally and integrally correlated with understanding of emotions and the resolving of emotional conflict. There is occasional decision making focused on self-understanding and understanding of others. Listening takes place on all levels and is increasingly directed to member responses. The content is significant only as the interpreter of the emotional state and as an aid to understanding.

## INTERNAL DYNAMICS

### Educational Groups

The members experience a degree of permissiveness. This is encouraged by the nonjudgmental atmosphere and interested listening. The members are also involved in cooperative planning and the making of decisions centered on the "here and now" of group goals and process.

In the balance between emphasis on content and emotion, the pendulum swings toward content. In the educational setting involvement is chiefly with content. Much of the individual member's satisfactions are results of his participation in the problem-solving process related to subject matter.

The leader offers considerable support, which encourages the participation of individual members. The concern of the members regarding another's participation or how he feels about it is almost entirely absent, unless he creates for them a difficulty in attaining ego satisfactions. Their listening then is centered on the quality of ideas in comparison with their own and others. The listening of members improves slowly, commencing with the contagion of the leader's concentrated and nonevaluative listening to each one. The member is more interested in the leader's unexpressed evaluation than in the opinions of the other members. As he grows in the ability of listening to others, his appreciation and understanding of their ideas and his own increase.

The members are stimulated toward involvement in several ways. The lack of extrinsic evaluation impels the member continually to reexamine his process and ideas. The discussion of process regularly conducted by the leader encourages insights and helps each to set levels of aspiration.

There is stimulation also from other sources such as direct contagion, association with ideas, and sometimes identification with the emotions of others and the developing sense of responsibility, belongingness, and adequacy.

Since silence is accepted as natural and productive, when verbalization occurs, it is more meaningful. The member's attempt to make his position and ideas clear is important to each. The assumption that each will contribute as he is able to encourages relaxation of each member to feel, think, and respond as he feels he has a contribution.

Reality testing, which is an integral part of group process, occurs in several contexts. The member is testing the old and new attitudes toward education. The novel aspects implied in the discussion of permissiveness, support, and stimulation are conducive to the development of new insights into his own attitudes and help in understanding others. He tests his attitudes, behavior, responses, and ideas on the spot and transfers to life outside the classroom those which he feels are adequate.


### Group Counseling

Those who have not had the opportunity to develop the skills, interest, and some sense of responsibility for the welfare of other members and the process of group functioning in general do not as easily move into the necessary interpersonal interaction of group counseling.

There is a deep level of emotional involvement which to be therapeutically useful must be based on trust and honesty. Such involvement leads to much concentration and careful listening, not only to the content, but even more importantly to its revelation of the speaker. In such a climate the ability and readiness to share oneself with others broaden and deepen. There is a high degree of support for the expression of creative differences. Support is also available in other ways. Members are encouraged as they perceive others to be maturing. They sense a deep relatedness as they discover that others have some of the same problems and find that others listen and try to understand them and their ideas and problems.

This type of relatedness is encouraged by the degree of acceptance, trust, and sincerity first on the part of the leader and then on the part of other members. The experience of this permissiveness enhances the safety of the group situation and its unrestricted choice of what is to be discussed.

Mutual support increases the possibility of discussion of the meaningful problems of members. In such a climate ability and readiness to share oneself with others broaden and deepen. Creative differences in values, ideas, and feelings are expected, accepted, and encouraged. Emphasis is on acceptance and understanding.

As in educational groups much of the stimulation or motivation arises from interest per se in the topic being discussed. Also stimulation increases with interaction and the expression of contrasting and differing viewpoints. In the former type of group there is an integral relationship between what takes place within and outside the group. Plans are made and ideas discussed which have a direct bearing and are carried out immediately. There is another and frequent kind of stimulation in group counseling. This is the stimulation of an experimental situation. There is an opportunity and expectancy that members in group counseling will experiment with certain ideas, attitudes, and solutions with other members in the group in order to learn their degree of possibility and workability. There is then a greater degree of isolation between the group's concern and the outside world. This degree of isolation is necessary at times in order to facilitate the concentration upon, and examination of, personal emotions. In educational groups the movement is back and forth between the practice aspect, planning, decision making, evaluation, and action phase, that is, putting plans into action. But in group counseling the action phase receives more emphasis, that is, the experimentation with group members' ideas, emotions, and attitudes, and is followed by generalizations, which become active in the outside world.

Acceptance of a wide range of ideas and attitudes is anticipated. This encourages one to describe and examine his problems. Since each is free to introduce his concerns and also responsible for doing so, expressions tend to be meaningful and genuine. Such expression is encouraged by each who discusses his problem. Each recognizes that he and others are helped most as he participates in the discussion.

The sense of well-being developed within the members stimulates them to increase their attempts to understand others in the group. The acceptance of, and absence of judgment concerning, their behavior, values, or ideas encourage each to know himself and his own position concerning the issues discussed by the group. The leader's support, which is accepted as a true expression, enhances the positive forces of becoming in each individual member.

The increased feeling of each with silence and ability to profit from it together with a comfortable free give-and-take attitude adds to the warmth and spontaneous expression of members on various topics. Discussions of attitudes and emotions occur in a natural relationship to the topic of discussion and are handled with sufficient ease and clarity to contribute to the member's understanding.

Each is motivated to test reality, since he recognizes this as an important means of gaining the necessary understanding of himself and others. In his reality testing he projects his conclusions into the outside world in order to gauge acceptability. His reality testing has become more serious. This is so because in reality he is in search of who he is and of meaning rather than trying to understand the feasibility and practicality of ideas and plans.

### Group Therapy

For the sake of clarity it is necessary to differentiate the major types. At least four types may be distinguished: One is the therapeutic social club, the purpose of which is to increase the member's skill in social participation. A second is the repressive-inspirational type, such as Alcoholics Anonymous, which mainly stresses the emotional support derived from group morale as a means of combating the vicious circle of damage to self-esteem, withdrawal, and further damage to the self-esteem. A third is psychodrama, which attempts to free the member's temporarily blocked spontaneity. In the fourth type, which has been described as "interview group therapy," analytically oriented group therapy receives chief emphasis. This last type is representative of the main stream of group therapy. Therapists differ widely also in their goals and procedures. Some are interested in cohesiveness, smooth functioning, and nondirective procedures. Others hope for as much emotional stress among members as they can handle without serious disruption, and they proceed analytically. Regardless of orientation all therapists desire to free the patient's spontaneity and capacity for emotional growth that he may become more comfortable, effective, and emotionally mature. Unlike group counseling, group psychotherapy is designed to help those who suffer, from those with minor reactions to situational stress to those who have severe neurotic character disturbances and psychoses. Some patients seek help; others are referred by counselors, medical practitioners, or psychiatrists.

Since they enter a situation for which they have only minimal preparation and less skill, they at first proceed to explore the situation as they endeavor to present themselves as they desire the doctor and group members to perceive them. During these sessions there are frequent inquiries as to procedure and attempts to appraise each other. As in other groups, and even more frequently, they escape into generalities and irrelevancies.

In other respects the members are more strongly motivated than those in other groups. They desire to get well. They also differ greatly from other groups in that many suffer from internalized controls in the form of guilt feelings and fears of criticism from others. Permissiveness is essential, and the therapist considers it an integral part of the therapy. His own attitude and the safety of the group lend certain belief to individual members.

The therapist also is supportive. The support differs from much of the support in other groups, since it is selective. The therapist is giving selective support to reinforce certain attitudes and behaviors. He uses it especially to reduce the annihilating loss of self-confidence suffered by many patients. Other forms of support are similar to those in other groups. The climate is nonevaluative. Each is helped to feel himself a member of the group. He shares the goals and believes that the group experience will help him to get well. Much support comes, as in other groups, through the concentrated understanding of the therapist. The member develops a sense of belonging through his recognition that his feelings and problems are shared by others.

Much of the motivation and stimulation comes from the individual member's desire to recover. Other forms of stimulation arise from antagonisms resulting from conflicting values, from rivalry for the therapist's attention, from association with the problems of others, from the perceived progress another member is making, and from the direct contagion of the situation.

The members are aware that the verbal expression of their problems clarifies and enhances the possibilities for recovery. There is an implicit understanding that emotions are to be examined in relation to the "here and now." Verbalizing becomes more common in the attempt to make ideas and emotions clear to other members and the therapist. The fact that the member is listened to with respect and understanding without judgment encourages verbalization.

Reality testing is a necessary and important aspect of therapy. In the group a member evaluates his ideas and performance by the acceptance they receive from the group. This helps each member to understand the other members and himself. Acting out, followed by the examination of his ideas and emotions assisted by the therapist, is an important means of realistically appraising himself. The relative directness and forthrightness of members' reactions helps each one to see how his behavior is perceived by others. He vicariously projects his new concepts into relationships in the outside world and assesses how these may be acceptable in the world.

Reality testing in group counseling and group therapy serves similar functions. In group therapy, however, the individual, being in greater need of the security of the group world in carrying through, finds reality testing more difficult and achieves it only gradually.


COMPARISONS

### Individual and Group Counseling

There are certain conditions favorable to therapeutic change which are unique or at least enhanced in the group. The permissive and accepting group climate, planfully encouraged by the counselor together with the motivation accruing from the group interaction, has especially beneficial results. Many resistances disappear, thus facilitating the verbalization of anxiety, guilt, and intrapersonal and interpersonal conflicts. Some of these find direct expression in the group, and others find acceptable outlets through sublimation. As well, the member's concept of himself is enhanced through the sense of belonging, support, and protection. Painful feelings of inadequacy, stigma, and isolation are relieved through the recognition that others have similar problems and they are all experiencing the same things.

The real-life situation inherent in the compresence of a number of others like oneself, each with his needs and behavior patterns, supplies many opportunities for acting out one's own attitudes and activities as part of the group experience. This increases the individual's awareness of his own functioning, while the reactions of the members and/or counselor promote insight into one's own motivations.

It may thus be concluded that group counseling has inherent potentialities for therapeutic change which are not included in individual counseling. Among these are (1) a community in which the person may test his evolving attitudes and ideas; (2) the motivation which results from the acceptance of peers and the experiencing of his changing attitudes; (3) the skills of communication with others, which improve his possibilities of developing genuine interpersonal relationships; (4) the encouragement which follows from the participation of others in trying to resolve their conflicts; (5) the acceptance and understanding of peers, with the resulting sense of safety and belonging, which support the process of introspection and expression of feeling in depth.

Group counseling progresses to the real situation through reality testing in the group, whereas individual counseling awaits the opportunity for practice which may not take place in the outside world. The group experience encourages a sense of equality, commonality, and responsibility. Overemphasis on the individual denies an important facet of human behavior: that the group is both a supporting and an impelling force. It can also provide what Buber describes as the opportunity to exist as a genuine "We." The counselor's emphasis on individual counseling may deny this growth of the person. The potential to become a real person is only fulfilled in relationship with other persons.

It is unwise, however, to conclude that group counseling should replace individual counseling. Variables little known and intangibles which are always present in interpersonal relationships and individual decision making suggest that one may be effective in some situations and the other more effective in other situations. Both are necessary, and each is significant in its own right. They are of course not in competition, and neither should be considered an adjunct of the other.

### Educational Groups and Group Counseling

The generic development in educational groups is similar to that in group counseling. For example each requires keen observation, verbal and nonverbal interaction, listening, and concentrated thought. Successful outcomes in either are to a major degree dependent upon the development of these skills and as well upon certain attitudes and values such as a sense of belonging, an interest in others, and a sense of responsibility to the group as a whole and to each member in particular. To the degree that concerns involve much emotion and contrasting values the skills of listening, group maintenance, and group task functions become increasingly important. As in the drama, the more feeling and interaction in depth are required of the actors, the more their skills of communication must become automatic, requiring little directed attention. Members who have not yet become psychologically comfortable in the group and who have not developed the ability to listen, assimilate, clarify, and reflect upon many points of view as they are expressed, to differentiate among them, and to integrate them are to an important degree unable to contribute to, or benefit from, group counseling.

Although a greater degree of self-insight and reorganization of personality may be expected in group counseling, this does not necessarily occur. A student writes in an anonymous self-report, "I never realized before just how hard I tried to please those in authority. I need to become more self-critical, to become more creative. In this way I will be better able to help others learn more of themselves." This was following a content-oriented discussion in an educational group. But it could be just as applicable following a session in group counseling.

## Group Counseling and Group Therapy

Group therapy incorporates group counseling, but, it also may include further stages. The overlap is to be expected, since regardless of the purpose of the group the persons enter with the same fears, uncertainties, and habitual sensitivities to strangers and strange situations. Unless of course they have had previous experience of some duration in "true groups." They proceed through the same initial stage in which communication is dominated by primitive ego functioning. The tasks in each group, as well, are similar. They are the resolution of dependency, ambivalent in nature and focused on the counselor or therapist. Also there is the crystallization and movement from identifications into more genuine relationships among members, in which each is perceived as a person. This promotes a corresponding individuation of the member as a whole.

In both kinds of groups communications flow freely among members with such accompanying overtones as a deepened respect, awareness, and sense of responsibility to one another and the process. Frequently both group counseling and group therapy will conclude in this stage. This experience is generally highly satisfactory, especially with heterogeneous groups with mixed syndromes and inability to love in a mature manner.

But for those groups where individuals have organized their lives on neurotic bases, a further stage, which evolves from the first, is necessary. At this juncture group counseling has moved into the stage generally referred to for purposes of description as *group therapy*. Success in this later stage requires to even a greater degree the group-centeredness of the well-integrated group. Since intelligence, communicativeness, and insightfulness become increasingly necessary, a low degree of these qualities in members presents some limitations. Also the characteristics and ability of the therapist play an increasingly significant role. It is almost disastrous if as a result of countertransference the therapist cultivates submissiveness and compliance on the part of the members. He must be a person who receives his ego satisfactions from the perceived improved functioning of the members. Again, it is now even more important that his reflections and comments be directed to the group as a whole, as though it functioned as a unit.

There is a transition finally and gradually into another stage in group therapy. The interdependence of all the members of the group undergoes revolution. Each of the members becomes a person in his own right. This reindividuation of the members enables each one to leave the group as a separate individual without neurotic needs.

Not all therapists, of course, conceive of group therapy only as an extension of group counseling. Some view group therapy as different in kind as well as in degree. They agree that what takes place in group counseling is therapeutic but do not consider this therapy. Durkin describes the position of many analytic group therapists when she writes, "Only reconstructive psychotherapy which resolves pathogenic conflicts and brings about basic character changes qualifies as psychotherapy." [1]

However, even analytic group psychotherapists consider that there are many principles basic to the several goals in group process. Such basic principles have been formulated after much study. As early as 1937 Lewin indicated the compatibility of field theory basic to group dynamics and psychoanalytic theory. The same year Brown systematically elaborated principles common to these two theories (see Chapter 2, under Conclusions).

Analytic group therapists have not been interested in group psychology, not even in Freud's presentation of it, but instead have devoted themselves to the application of psychoanalytic techniques to groups of patients. Slavson, though in a position to further convergence, since he kept abreast of developments in both fields, was so much concerned with therapeutic techniques, especially with those who should use them, that he drew a sharp line of distinction between the two disciplines. As late as 1960 Scheidlinger found the two fields of group dynamics and Freudian group psychology distinct but complementary. He described the first (group dynamics) as interested in the group, the other (Freudian group psychology) as interested in the individual; the first in the present, the second in the past; the first in the overt, and the second in the latent phenomena.[2] As Durkin has pointed out (see Chaper 2, under Conclusions), these differences are now merely a matter of emphasis.

[1] Helen E. Durkin, *The Group in Depth,* International Universities Press, Inc., New York, 1964, p. 98.
[2] S. Scheidlinger, "Group Process in Group Psychotherapy," parts I and II, *American Journal of Psychotherapy,* vol. 14, pp. 104–120, 346–363, 1960.

## CONCLUSIONS

There are significant commonalities among all forms of group process. All groups depend heavily on the quality of listening of members
and leader. All groups require information giving. It is perceived,
according to the purpose of the group, as a means or, to a greater
degree, as an end. Regardless of the purpose, group process depends upon clarification, reflection, questioning, linking, and synthesis to give it meaning and a forward movement. To function fully
as a group, all groups require a three-way interaction process.

Equally important are the differences among groups. These
dissimilarities are a function of the diversified purposes of each
group. Because of these varying purposes the emphasis in each
group differs significantly from that in each of the others. The
explicit and implicit purposes for which the members assemble to
become a group influence the manner in which they endeavor to
proceed.

Regardless of the purpose of the group it cannot immediately
become a therapy group or an educational group. It will move toward
its goal in relation to the experiences, skills, insights, and openness
of the members. The process is dynamic and therefore always in a
state of becoming. This process of becoming varies with groups.
Different groups do not become adequate in their development of
process skills at the same rate. Intelligent evaluation of the process
is assumed to accelerate the becoming through the effective use of
skills.

The vitality of the process is dependent upon the interest of
the members in terms of their willingness to be involved, their sense
of responsibility toward each other and toward the progress of the
group as a whole, together with their perception of their personal
need satisfaction.

Reality testing is recognized as an important aspect of all
groups. In individual counseling and educational groups reality testing is carried out chiefly outside the relationship. In group counseling
and group therapy it operates chiefly within the group. In all situations reality testing is the nexus of the change process.

In all groups involvement is considered necessary to their dynamic functioning. All leaders depend on certain common conditions
to enhance the involvement of the members. Such conditions are

acceptance, permissiveness, and respect for each member as a person. The theories upon which they operate to develop these conditions vary widely. The meaning attached to these labels describing the condition may also vary in its connotation from leader to leader.

One very hopeful sign of progress is the respect each leader has for other leaders whose assumptions and methods may differ from his own. Various emphases are recognized as necessary to accomplish different purposes. The significance of the group is a function of how well the purposes of the group are attained.

# 3

## CONTRASTS IN
## THEORY AND PROCESS

*Any analysis of group processes at this stage in their development may be subject to radical change with the passing of time. Nevertheless analysis is necessary to clarify the present situation if progress is to proceed intelligently. For the most part the authors of the various processes are ready to emphasize the tentativeness of both underlying principles and the processes themselves. Each author views his particular theory as making a significant contribution in the field of learning interpreted as psychological becoming. This continues although great variance exists among them regarding the very aspects of what they themselves consider to be crucial determinants. However, it is encouraging to note also the similarity with reference to what each protagonist considers crucial.*

Most elusive in the varying treatments of process is the basis for the procedures described. Although all recognize that some psychological theory of personality and behavioral change underlies the process, there is apparently much less interest in and concern with the psychological and other foundations on which the process rests than with the process itself.

Implicit in, and sometimes made explicit, is the recognition that the final interpretation and working out of the theory become an individual matter. The process is unlikely to be more permissive or structured than is comfortable for the leader. The leader is most authentic and helpful to the group when he is genuine. Other things being equal, a dominant person is a dominant leader, and an accepting, trusting person is an accepting, trusting leader. Rogers sums it up in this manner: "If he behaves in some way that is not natural for him, simply because he feels that he should do so, this is quickly sensed by the group and damages the group atmosphere." [1]

The most influential types of groups, especially from the viewpoint of educators and counselors, are the authoritarian group; democratic group; group-centered group; national training laboratory group, or T group; and basic encounter group. These several types of groups represent the various current viewpoints on educational and group-counseling possibilities. Each may conduct marathon (continuous process over an extended period of time) and sensitivity training. Although assisting members to be sensitive is one of the implicit goals of all processes, the nature of the training varies with the nature of the group.

For purposes of discussion the various types of groups are organized under the headings of Single-theory Approaches and Multiple-theory Approaches. Those discussed under the first heading are authoritarian, democratic, and group-centered groups, and under the second heading T groups and basic encounter groups. The first three are assumed to be primarily based on one theory of learning and a method consistent with its assumptions. The two in the second group are based on more than one theory of learning and several methods necessary in the implementation of the various theories. All groups have some theoretical input or content, and each to a varying degree is therapeutic. Some, therefore, are considered to be prima-

[1] Carl R. Rogers, *Client-centered Therapy*, Houghton Mifflin Company, Boston, 1951, p. 401.

*rily educational because of the emphasis on learning content; others, primarily therapeutic because of the emphasis on self-understanding of others and resolving of conflicts. During a single session any type of group may move back and forth along the continuum between education and therapy. However, a survey of the total session reveals a decided emphasis toward one end of the continuum rather than the other.*

# 5

# ANALYSIS OF GROUP PROCESS: SINGLE-THEORY APPROACHES

## AUTHORITARIAN

Among the groups with single-theory approaches the authoritarian has the longest tradition and is the most common. Authoritarian leadership and authoritarian groups have characterized much of the teaching and counseling effort.

### Purposes and Goals

Aggregate or authoritarian groups are organized as educational groups to secure ideas and make decisions. As therapy groups the purposes range from preventive mental hygiene to significant personality and behavioral change. Authoritarian methodology is widely used in many settings in the training of teachers, counselors, and employees.

### Process

A status leader appointed from without the group assumes responsibility for leadership of the members. He plans the content and decides the methods and times of presentation and the rewards or punishments to be used. He presents in lecture form or by other media—maps, charts, films, tapes, etc.—the content which he believes the learner should know. Through discussion he plans to lead the members to his predetermined conclusions. He tries to improve the experience of others by giving them increasing quantities of information taken from books and other sources on an ascending scale of academic or psychological difficulty. He may confuse quantity of secondhand information with quality of behavior.

### Leadership

The authoritarian leader plans for the group by setting forth its purposes and objectives and the methods to be used in attaining them through lectures, explanations, and directions. He directs the group through evaluative comments, interpretations, and suggestions, and by interventions in the process. Through ongoing and terminal rewards and mild punishment he hopes to assure the direction of the group and the outcomes. By such procedures the leader centers control in himself. He assumes that his knowledge and decisions are superior to those of the group and perceives that his function is one of directing the group members toward the fixed goals. He expects a high degree of conformity, since he assumes that the group is inexperienced, untrained, and unintelligent about, or even incapable of, dealing with the problem. A good authoritarian leader is forceful, energetic, a good organizer and planner, firm, kind, and successful in securing the cooperation of the members.

### Membership

Members react in various ways according to their past experiences and their openness to new experiences. Some welcome the security which the structure encourages. They are apparently willing to cooperate and relinquish their right to make decisions regarding their involvement in exchange for the rewards offered for good behavior. They also relinquish to the leader their responsibility for the success of the enterprise. They may take a cooperative stance or react with passivity, conformity, withdrawal, or "apple polishing." Others who are more secure and more open recognize that they are sacrificing their right to share in the making of decisions and as a consequence may become restrictive in their response or sabotage the plans, suggestions, or requirements set forth by the leader. A few unable to control their aggressive feelings may project them toward other members, toward the leader, or toward the prescribed conditions. Counterhostility may result or cliques form which undermine the leader's authority. The members are unlikely to develop much sense of responsibility or caring for one another. Each member is an object to the others, a means of making it possible to satisfy his own needs. The lack of trust in one another is not helpful to the development of a psychological climate conducive to mental health.

### Forms of Expression

The authoritarian process takes many forms of expression and claims, as it should, its fair share of usefulness in the helping relationship. It receives a high preference in classrooms at all levels of education. It is also used extensively in all forms of industry, government, and community living. It is unfortunate that many who use it hesitate to name it correctly. They apparently prefer to view their leadership as democratic. The pseudodemocracy which results is unjust to both authoritarianism and democracy. An example of what too frequently takes place in industry is given by French, Kornhauser, and Marrow. Describing this dilemma they write: "Under these circumstances, democratic cooperation is at best a euphemism, and at worst a deceptive make-believe process. Sometimes management is deliberately using the attractive symbols of democracy, participation, man-to-man discussion, group decision, etc., to create the desired atmosphere within which it can smoothly manipulate the attitudes of its employees, retain their loyalty, and still run the business 'as it should be run' without irritating interferences from below." [1]

[1] J. R. P. French, Jr., A. Kornhauser, and A. Marrow (eds.), "Conflict and Cooperation in Industry," *The Journal of Social Issues,* vol. 11, pp. 44–45, 1946.

Another expression of the authoritarian process is seen in analytic group therapy. In this process the members come to an expert authority for personal help requiring the examination of unconscious motivations. The therapy group is not expected to develop or have a goal of its own, at least not until much therapeutic work has been done. Any group decision is an assent to the requirements, suggestions, or directions of the therapist, in whom they have placed their confidence. The members have surrendered to him the right to make decisions, especially those concerned with process. Competition among members is encouraged in order to activate conflict, since it is deemed essential that members freely express their socially unacceptable feelings. Neurotic transferences are analyzed by the therapist, and group cohesiveness is not encouraged, since it may prevent members from venturing to develop more realistic and satisfying relationships outside the group.

Still another expression of the same process is that of its use by behavioral science. This process views counseling as strictly a process using the association theory of learning. Krumboltz [2] outlines four general approaches applicable to counseling: (1) operant conditioning; (2) imitative learning; (3) cognitive learning; and (4) emotional learning. The process relies on some form of reinforcement, such as verbal reinforcement, the use of such models as tapes, video-taped television presentations, and anxieties and fears as illustrated in the work of Wolpe [3] and Lazarus.[4] Krumboltz places importance on the client's deciding his goal. This, however, becomes exceedingly difficult if a goal for him is already in the thinking and reinforcements of the counselor. In a group situation, a heavy responsibility rests with the counselor to know the timing and each individual sufficiently well to perceive those responses and behaviors which need reinforcement. One of the main emphases of the approach is the use of specific techniques to accomplish specific goals. On the other hand, who decides what is best for the counselee who does not realize he needs counseling, or who does not have any goals, or whose goals

[2] John D. Krumboltz, *Revolution in Counseling,* Houghton Mifflin Company, Boston, 1966, pp. 13–20.
[3] J. Wolpe, *Psychotherapy for Reciprocal Inhibition,* Stanford University Press, Stanford, Calif., 1958.
[4] L. A. Lazarus, "Group Therapy of Phobic Disorders by Systematic Desensitization," *Journal of Abnormal and Social Psychology,* vol. 63, pp. 504–510, 1961.

are destructive? In such situations, and there are many, would it not become the responsibility of the counselor? The counselor, then, primarily plans *for* rather than *with* the counselee.

Regardless of the method of conditioning the focus in the group process is on the leader. Improvement in the group members is a function of his insights and skills. He develops a climate of permissiveness and acceptance and expresses an interest in each member. Those who favor the Dollard and Miller assumptions over those of Wolpe and Salter endeavor to reduce fear and anxiety through the development of this climate. They assume that when an antisocial or other remark is made by a member and accepted by the therapist, the process of extinction is set in action.[5] Those who follow Dollard and Miller in their thinking hope through their various methods of reinforcement to remove symptoms, which they conclude is the means of curing the neurosis. Those who use verbal reinforcement of positive cues place emphasis on labeling, discrimination, and generalization. Therapists vary greatly in the emphasis placed on discrimination as compared with automatic conditioning. The emphasis on a verbal-rational approach focuses attention on the intellectual to the neglect of the affective elements. Dollard and Miller of course recognize the inadequacy of an overemphasis on the intellectual and state that they "are not advocating any mere intellectualization of the therapeutic process." [6]

The group members following the lead of the therapist are inclined to reinforce what they consciously or unconsciously perceive is desired by the therapist. They become aware of what receives a verbal reward from the therapist and may to some degree inhibit what they feel he may not wish to hear. To the extent that this takes place, it may be questioned whether or not extinction of regressive thinking and behavior actually takes place or whether the whole may assume the aspects of play acting. Since each member comes to desire approval from the therapist, he becomes less aware of what each other member is contributing and does not give or receive the help which otherwise may have been possible.

One of the chief strengths of reinforcement counseling is its focus on specifics. The practice of dealing with what the counselee

[5] J. Dollard and N. E. Miller, *Personality and Psychotherapy,* McGraw-Hill Book Company, New York, 1950, p. 307.
[6] *Ibid.,* p. 303.

perceives as his difficulty, even though it is symptomatic of a deeper problem, should not be passed over lightly. One of its chief limitations follows from the inherent weakness of the reinforcement theory itself. Whatever adequacy it may have is limited to those problems which yield to anxiety-reducing and drive-reducing procedures.

### Theoretical Bases

Authoritarian leadership is based upon association theories of learning. Attention is focused upon the relation between persons and things. The associationist takes an external objective approach to behavior. The action of the group member is perceived as a function of the externally controlled stimulus. The center of the field of new experience is outside the member and within those things in the environment which can be measured. Change in behavior is the result of learning the connections and interrelationships which exist in conditions outside the learner. These he learns from authority figures, teachers, counselors, and employers. Movement, then, in the field of the individual or group is directed by ideas, meanings, and values inserted into the psychological field by authorities at the outset to control behavior. The locus of evaluation resides in the authority figure, and the individual group member uses psychic energy in trying to discern and move in a praiseworthy direction.

Each member has discreteness but lacks uniqueness. He is expected to be motivated by the leader. Conformity is valued. Variability in any degree is unwelcome. The member feels adequate and worthy only if the leader indicates that he perceives him as such. He tends to relinquish his personal capacity to evaluate and reflect and may gradually become unable to exercise this potential without great difficulty.

### Considerations

Certain considerations are inherent in this approach: (1) The members may not become sufficiently involved to receive more than minimal benefit. (2) The members may not be able to develop the independence and initiative necessary to cope with situations within and without the group. (3) The degree of permissiveness possible in this structure may not accomplish the purpose hoped for by the leader.

The leader's reasonable success could have the following results: (1) The members have more information upon which to base decisions. (2) Members may make phenotypical changes in return for the positive reinforcement from the leaders. (3) Members may also introject suggestions and ideas of the leader and later carefully consider them, deciding to develop new directions. (4) Members may become more dependent upon an authority and less interested in developing ability to solve their problems independently.

The leader assumes that the group members are capable of, and interested in, quality interaction. He helps them clarify their interests and goals and select a topic or problem of mutual concern.

## DEMOCRATIC

### Purposes and Goals

Democratic group functioning is focused on the growth of the whole person. Its purpose is the development of the potentiality of the individual to work on his own needs. It does so by helping each member to locate, understand, conceptualize, and direct his energy intelligently. It assumes that the origin and control of his behavior is within, despite the fact that he is affected by external conditions. A further purpose is to help each member to respect his recognition of needs and his ability to work toward their satisfaction. Also the leader hopes that the abilities of the members to learn from one another through listening and interaction will improve. The goal is to assist each member in attaining better understanding of himself, other members, and the process in which he is involved. It is hoped also that he will become more mature and responsible in his relationships and more able to use the environment to work toward a socially constructive outcome.

### Process

The process is open and developmental. The teacher or counselor removes or opens the closed ends common to aggregate or authoritarian groups. Leader and members handle their experiences cooperatively. They explore together the area of concern in order to locate the foci of interests, decide the direction and plan of work, and determine how they will perform responsibly. The leader as a member of the group has the same rights and privileges as others. He does not abdicate nor does he assert himself but makes the quality of his experience available. They accept him as they do one another for his intrinsic contribution to their mutuality.

If it is primarily an educational group, the leader entertains a broad perspective and meaning of the subject matter. Cooperative planning may result in a different approach or a change in the content. The leader is psychologically adjusted to this possibility, since he believes in the capacities of the members and has respect for their judgment.

The leader assists them in the fulfillment of their area of need. His acceptance aids them in their evaluation and selection of those learnings which they consider are sufficiently valuable to keep. He helps each to make his best selections, but he does not use his influence to direct.

The leader should find the quality of his efforts reflected in the better need fulfillment, the higher operational unity, and the more adequate interpersonal behavior of each member. Ideas are considered most valuable when they help to contribute to such outcomes.

Evaluation of the process in each discussion is considered a necessary and integral part in the development of the group. This is usually performed through the remarks of the observer, the comments of the member who is the leader of the discussion, and the cooperative discussion of all. The process is examined at various levels. The actions and reactions of members which help the group in its progress are clarified, and possibilities for improvement are considered. This is a cooperative analysis and resetting of goals in which the teacher or counselor participates with the group members.

### Leadership

The democratic leader engages in cooperative planning in accordance with the freedom within the situation, his own security and experience, and those of the group. Since the experiences of many would-be democratic leaders have been in authoritarian climates, the aspiring leader wisely begins by recognizing the influence of these conditioning experiences and accepting the fact that he is an authoritarian in an authoritarian culture. He should also recognize that since the culture is oriented toward a marketplace-orientation competitive way of life, democratic procedures may seem unrealistic and almost invariably will be met with opposition. Like the authoritarian leader, he assumes that the group members are capable of, and interested in, quality interaction, and he helps them clarify their interests and goals and select a topic or problem of mutual concern. He strives to develop and respect their evaluative abilities. The controls and direction are those cooperatively developed and accepted. Together they visualize alternatives, project themselves into ensuing situations, and make decisions.

Unlike the authoritarian leader his need satisfaction is not derived from his controlling, directing, informing, analyzing, or making suggestions but from indications of improvement of thought and behavior in the members. He encourages this improvement through listening, questioning, and reacting, and by reflection, clarification, and synthesis. In this manner he helps the members to do situational thinking, assuming that free, thoughtful reflection and interaction produce better insights and decisions.

Permissiveness and acceptance when used by the democratic leader have a broader framework than when used by the authoritarian leader. Within the democratic framework the members have the opportunity to make many and more important decisions. In fact they may make all decisions for which they can demonstrate responsibility. However, the framework is established by the leader and varies with his ability both to extend freedom to the members and the "unfixed ends" in the particular situation.

Those who accept the view of democratic cooperative planning consider good leaders to be those who facilitate an environment in which a sense of responsibility toward, and caring for, one another is nurtured. He encourages freedom of expression, respects each individual as a person, and concentrates upon trying to understand the individual and the meaning of his verbal expression. He is a resource person and through the extension of leadership and planning to the members of the group contributes to their develop-ment.

### Membership

The members discuss freely with one another the topic under consideration. Each is considered to have a contribution to make and is encouraged by the absence of evaluative comments from either members or status leader. The members become willing to consider the points of view of others and to alter or modify their own thinking accordingly. They increase in their understanding of, and willingness to arrive at, conclusions through a consensus. Also they are encouraged by the leader and the group atmosphere to expect and facilitate creative differences of expression. The status leader gradually is accepted as a member, a different one but similar to themselves in that they agree or disagree with him as their critical thinking suggests. The discussion is led by one of their members who has volunteered in advance in relation to the time and topic. All feel some responsibility to bring ideas to the discussion and to increase their ability to do so. The status leader of course also brings ideas, but these are presented, as are others, only in relation to the particular facet of the topic currently under consideration. All learn to express more, using fewer words as they become aware of the importance of sharing time as a part of the helping relationship. The interaction is three-way, members to one another, members to leader, and leader to members.

### Forms of Expression

The democratic group process is used in classrooms, industry, recreation, business, churches, schools, and clinics. Great variation exists in the degree of cooperative planning and decision making which is encouraged. When leaders become threatened and insecure regarding the process or perceived outcomes, they are inclined to move toward the authoritarian end of the continuum. Much becoming is necessary before an authoritarian leader becomes democratic. Confusion exists in that democratic functioning is sometimes perceived to result entirely from the development of skills rather than also through becoming a democratic person.

The assumption that groups have proceeded democratically when actually they are a hybrid of authoritarian and democratic has militated against the exploration of what truly democratic groups can accomplish.

### Theoretical Basis

Democratic process is based on the field theory of learning. Since the field is composed of persons and objects, there are three possible relationships—objects to objects, persons to objects, and persons to persons. Whereas in authoritarian groups the emphasis is on the relationship between persons and objects (ideas, plans), in the democratic group the emphasis is upon relations between persons. In accord with field theory as generally conceived the democratic leader takes an integral-self approach to behavior. He considers the member's behavior as a function of his individual perception or meaning of a situation at the time of response.

Each member is the center of his own field. Through free and open interaction each may understand others better; experiences are clarified and individual organizations are improved. The unit of learning, then, is primarily the member facing his own situation, growing out of his needs as he perceives them. His progress is assisted by the emerging intelligence of the members operating as an organic group in areas of their need. The psychosocial process of interaction is the most important single factor in the determination of the member's possibilities of becoming.

It is accepted that no one has immutable perceptions, meanings, or values which are superior in quality to those of another member. Feelings, thoughts, and responses of each are data for intelligent consideration. Through interaction dynamic energy is used in a fluid wholeness toward each member evaluating his own major process experiences. Through interpersonal relations in the group each member creates new meanings necessary to the reconstructive development of his field. As he progresses, he increases the quality of his differentiations.

As a result of interaction of group members open to change, the field is a fluid whole always emerging or becoming. Improvement in each member is the outcome of qualitative interaction.

It is evident, then, that the democratic leader believes in wholism, the theory that all behavior emerges from the dynamics of the whole at all times in its development. It is assumed that the members continue their differentiative development while maturing their integrative unity.

### Considerations

Certain considerations also attend democratic functioning. The leader moving away from his authoritarian conditioning, as he must do, may experience difficulty in the following: (1) the recognition of "unfixed ends" and utilization of them for growth purposes; (2) believing that group members are capable of, and interested in, critical thinking concerning their problems; (3) developing the members' abilities to evaluate and accepting their conclusions; (4) encouraging member interaction, essential to cooperative planning; (5) developing situational thinking as a prerequisite to democratic planning; (6) assisting members to change their stereotypic concept of the leader's role.

## GROUP–CENTERED

### Purposes and Goals

In the group-centered process the emphasis is on (1) the release of the group's potential capacities and (2) the development of the members' independence and self-responsibility. These purposes move forward through the leader's assistance to the group in working out its own adjustment and in assuming responsibility for outcomes.

The goals determined by the members vary from group to group. For success the goals of the group generally require the following conditions: (1) an increase in participation, (2) a decrease in barriers to free communication within and among the members, (3) a nonthreatening climate and genuine acceptance. The leader in part facilitates the development of these conditions through his genuine caring and belief in the capacities and values of the members.

Group-centered groups accomplish the following objectives

reasonably well: (1) skill in critical thinking, (2) ability in cooperation, (3) a degree of sensitivity to the feelings and needs of others, (4) self-reliance and responsibility to oneself and others, (5) understanding of self and of the group-centered process.

### *Process*

Group-centered process holds new experiences for the members. Each learns what it means to give and receive emotional support and understanding in a special way. For many, distortions of self-perception have taken place in a group, but here in the context of a very different group the self is redefined.

Each of the members experiences a climate in which he can redevelop his own value system with a minimal imposition of the value system of the leader. The leader is in fact careful to support this primary right of each to determine his own way of life. Another important aspect of the process is that the member is not only a giver of help but a receiver as well. He has the opportunity for achieving a balance between self-independence and realistic dependence and at times a responsibility toward others.

The leader initiates the members into a permissive, accepting situation in which they assume direction for the goals and process. He does this not by giving direction or presenting plans but by indicating that the group can develop and follow its own leads. Some groups are able to get started almost immediately, but most groups have considerable difficulty.

The process moves through *themes*, which is the name given to a topic and point of focus in discussion which has a clear beginning and a clear stopping. There may be one or several themes in any session. Some themes are of short duration; others reappear in session after session, recurring with added and deeper meaning. A theme which was dropped may be reinstated and elaborated. The general movement in themes is toward greater detail and deeper emotional response.

The process is somewhat predictable. It consists of both positive and negative elements. Elements considered positive are those which show positive attitudes toward self and others, and positive insights and planning. Within each session and within the whole experience positive attitudes increase, reaching their highest points at the end of individual sessions and in the final sessions. Negative elements have a different pattern.

Negative elements are expressed in the form of nonparticipation, defensive remarks, and negative attitudes toward self and others. Within each session some of these elements are present, generally more at the commencement of the session than toward the end. These negative elements increase gradually until they reach a climax, after which they consistently decrease. In the last sessions negative elements have become quite minimal.

As might be expected, there are always problems to be considered. In fact there are apparently many problems remaining at the close. This of course may be an indication of its closeness and resemblance to daily living. The group experience differs from individual therapy, since it blends into life itself more easily and naturally.

Even with leaders who have become group-centered persons in belief and action, all members benefit in varying degrees and some much more than others. In general those who benefit most are apparently more able to focus on their own and others' problems of living and more interested in doing so, and become more involved and responsible in helping the other members in their understanding of them. Those who benefit least focus more on intellectual problems and are more prodding in their interaction with other members. They avoid focusing on their own perceptions and feelings.

An important aspect of the process often escapes notice: the possibility of releasing the therapeutic potential of the group itself. As the number of sessions increases, some members develop the ability to facilitate, and do so both verbally and nonverbally, the conditions which help others to gain insight and to feel supported in their efforts toward gaining self-understanding and understanding of others.

### Leadership

Group-centered leadership is difficult to attain. This is to a large degree because the leader must be able to believe in the capacity of the group members to select, plan, progress, and evaluate outcomes. Most difficult to believe and act upon are the following: (1)

that the group members are able to and will evaluate, (2) that their evaluations will further the progress of the group, (3) that in so doing they will increase their intelligence regarding interpersonal relationships.

The leader listens to understand the meaning of each member's contribution. His interest in each member is conveyed through his genuine warmth and empathy and his nonevaluative attitude. He clarifies, reflects meanings, links members' ideas, and synthesizes. He receives satisfaction from indications that the members are developing their potential capacities, becoming more independent and adequate, with an increasing sense of responsibility. To attain these outcomes he encourages the following conditions: (1) an increasing opportunity for participation, (2) the absence of barriers to free communication within and among all the members of the group, and (3) a nonthreatening, accepting psychological climate.

It is evident that the performance of the group-centered leader is unique. His beliefs about the members and process are different from those of leaders of other groups. Of prime importance is his attitude toward people. Through his interaction with the members, he conveys the confidence he has in the group members and in their ability and willingness to be responsible for themselves. Research has shown that the leader's acceptance of what is said, his reflection of the meaning of the content, and his clarification of feeling are the most useful kinds of responses. Such leader behaviors assure the members that he is genuine, lower the threat, and give some release to those members, especially, who are trying to understand themselves.

Helpful leadership develops slowly. Not only must the leader become skilled in spacing and timing, but frequency of participation is also important. The leader is not passive; he is a participating member. But his participation must facilitate interaction and insight, not intrude, direct, or dominate. This is especially important in the early development of the group. Later the risk of his having too great an influence is greatly diminished, almost nonexistent.

### Membership

The members slowly learn how to listen. They discover that the kind of listening abilities developed in an evaluative, competitive environment are an impediment to understanding within a nonevalua-tive framework. They gradually come to know the true meaning of acceptance, since they experience listening and being listened to regardless of the nature or length of their contribution, and as caring and respect develop, they are able to express their creative differ-ences, discovering that differences in values, attitudes, and expres-sions can add depth and perspective to their understanding. Silent periods become acceptable and more comfortable. Members report that they become able to respond to one another and use more readily the skills of clarification, reflection, and summarization as necessary. Distributive leadership emerges and becomes a natural pattern. Members improve greatly in their use of time and in their ability to focus on various aspects of a problem. They grow in spon-taneity both within and without the group. They apparently experience a greater sense of adequacy.

### Forms of Expression

Self theory is applicable to all forms of interpersonal relation-ships. Its use is limited at present by inability to believe in the group-centered or client-centered principles of interpersonal relationships. To perform truly as a group-centered person usually requires time and such change of personality in depth that the amount of becoming is difficult. Therefore it is not surprising that there are pseudo-group-centered groups just as there are pseudodemocratic groups. Group-centered principles have proved useful in all forms of education, management, counseling, and therapy.

### Theoretical Basis

The theoretical basis of group-centered functioning is self theory. Its basic assumption is that the self has a single goal, that of realizing itself in accordance with its nature. It expresses itself through a creative biological urge which motivates a continuous striving against most difficult odds. The rationality of the organism is considered dependable and oriented toward constructive develop-ment. The development is through differentiation and expansion, the individual becoming progressively capable in decision making and more autonomous.

This increasingly constructive development is a function of the individual's perception, knowledge, and symbolization. Added to these is the satisfaction of ego needs.

Foremost in the individual's growth is the nature of his perception. He plans and makes decisions in terms of reactions to the experience of his perceptions. The quality of his perceptions bears a direct relation to the internal and external inhibiting or releasing forces which he experiences. Unless he is too much inhibited, he checks his tentative impressions against other sources of information. His perceptions take place on both the conscious and subconscious levels, and both levels are able to affect the resultant behavior.

Knowledge is necessary to enable the member to distinguish between more and less mature ways of behaving. Some of the most useful knowledge is assumed to result through interaction with the leader and other members. Interaction helps the member to understand, appreciate, and develop values. Some values may be introjected and distorted in the process. It is hoped that in an accepting and nonthreatening atmosphere distortion will take place less frequently. The assumption is that when values are "clearly perceived" and "adequately symbolized," the member will make a constructive choice, increasing his growth potential. It is further assumed that it is possible for the member to know himself better than he can be known by another even with the utilization of the best methods and instruments. The member's self-reports are considered the best means of understanding his behavior.

The extent and character of the process of symbolization influences the character of the individual's development. Members vary greatly in their ability to assimilate on a symbolic level without distortion. How well experiences can be assimilated into a consistent relationship with the self, on this level, depends on the degree of threat experienced. Threatening ideas, especially in a nonaccepting climate, become extremely difficult to assimilate without narrowing and distortion. Recognizing this the leader is constantly alert to reduce threat and thus increase the possibility of the member's consideration of ideas and feelings, which is necessary to his development. Some behavior does not depend on symbolization.

All members have ego needs. One set of needs derives from the desire to be accepted and respected by others. Some conclude that this is possible only in relation to one's appearance, behavior, quality of work, or degree of conformity. They have a great need to be well liked. A second set of needs derives from the desire to be useful, to be of service, to help a cause or a friend, or to be involved in a constructive undertaking. Such a person may be respected by others but remain dissatisfied because this set of needs is not met. Introspection becomes an instrument for assessing one's relation to this need satisfaction.

Further assumptions focus on the conditions of change, therapy, and growth. It is assumed that the safe, genuine climate in which the leader completely accepts the member facilitates change and growth. In this climate it is expected that the member will perceive, focus, and examine experiences formerly disowned and considered inconsistent with the structure of the self. His attempts to do this greatly increase his understanding and acceptance of others. The process of movement from the safe, comfortable behaviors to the threatening unsymbolized or wrongly symbolized experiences is slow, with numerous setbacks, but once commenced is carried forward with steady persistence.

### Considerations

Both the leader and the members become increasingly aware of the difficulties involved in becoming group-centered persons. Competition and evaluative attitudes are replaced only by understanding and acceptance through time and much effort. When the group forms, only a minority willingly and enthusiastically desire a group-centered group. Many have been so conditioned in authoritarian patterns that they feel insecure in another. For some members the leader's method is confusing and disturbing until they lose stereotypic leader image and accept the leader as a member of the group. When he is accepted, his ideas receive the same consideration as those of other members. Increasing member participation develops only within the accepting climate; it cannot be verbally encouraged or forced. As the group develops, there is a marked improvement in concentration and listening; a greater understanding of, and progress in, evaluation; an increase in spontaneous expressions of both ideas and feelings; and a growing sense of responsibility for the welfare of others and the progress of the group.

The question often asked of group-centered procedures is, Do the members become sufficiently involved for genuine change to take place? This question is important in the consideration of any group method. Anyone considering group-centered leadership should ask himself if he is interested in, and capable of, becoming a group-centered person. Also, beyond being capable, does he have an ontology? When he fails, will he assume it is because of his inadequacy in developing the necessary psychological climate? Or does he believe that man has human freedom, that he does not necessarily live by cause-and-effect relationships?

## THEORIES AND ASSUMPTIONS

### Principles of Learning

Each of the single theories of group process rests upon a different theory of learning. In the authoritarian group the leader, who expects intellectual assimilation to produce change, uses the learning principles of association. Improvement in learning is a change in the response system by deliberate or unconscious linkage or association of new stimuli with old or new responses. Integration is expected to result from the external explanation the leader adds to the internal reality of the group members. He assumes that he can correctly understand the significance of the presentation made by the member and that the member will correctly understand the significance of his interpretations. He expects that the member will intelligently and correctly accept the levels of aspiration set for him by the group leader. Most authoritarian situations have some unstructured aspects. Some members may be sufficiently safe and independent to examine their experiences and to decide which they will genuinely accept and to which they will give only token allegiance. The former become the significant change agents, although whatever change appears to take place the leader may conclude is due to genuine acceptance whereas it may be phenotypical change based on expediency. Other members, more dependent and inflexible, may introject the ideas, desires, and attitudes of the leader and later forget even their derivation, believing that they resulted from their own doing. The assumption that involvement chiefly on the cognitive level with only minimal and incidental involvement on the conative and motoric levels is sufficient to induce genotypical change is open to question.

The democratic group is based upon organismic field theory. This is described as the response of the whole organism to the total confronting situation in order to reduce tension in the direction ot life fulfillment. Meaningful interaction in a cooperative setting is assumed to release in the group a latent, emergent quality of whole-ness previously unknown to any member. Learning thus is the product of living in mutual interaction with others, so that everyone can improve his quality of behavior. The democratic leader, then, assumes that learning or behavioral change results through the member's interaction with his environment, during which process both are modifying or changing each other. The democratic leader assumes that each member learns what he selects and accepts, and to the degree that he acts upon it. To be genuine change is consid-ered to necessitate the involvement of persons on all levels and on each level at one and the same time. Instead of the assumption that the member learns chiefly or only from the leader, the democratic leader encourages distributive leadership, believing that he and others learn from one another. Such a process challenges the leader to believe unreservedly in the capacities of the members and to rely upon their judgment in the solving of problems which he and they select. The locus of evaluation rests with the members and the leader in cooperative interaction.

The leader does not override or by any means whatsoever try to manipulate the decisions of the group. He does, however, assist them in recognizing and weighing alternative possibilities and pos-sible outcomes. This he accomplishes not through evaluation but through questions and the presentation of relevant information. He is prepared to accept and support ideas and solutions inferior as well as superior to his own.

The group-centered group based on the Self Theory of Carl Rogers places implicit faith in the capacities of the members and their motivation to move toward constructive solutions in a psycho-logically healthy manner. The democratic leader may from time to time feel a responsibility for trying to improve the quality of the process through broadening the perspective and supplementing the criteria for making judgments, whereas the group-centered leader primarily feels responsible for encouraging a psychological climate conducive to the development of acceptance and the enhancement of the self-concept of the members. He assumes that members will become involved and will perform more constructively and creatively as they feel safe, accepted, adequate, and in touch with what they believe are their real values. To assume that given the right psychological conditions members will develop a sense of caring and responsibility for one another and together will relate to one another and the leader in a constructive, cooperative fashion is a distinctly unique assumption.

The uniqueness of the group-centered approach lies in the assumption that "man's behavior is exquisitely rational moving with subtle and ordered complexity toward the goals his organism is endeavoring to achieve." [7]

Self theory emphasizes that total involvement is the concomitant of the noncompetitive situation in which each member is a person in his own right and perceived as adequate, worthy, and interested in his own development and that of the group. The extent of feeling of safety and adequacy is assumed to bear a direct relationship to the degree of involvement and ensuing behavioral change.

Each one of the single theories requires the learning of new skills. This fact is most clearly seen in the different functions of listening, and therefore listening skills required, in each of the three.

### Leadership Demands

The most significant and far-reaching contrasts are in the demands of leadership. Since most situations during the formative years are authoritarian, leaders are generally much more comfortable in authoritarian roles, since they are by conditioning if not by conviction authoritarian. For leaders to become truly democratic is a task of some magnitude requiring strong motivation, basic convictions, patience, open-mindedness, training, experience, and more time than is generally deemed necessary. A leader may succeed in becoming democratic but fail in becoming a group-centered leader. He may fail for a number of widely different reasons: (1) He may

[7] Carl R. Rogers, "A Note on the Nature of Man," *Journal of Counseling Psychology,*" vol. 4, p. 202, 1957a.

continue to think about a member without becoming able even minimally to understand his frame of reference. (2) He may even with effort fail to believe sufficiently in the capacity and/or goals of a member to be able to permit him the freedom to make decisions and to feel himself a person; that is, the member may still remain an object to be benevolently directed by the leader. (3) The leader may remain unable genuinely to respect a member as a person. It is Rogers' belief that "a person can implement his respect for others only so far as that respect is an integral part of his personality make-up."[8] (4) He may be unable to gain satisfaction from his leadership by seeing others develop rather than through personal aggrandizement. (5) Despite his good intentions he may not be able to relinquish his "downstage" position; to move from leading actor to stagehand may not be possible. (6) Unable to transmute his psychological needs he may continue to interpret and evaluate. (7) He may discover that he is incapable of really caring for the members, that to accept the responsibility for caring or to become open enough to himself to be able to accept others is outside the scope of becoming.

To become a group-centered leader is not an easy task. It is one which any aspiring group leader should ponder carefully before deciding to enter into a new way of life so different, perhaps, from what he has known.

### Membership Demands

The essentials of membership differ with each group. In the authoritarian group the members listen to the leader for the purpose of recording his ideas, and only infrequently and casually to one another. They do not listen to react, to take issue with, or in some manner modify the leader's comment. They listen to learn his ideas, since the outcomes they desire depend upon knowledge of his ideas, position, or point of view.

The members are not expected or encouraged to supply information or to take a critical attitude regarding the leader's position. They are therefore passive, conforming, and obedient, or if they have

[8] Carl R. Rogers, *Client-centered Therapy,* Houghton Mifflin Company, Boston, 1951, p. 21.

more or dissimilar information or differ in their conclusions, they rarely if ever communicate these to the leader.

Each member is expected to learn from the leader, but it is not anticipated that he will learn from the members, and he does not learn much from them. Opportunity to learn the skills of communication is almost entirely lacking. The member's motivation for participation is centered in the rewards offered by the leader.

Membership in a democratic group is a very different experience. Members listen to one another as well as to the leader. They do not listen only to hear and accept but to weigh, consider, and compare. They present information, ask questions, evaluate, summarize, and conclude. Each expects to learn from all the others. Likewise the leader expects to learn from the members. All assume that the outcomes will be cooperatively determined and that these will be improved and enriched through sharing.

Listening in this environment requires more concentration, more openness to ideas, and a greater sense of responsibility for both means and ends. Members listen not only to hear what is said but to understand the meaning. In this environment they gradually realize that they are involved with others and that each affects the others in the process of thinking, planning, and acting together.

Membership in the group-centered group has dimensions beyond those of the democratic group. This is because of the added responsibility the members have for the direction, maintenance, and decision making. Whereas in the democratic group the leader functions as a special member and assumes some responsibility for all aspects of group functioning, in the group-centered group the members assume this responsibility. The leader here assumes a different responsibility. It is the responsibility of trying to initiate, maintain, and enhance a pychological climate in which the members can carry out these responsibilities more efficiently.

Members listen not only to hear and understand the meaning of what is said but also to try to gain some insight into what it means to the contributor. Since the members rely on one another for the progress of the group, they become more sensitive to the interaction taking place and the direction of the discussion.

Members sense their responsibility and try to develop their

skills of analysis, summarizing and linking ideas in order to aid the progress of the group. The situation demands as much involvement as they are able to give, and their interest increases as they gradually and progressively realize the challenge to their ability to understand and share with one another.

# 6

## ANALYSIS OF GROUP PROCESS: MULTIPLE-THEORY APPROACHES

Several theories of group process are based on more than one theory of behavioral change. Representative of these are the T group and the basic encounter group. Each emphasizes permissiveness and acceptance. Although this emphasis resembles that in self theory, it is a permissiveness and acceptance restricted to the purposes of the setting as viewed by the leader. The main emphasis of the process is leader-directed and somewhat controlled. To the degree that this is the case it becomes more analytic and authoritarian, using association theories of learning. There is also some cooperative planning, limited generally to the consideration of necessary input of theoretical content. How much of each of these approaches is emphasized is in part a function of the past experiences and operational beliefs of the leader.

# T GROUPS

Any discussion of T group theory and practice must be considered tentative and of the nature of a progress report. Much change has taken place in assumptions and practice since its beginning in the late forties. Those who have been closely involved in it over a period of years perceive it as a series of points of view, fragments, and constructs which could have great potential in usefulness and in theory building. Gibb, Blake, Bradford, and others who report their conclusions in *T-group Theory and Laboratory Method* each focus on what are considered the critical elements in theory and process. They also hold certain assumptions in common such as the ambivalence with which members in general approach learning and change.

### Purposes and Goals

The members participate in the development of a group which enables each to grow. They have the opportunity also to learn about groups, about larger social systems as well as about themselves and their interpersonal relationships. Awareness and understanding improve the quality of participation, but each member tries to integrate his "inner" and "outer" needs. To do this he must learn the skills requisite for understanding and responding integratively, adaptively, and responsibly to another. These skills also assist each person in changing the structures of his environment. The general focus is on the development of behavioral skills "to support better integrations of intentions and actions."

There are other objectives. Among these is greater ability to perceive and to learn from the consequences of one's action through attention not only to his own feelings but also to the feelings of others. A second objective is the clarification and development of concepts and theoretical insights which aid in the understanding of group functioning and its relation to personal goals and values.

A third goal is in part reached through the input of content. It is generally agreed that cognitive input is necessary, but there is much less agreement with reference to its substance, frequency, and method of presentation. It is usual to present three kinds of theoretical materials: (1) individual and small-group dynamics, (2) community and role dynamics, and (3) behavioral change, change agents, and application. Considerable differences exist concerning the effects of conceptual presentations upon the members' learning. Some fear they lead to intellectualization and the avoidance of emotional problems. Conceptual inputs were at one time ideological as well as descriptive. Later they became descriptive; now there is again a trend toward the philosophical.

### Process

Certain emphases are highlighted in this method: the integration of scientific and democratic values in group building, the use of ambiguity and frustration as a means of encouraging optimal involvement, the interventions of the trainer, the focus on the "here and now," and the use of cognitive input.

With the recognition that democratic ideas if taken seriously also become value commitments, emphasis is placed on the cooperation of members in the definition and solving of problems. It is apparent that to do this scientific knowledge and methods applicable to group functioning are necessary. It is assumed that the commitment to the democratic process of solving problems by those affected by the solution and that the use of scientific knowledge in doing so enhance the opportunities for change.

Decisions are reached by consensus, but psychological consensus at any time is not necessarily considered right. However, certain safeguards ensure only minimal risks. One of these safeguards is access of each member to present relevant ideas from within his own framework of values. Another is the reduction of all barriers to free participation. These are recognized as the rights and responsibilities of members to participate in methods which facilitate learning.

Much attention is given to overcoming the passivity often attendant upon formal learning. The total involvement of members is recognized as prerequisite to behavioral change. Ambiguity and frustration are used as a means of increasing individual involvement. The structure in the T group is minimal. The members are told that they can learn by the observation of others and the analysis of experiences in the group. The trainer usually refuses to become a group member or to act as a discussion leader. He offers to help in the utilization of their experiences for learning.

The usual referents such as agenda, procedures, expectations, or requirements are not provided. There is thus created a kind of social and operational vacuum. With ambiguity come mounting tensions and frustrations resulting from what is perceived as lack of progress.

The trainer intervenes in order to effect the members' examination of what is taking place in the group. He intervenes to clarify, interpret, make suggestions. He may also report his own internal feelings if he perceives that this may be useful. For example, a trainer may comment on the attention given to the "there and then" problems of members as compared with discussions of present problems in the group. He may add that some members have said that they do not wish to discuss present group problems and that this seems to present a dilemma to the group. At another point he may mention that perhaps not everyone is ready to discuss the present happenings in the group, or wants to, or feels that he can do so, and that for the group to insist on this would be to utilize conformity pressure.

Another concern has been the degree of emphasis to place on the "here and now" of the group experience in contrast to the "there and then." Should the "here and now" receive the primary and only emphasis? Is there a place for the "there and then," and should it be considered in relation to the "here and now"?

The general conclusion is that immediate experiences of participants are the basic ingredients for learning. Motivation to do so comes from the incongruity of the members between their expectancies and the actualities of the group experience. Learning experiences are increased as the members become more involved. It is accomplished through the data each provides, followed by the personal and collective analysis of this data assisted by the trainer. The members' release of significant "here and now" experiences provides the material also for conceptualization, practice, and generalization.

When the time is appropriate, attention is also directed to the similarities and differences between the laboratory island and work and life at home. The purpose is to assist members to use insights gained in the laboratory in the situations at home.

There are other related foci, especially the challenge to reassess the adequacy of one's value orientations and social perspectives, to

become more competent in the use of skills of inquiry and evaluation, to accept the responsibility of reducing internal barriers, and
to become able not only to give help but to receive help from others.

As discussed earlier, the problem of how to supply the necessary cognitive input has received continuing attention. Several
methods are used. One of these, the use of lectures to members of
all groups en masse was described earlier. To assist in self-study,
self-rating scales are used before the groups are formed, near the
end of the workshop. Each member compares the results, and
changes are discussed in the group. To provide more data for the
the understanding of the group process, each session is taped and the
tapes are listened to on a voluntary basis. Other methods are used to
increase understanding on the emotional and cognitive levels. The
most common are the use of paired interviews, of small groups
formed for this purpose, and of voluntary individual consultations
with the trainer. There are of course many informal small-group discussions outside the regular meetings.

The building of an effective feedback system in the group is
considered a necessary condition for valid learning. The term *feedback* is used to signify verbal and nonverbal responses from others
to a unit of behavior provided immediately following its presentation
to the group. The initiator of the behavior is assumed capable of
perceiving and utilizing the reaction. Nonverbal feedback or reinforcement may be useful in the early life of the group. Verbal feedback should await the development of mutual trust and a pattern of
interchange of support from person to person.

The development of the conditions in the group whereby effective learning may take place through feedback is difficult. Attempts
are filled with latent anxiety, and the skill needed to evaluate constructively is slow to develop. Groups come to recognize that a climate of helpfulness, the support of group members, and their
sensitivity and alertness to destructive feedback are useful safeguards.

### Leadership

The leadership of a T group is a complex and multidirectional
task. It is an ever-changing emergent blend of many facets and elements, artistic, technological, professional, scientific, and intuitive,

and not least the personal values and beliefs of the trainer. Some trainers lean heavily toward the action research concepts, others toward organization and mental health concepts, and still others toward the clinical and psychiatric positions. Regardless of his orientation the trainer endeavors to develop an effective learning environment for all the group members.

The trainer confronts several problems related to both purposes and procedures. There is the problem of orientation: Will the group be oriented toward skill development, therapy, or behavioral change? A second will be use, and if so to what degree, of feedback, role playing, simulation experiments, or data-gathering instruments. Other problems are, How much does he work with the "here and now" and how much with the "there and then"? With what feelings does he work and at what level? To what extent does he rely on the emergent qualities of the group, and to what degree does he assume responsibility for their direction and guidance? Basic primarily to his introspection concerning himself are the questions, How willing is he to understand himself, and to what measure can he be open concerning his motivations, beliefs, attitudes, and feelings? How great is his need to protect the members and himself?

The way he answers these questions determines in large measure the character of his trainer performance. It will influence especially the kind and frequency of his interventions. Some trainers remain outside the group, take no part in the discussion of content, and serve the group chiefly as process analyst. This they do by analysis, questions, and suggestions. The rationale for nonparticipation in topical discussions is directly related to the following probabilities: The trainer believes that if he did participate, eventually his participation would determine the content and also the members would come to know the topics of most interest to him and would move the discussion either away from or toward these topics. Regardless of these possibilities he reasons that he facilitates process analysis when he does not become involved in content ideas.

Other trainers take various positions with reference to their place in the group, the freedom given the group, and the kinds and number of interventions. A small minority enter the group as members, but these generally conclude that by so doing they greatly decrease the effectiveness of their interventions. The majority withdraw from the group and thus induce member tensions and frustrations. These in large measure result from the accompanying ambiguity and lack of satisfactory procedural organization. This method is believed to increase member involvement greatly. Their interventions have a dramatic effect and receive member attention.

Still others enter the group at one or more of its work cycles, that is, its planning, acting-observing, process analysis, or generalization stage. While some trainers conclude that they are effective as a special member participant in some phases of the group, others reject this procedure, feeling that member involvement is decreased and the dependency of members on the trainer greatly increased. All trainers make continuing professional attempts through their performance to facilitate concern resolution, group growth, personal growth, and defense reduction.

### Member Reaction

The usual initial reaction to the lack of trainer direction and resultant ambiguity is one of frustration and the display of some aggression toward him. Members wonder how they are going to learn unless the trainers do more. They do not perceive trainer interventions as supplying the help which they consider is needed.

The second stage is generally one of more realistic discussions. These take the form of brief efforts to look at group process interspersed with discussion of general topics.

Following the initial stages many groups face a sharp cleavage. Some of the members are disturbed and threatened or bothered by efforts of other members to understand member interaction and individual member behavior. On the other hand, some members realize that problems must be faced and interaction studied and understood in order that problems of communication, decision making, and standard setting can be explored and studied. The group experiences difficulty in moving from the discussion of "there and then" topics to a discussion of "here and now" happenings taking place in the group.

The difficulty centers around the problem of feedback. Even those who feel that feedback is necessary to learning are apprehensive concerning the use of it. Their apprehension focuses on the concerns. They are afraid that some may be hurt by such interpretation of action and feelings. Also the members feel that they lack the skill to participate in such a manner. Even when the trainer opens up group issues and reports his own feelings, they hesitate to use his behavior as a model. More candid conversation awaits the development of intermember trust.

As fears subside and trust develops, members experiment in discussing the current issues in the group. As they sense one another's support, they participate in better listening, and cooperative thinking and problem solving improve. Members report that the progress at this stage seems to happen almost unnoticed. They sense the necessity to maintain a balance between meeting individual needs and continuity on group tasks and come to recognize that several group goals can be accomplished during the same period.

In the ending stage the members feel that they understand one another and are accepted. Empathy and cohesion are high. The last meeting is a sober reflection on the route by which they have come.

### Forms of Expression

T groups are increasingly used in programs of management development for in-service education to help resolve the difficulties of the individual today within an organization of bureaucracy. These are the difficulties of communication, interpersonal relations, belonging, and loneliness. With increasing numbers of people employed by big business, management is recognizing the need for more human relationships within our bureaucratic structures to permit meaningful interpersonal exchange.

T groups are used in training management and supervisory personnel, those who must work through people to accomplish the task. This is called a *horizontal slice,* that is, individuals are selected from the same level but from different components of a firm. The *diagonal slice* is a training group of individuals selected from different levels in order to expose them to others above and below them in the hierarchy.

The training group is also used extensively in preparing professionals in helping occupations, such as the conference for the training of personnel to work with the educationally disadvantaged held at Boston University in 1964. Gradually the use of T groups is being applied to the socialization process of children, youth, and college students as well. Finally, the Peace Corps and other agencies that work overseas have implemented the T group approach for furthering understanding in cross-cultural situations.

The objective of the T group theory is to improve the quality of membership in various agencies or associations and in participation in human affairs in general. Individuals involved as participants come to understand their internal needs, values, perceptions, and resources and to integrate their needs with external demands. They also become aware of the opportunities and expectations of the social climate in which they function.

### Theoretical Basis

The approach relies heavily on various theories of learning. These theories are elicited from several disciplines. The approach is described as "a cross-professional and cross-disciplinary approach which attempts to draw relevant aspects from various approaches and to develop a more integrated model of social technology for facilitating learning." The desired direction of the learning experience is "toward a more integrative and adaptive interconnection of values, concepts, feelings, perceptions, strategies, and skills."

Members come to the laboratory experience with many values, concepts, and behaviors derived from experiences in various types of groups. They are involved, then, not only in learning the new but in the evaluation of the past in relation to the daily laboratory experiences. This requires individual confrontation of old patterns of thought and behavior in light of the new, and the examination (in themselves and others) of feelings and possible motivations.

Learning results from the interaction of each member with others. The member develops abilities to take initiative in both giving and receiving. In this development he achieves to some degree a self-identity which is active, reflective, and engaged in realistic, collaborative relationships.

Another area of learning is the development of independence toward autonomy in interdependence. The laboratory offers the individual help and support in examination of the nature of his authority and peer relationships. His tentative expressions of new behaviors signaling growth are expressed in the group. His possibilities for learning in this and other areas are heightened as he and others consider the contrasting and frequently contradictory demands of the laboratory group in comparison with the demands of other groups.

The focus of the learning experience has two dimensions: First, the method is planned to encourage each member to test the reality and depth of his conscious dissatisfactions. The second dimension follows from the first in the provision of situations in which the member recognizes and confronts dissatisfactions not previously perceived.

### Considerations

There is solid agreement that learning is an active experience; further, that one learns what he chooses to accept and act upon. Conditioning influences of the past are considered to be a handicap to learning; hence the emphasis on reeducation. The theoretical learning theory remains the same. It is authoritarian association learning with some overlay of pseudo self theory. The differences between the old learning and T group learning are the conditions under which learning is considered to take place and the emphasis upon the examination of the interpersonal events of the process as it takes place. Each member is considered to be a reactive individual. The problem is to induce him to react in such a way that he will become sufficiently involved to learn.

To ensure the degree of involvement deemed necessary the members are introduced to a mildly traumatic situation. The ambiguity, frustration, and apprehension created are assumed to be a necessary prerequisite to learning. This state is relied upon to reduce inhibitions and promote regression considered conducive to exploration of their psychological conditions. Such a procedure is expected to produce aggressive attacks, overt and covert, and directly and indirectly expressed. It is assumed that members in general have aggressions which need expression before positive learning experiences can take place. Although the members are considered normal, it is assumed either that positive, cooperative, democratic, and sensitive persons are not enrolled in the group or, if they are, that they are not genuinely so normal and need to regress in order actually to progress. Persons who have found normal and useful outlets for their aggressions and hostilities and are genuinely caring, responsible persons are unlikely to find the process self-enhancing in its early stages.

Since the process is basically authoritarian, the trainer carries a heavy responsibility for the development of the group, individually and corporately. His interventions are determinative in the progress of the group and must be carried out with great depth of insight and skill. This can be attained only by those who have had adequate psychological training and much experience. The group member has little opportunity to develop any leadership skills, and therefore the trainer has little previous opportunity to develop the skills before he becomes responsible for a group.

This may be one reason for the great variation in the methods of leadership used among trainers. Their variation in performance is also a function of their beliefs about the nature of man and how behavioral change takes place. Interestingly enough they apparently all agree that a climate of interpersonal understanding, support, and trust with some degree of responsibility and caring is necessary for worthwhile member changes to result.

Regardless of the variation in methods, trainers assume that the basic theory underlying the T group process is Lewinian. It is difficult, however, to reconcile this theory with the methods used by trainers to involve the members and to encourage behavioral change. Trainers in general interpret, question, suggest, and encourage. That is, they perceive themselves as taking a very active part in bringing about individual and group change. At this point one might sincerely question whether this is Lewinian, since one of the tenets of his theory is that an individual genuinely changes when he is free to do otherwise. Although in many respects the methods used bear a close resemblance to the above-mentioned theory, there appears to be a lapse at least in this one respect.

The Lewinian position that involvement of persons on the cognitive, conative, and motoric levels is necessary for genuine change to take place is apparently accepted and used by the trainer in his process efforts. However, when the need for information on the part of the members is considered necessary for progress, the method is changed. Groups en masse listen to a lecture on the concepts the trainers decide that they should hear. They assume apparently that a person is totally and sufficiently involved in listening to a lecture to integrate and use it (change) in relation to the concepts heard.

Such a departure from the method they claim so necessary in the group process itself is difficult to understand. Have trainers themselves been so conditioned in authoritarian one-way learning relationships that this inconsistency passes unnoticed?

It may be that from the viewpoint of the trainers these inconsistencies do not exist. It should be recognized that the lecturer (trainer) is engaged in this activity in the same one-way authoritarian relationship as when he is engaged in the group process with the group. He is therefore consistent and performing apparently in agreement with what he believes. The better and truer explanation is no doubt that various theories are used regardless of the contrasting differences in their basic assumptions if and when they seem to fit what the trainer does on the basis of expediency.

This performance, it should be noted, is not the result of a study made of the several theories of learning and the selection of the best from each or several of them to be integrated into a method. It is rather that trainers were engaged in an experimental approach who only later examined what theories they had used; that is, the approach is not eclectic in the usual meaning of this term.

## THE BASIC ENCOUNTER GROUP [1]

### Purposes and Goals

This type of group experience is intensive. Its method is designed to facilitate a high degree of member-to-member involvement. Through dynamic open interaction it is expected that each member will achieve understanding of himself and his relationship to others more accurately, that he will change in his personal attitudes and behavior, and that he will subsequently relate more effectively to others in his everyday life situation.

As indicated by these expectations significant personality changes are hypothesized as outcomes of this experience. This is predicated chiefly upon the unstructured highly emotional interaction concerned with the ongoing experience of what is currently taking place in the group.

[1] Based on Carl R. Rogers, "The Process of the Basic Encounter Group," in James F. T. Bugental, *Challenges of Humanistic Psychology*, McGraw-Hill Book Company, New York, 1967.

### The Process

The process is complex and varies to some degree with different groups in relation to the openness of the members and their ability to tolerate ambiguity. It varies also with the leadership, that is, in the degree to which the leader himself is open, believes in the capacity of the members, and is able to trust them to progress in their relationships. Rogers views it as a "varied tapestry" but within any one group discerns certain patterns. Based upon tape recordings and personal reports he lists these as tentative: (1) milling around, (2) resistance to personal expression or exploration, (3) description of past feelings, (4) expression of negative feelings, (5) expression of and exploration of personally meaningful material, (6) expression of immediate interpersonal feelings in the group, (7) development of a healing capacity in the group, (8) self-acceptance and the beginning of change, (9) cracking of facades, (10) the individual's receiving of feedback, (11) confrontation, (12) the helping relationships outside the group session, (13) the basic encounter.

The process is relatively but not completely unstructured. The members choose the goals of the group, and each decides his own personal direction. As the leader determines necessary, some cognitive input is presented. This content material is presented outside the group session, generally in lecture form. The experiences, especially the initial ones, are planned to provide ambiguity, uncertainty, and lack of leadership direction as a means of increasing involvement on the part of the members. It is expected that the members will move through confusion, uncertainty, frustration, fractionation, and discontinuity to a climate of coherence, trust, and some feeling of mutual responsibility.

### Leadership

The leader perceives himself as a facilitator of thought and feeling on the part of the members. He performs from within the group but not as a member of the group. On the one hand he is permissive, especially in the initial stages, and on the other hand he is interpretative and evaluative. Also, as he thinks necessary, he uses questioning to encourage deeper exploration of the problem by the one presenting it. At times the dialogue is between the member and other members. Other members also are quite interpretative and evaluative. At times they even demand that the member continue exploration of his feelings.

The degree to which the leader is authoritative and analytical depends of course upon his personality needs and his beliefs regarding what makes for a useful therapeutic experience. Those who are themselves more democratic or client-centered personalities would be expected to conduct the group differently from one who is a benevolent authoritarian at heart. The leader who has become from conviction a self theorist and is truly a person believing in its tenets will not conduct a group as a basic encounter group as herein described despite the official label which designates the course or experience.

### Membership

Members in general are expected to be more or less disturbed by the lack of structure and goal-directedness of the situation. This situation is counted on to shake the members from the passive state which otherwise is assumed to exist if the leader provides security through structure and the setting of goals. Greater involvement of the members is the anticipated outcome of the fluid and ambiguous environment. Such an environment affects the members in various ways but forces each into some kind of confrontation with the others. Eventually it is anticipated that the total situation will generate the expression of negative feelings toward one another, the leader, and the purposes of the group. Thus the leader assumes that the stage is set for genuine exploration of personal and interpersonal feelings and development of insights leading to personality change.

The members gradually move in their dialogue from talking of the past or situations outside the group to dialogue concerned with what is taking place within the group. This is frequently referred to as a movement from a discussion of the "there and then" situations to the "here and now" situations.

It is assumed that after the members have attacked one another and have broken through one another's protective defenses, they will gradually change in their attitudes from the negative and critical to the constructive and helpful.

The evolution of this process increases the pressure on each member to open himself to the group, not only to gain self-insight, but also to remain a respectable and respected member. Those who have revealed themselves are not in a mood to permit a more sensitive, more inhibited, or more threatened member to progress at his own rate. Also, once he commences to discuss his fears, anxieties, concerns, he is not allowed to stop or hesitate or even proceed as he feels he would like. The leader or members question, probe, "push" to get the complete story or cause him to come to grips with the situation. He probably concludes by telling all, but is he really at one with himself? Has the split that was within been overcome? Or will the "healing" of the members who pressured him to reveal himself be able to restore him to himself?

It should be recognized that in the early stages members are not performing in this manner because they feel some responsibility for one another. In this as in other groups, a genuine feeling of responsibility for one another develops late in the process.

### Forms of Expression

This experience takes many forms as indicated by the labels, for example, workshops in leadership, in human relationships, in counseling, in education, or sensitivity training in human relationships. There is a great deal of diversity among them with reference to purposes and duration. Their chief commonality is that all are planned to facilitate an encounter between persons in a group environment. Purposes of the groups may vary from the educational one of learning skills in human relations to the therapeutic one of self-understanding and understanding of others especially in relation to maladjustive patterns of behavior.

### Theoretical Bases

This method has several theoretical bases. The most common theories on which intensive group experience is based are Lewinian and client-centered, but these are heavily overlaid with gestalt therapy and various brands of psychoanalytic theories. Which theories receive greater emphasis in the conduct of any one group is dependent upon the theoretical assumptions of the facilitator. The multiple theoretical bases of operation are only as multiple as the facilitator actually is. It may be that for most facilitators the chief basis is authoritarian and analytic with some simulated overtones of self theory. The members soon recognize that the acceptance and permissiveness is limited and conditional. The differences in the theoretical approaches revolve around the facilitator's beliefs with reference to the conditions necessary to assume a high degree of involvement on the part of the members. Although facilitators generally accent the Lewinian organismic and field theories, they also apparently assume that cognitive material on group phenomena presented in lecture form will be integrated and used in the progress of the group learning experiences. They retain an implicit belief in association learning, which in large measure is in conflict with the chief emphasis in the group process itself. This inconsistency, or conflict, in assumptions apparently is unrecognized.

### Considerations

The facilitator increases the possibility that involvement with one another at some depth and within a limited space of time will take place. This he does by insisting that reactions to one another in relation to the "here and now" of the group experience take place at once. No one is to avoid or refuse to interact. He anticipates that the group will move through stages, namely, descriptive personal comments with emphasis on past experience, beginning reactions to one another concerning current statements of members, explosive interactions of a negative and/or aggressive nature—the "pressure cooker" stage, and the reconciliation and positive interactions sometimes referred to as "the love feast."

The facilitator then anticipates that the members will gradually become negative in their verbal comments and that this negative action is a prerequisite to the healing action of progress. If this becomes, as it apparently has, the expected pattern of these groups, then may not the leader create such an expectancy in the group, and may not the members engage in negativism, since this is what they have come to believe is expected?

The assumption that all members will need and benefit from this kind of process should be reexamined. Will those who have a genuine personal center, a sincere respect for themselves, and constructive expectancies concerning others benefit from this kind of process? May they find it unnecessary to become emotionally, defensively, and aggressively involved? Could it be that interpretations others make of them have only a minor effect? And those which they perceive as having some merit may be accepted and may not call forth a defensive reaction? It could be that because of their ego strength and self-respect they may reflect upon it and decide on its validity quietly and unobtrusively. Could it be that certain individuals are capable of this and are not in need of, or are not especially assisted by, first reacting in a somewhat hasty, impulsive, unexamined, irresponsible, and emotional manner? May the early and middle stages be irrelevant for some, perhaps the more so-called "normal" members of the group?

# 7

# GENERAL SUMMARY AND CONCLUSIONS

## THEORETICAL SIMILARITIES

Both single and multiple theories of group process are concerned with genuine change. Also their conclusions agree that involvement is necessary for change to take place. All, with the exception of analytic group therapy, are used with normal or near-normal populations. All use a circle or other seating format which increases the ease of interpersonal interaction. All assume that the members need cognitive input for best results. All are concerned with the degree to which learnings transfer to other situations. All agree that the groups should be small, under twenty persons. All emphasize permissiveness as a necessary constant for behavioral change, although its meaning differs in the context of the various processes.

## THEORETICAL DIFFERENCES

Contrasting theoretical differences exist among the various kinds of group processes. They differ most significantly regarding assumptions concerning (1) motivation, (2) involvement, (3) learning, and (4) leadership requirements. All these are discussed in this chapter except the differences in assumptions regarding learning, which were discussed in Chapters 5 and 6.

### Motivation

Major reliance is upon extrinsic motivation in all theories except the democratic and group-centered theories. This type of motivation is accomplished through leader intervention in such forms as goal setting, reinforcement, and interpretation. Through these methods the members are conditioned to interpret progress as congruence between their perception of the leader's guidance and their performance in the group. The leader perceives his responsibility to be one of analysis, planning for the group in terms of this analysis and implementing his conclusions in the most acceptable manner in the group. He thinks about the members and how best he can encourage progress.

Leaders using democratic or group-centered methods perceive the members differently from leaders using other methods. In each of these the members are perceived as capable, interested, and responsible. The democratic leader plans with the members in terms of their interests. He assumes that their participation in setting goals and planning methods of realization generates the motivation necessary for accomplishment of the undertaking.

The group-centered leader also relies on the members' abilities to plan and execute their plans without his direction or reinforcement. The motivation derives from the fact that they are engaged in fulfillment of their own plans. It is intrinsic in nature.

### Involvement

All theories recognize the need for member involvement. Their methods for securing involvement differ. In the authoritarian process the leader relies upon rewards, reinforcements, or the lack of these as a means of involvement. Praise, grades, promotions, relief from neurotic behavior patterns—all are assumed to be the means for involving members to the degree necessary for change.

Democratic procedure relies on the involvement of the members resulting from discussion of what is cooperatively chosen. The leader as a special member of the group participates by questions, supplying information, clarifying, and summarizing for the purpose of helping to identify what they as a group would like to undertake.

Group-centered process based on self theory assumes that the individual's intrinsic motivation for self-understanding and understanding of others is dependable under certain conditions. These conditions are considered to be unconditional acceptance and positive regard, a psychological climate in which each is encouraged to become a person in his own right. This climate, when genuine and accepted as such by the members, is one in which there is a high degree of trust and readiness to react and be oneself without fear or defensiveness.

The involvement thus secured in these groups is deemed insufficient both in degree and kind for the purpose of reeducation by T group and basic encounter group theorists. They encourage a different kind and greater degree of involvement by the promotion of ambiguity and frustration cultivated initially by absence of trainer goal setting and supportive leadership. They depend on these conditions to cause a confrontation or encounter between and among members. Such an encounter is expected to result in the expression of aggressive and negative feelings toward the trainer and one another. Such interaction is viewed as a prerequisite to supportive relationships resulting in positive behavioral change.

### Leadership Requirements

Leadership requirements for the several groups vary greatly with reference to both the function of the leader and the personality characteristics he must have so that there is a healthy congruence between what he is and what he does. In the authoritarian, T group, and basic encounter groups he functions as the dominant, planning, guiding force. He interprets, evaluates, suggests, and rewards. He makes decisions about and for the group without consultation. He decides the necessary input, also the time and manner of its presentation. Within this framework he assumes major responsibility for the progress of the group. He develops skills in analysis and in perceiving the critical and most useful times to intervene. He is not a member of the group and does not participate in using himself as a model of involvement. His functioning does not require deep or basic personality change. He can be successful and remain a representative of the authoritarian culture. Since the members are accustomed to and adjusted to authoritarian personalities, he does not present to them problems in understanding except when he frustrates them because he does not provide direction in the way they have come to expect it.

The leader, trainer, or facilitator derives his satisfactions from at least two sources: One source is the satisfaction which comes from recognition of his skills and abilities in facilitating group progress. Since he assumes that the forward movement of the group is chiefly dependent on him, this may well be a very great reward. Since he interprets the progress of the group as a reflection of the quality of his performance, he receives further ego satisfactions when progress is evident, or he is disquieted somewhat when it is not, because he perceives it as a failure on his part. Further satisfactions are no doubt present as he understands more about an individual member and when that member progresses.

The group-centered leader within his framework of acceptance and expectations is satisfying different needs. The need to demonstrate his analytic interpretative ability and his need to direct, control, and plan for are far removed. His satisfactions come when he is able to extend freedom to others and when they demonstrate responsibleness. He receives satisfaction when there is evidence that a member or members are moving toward freer communication and better understanding. His satisfactions come from the recognition that they are pleased with their own self-understanding and better interpersonal relationships. His satisfactions derive from seeing what is happening to members for their own sakes and not also for what it does to his feeling about himself as a group leader. The last, when it comes, is incidental, at the bottom of the list of need satisfactions rather than at the top.

It is now evident that T groups and basic encounter groups, when compared with the group-centered group, differ fundamentally in their theoretical bases and methods of operation, and the leaders have different beliefs about the therapeutic process. At this stage, if ever, no attempt should be made to compare and evaluate their efficacy. Much creative effort is being used in endeavors to improve their possibilities and increase their potentialities. Each has experienced success and failure in helping individual members. It may be that the character of the most useful group experience varies with the needs, background, experiences, and values of the individual person.

For the professionally involved person there remain some unanswered questions and problems. Representative of these are the following: Which theoretical basis is most in congruence with my beliefs and personality as a leader? Which method is most in congruence with my natural method of working with groups and supplies some of the necessary satisfactions in my work? Which do I believe is most conducive to the kind and degree of involvement which I perceive as necessary to progress? Which process best prepares participants to become intelligent and skilled members and leaders in their work and social and family relationships? If the course is offered in a university as part of an educational sequence of preparation, which is most useful to educators, nurses, counselors, and others in its transfer value to their professions?

Further questions which confront the decision as to theory preferences revolve around the following queries: Have we been so conditioned that only a dramatic change in environmental expectancy causes us to ask who we are and where we are going? Have we become reactive objects rather than existential beings? Is thinking concerned with the meaning of life, or are our own values and responsibilities so remote from our experience that thinking concerned with expediency and present immediacies—for example, reacting, getting, spending, and enjoying—are the only reality we know?

How do we become able to care for another? Must we have and express our doubts, fears, negativisms, aggressions, and even hostility to these others and receive theirs in like manner as prerequisites for caring? Must these fears and counterfears, dependencies and counterdependencies, aggressions and counteraggressions be drained off in order to recognize what we are in depth? Is it possible that these may through clarification and understanding evaporate, be sublimated, or be transmuted into positive perceptions in a continuous, genuine, and completely accepting group climate? Is there more than one way in which such a climate can develop?

These queries do not yield to easy decisions, and little agreement is to be expected. On the basis of what is comprehended about group life they remain challenges to our present understanding. Let us hope that we shall be too wise to draw conclusions on only pragmatic considerations.

It is also to be hoped that professionals will not be unduly influenced by the mounting degree of pragmatic activism and simulated caring, lacking depth and authentic change. Since it is generally acceptable that a caring, responsible psychological climate is a minimum prerequisite to genuine change, consideration should be given to the way or ways in which such a climate comes into being and the realization that such change is not purposely precipitated and also that it is not forced but develops.

This is perhaps the time to examine the meaning of guilt and grace. A beginning could be made in the examination and differentiation of societal and functional guilt.

## NEEDED—AN ONTOLOGY?

Much of our group counseling has proceeded on the assumption that the end justifies the means. However, we have conceded that any theoretical procedure differs with the leader, that his own personality enters into and in some important way determines or influences both means and ends. Should this insight be treated only as a concession, an idea in parentheses, or does it deserve more attention? Is there a place for the science of being or reality in our developing understanding? May we view interpersonal relationships in a distorted and superficial manner if we refuse to investigate and ponder the nature, essential properties, and relations of being?

Our present assumptions and methods are based on Freud's insights of the relationships in his model of superego, ego, and id. Freud concluded that aggressions and hostilities were common to every man and could not be completely eliminated. This aggression as considered in *Civilization and Its Discontents* is stored up by the weight of the superego and the cultural superego. The method of dealing with it is to recognize it, understand it, and express it verbally. This could be expected to be all that is necessary if the reality of a free self is only a myth. In Freudianism and apparently in many of present-day assumptions there is no need for ontology, since the self in depth does not exist. This is to assume that all guilt is neurotic guilt. Guilt then has only a horizontal dimension; it is the uneasiness experienced as the result of the fancied violations of arbitrary norms. If this point of view is accepted, the expression of each person's aggression and reconciliation is all that is needed to be free to care and to relate to one another in loving concern.

But if beyond this societal guilt there is what Tournier has described as "functional guilt," the situation calls for more than acceptance of others. Should we not consider the sense of guilt which results from the self's violation of norms accepted by it as valid and validated by the experience of others? Is there not this reality which Tournier has termed functional guilt and Tillich the "transmoral conscience"?

May it be that those who, following some forms of group experience, conclude that they were less than helpful have not been enabled to understand and cope with this "functional" guilt? Those who have a "sensitive" conscience may need a kind of experience which offers support to contemplation and reflection which is not in accord with the expectancies or character of other groups. Some groups may offer much help in the area of the "how" for future behavior. Could It be that the real difficulty is not the "how" of future living but that first there must be the "why"?

After some self-understanding and understanding of others has taken place, the individual still has the problem of the dedication of his energies to something beyond and greater than himself. The question becomes, What kind of group experiences are most in accord with the possibility of coming to grips with meaning in life, extending beyond the egocentric self, and the commitment of oneself in constructive activity?

New lines of development would require that we give serious study and thought to ontology. It is necessary to become concerned with such matters as conscience, guilt, truth, freedom, and inner freedom. Without decreasing attention to environmental forces it is essential that we increase attention to the actualization of inwardness. Each of us must accept the fact that he is responsible for his own decisions. The age in which we live is influential but must not be given as a reason for our behavior. The basic concern is what can be done to help persons to develop the potential of depth and self-examination in relation to values beyond egocentric concern. How can we assist one another in becoming able to care and to be responsible? No group or society can do this for anyone, but it can accept the fact of a personal valuing center. Then, through information gained through open-minded and responsible research, leaders of groups may secure the insights which would assist them to become more able to understand and encourage a climate in which the person develops the inwardness to communicate meaningfully alienation, guilt, and love.

The group process which is most useful is one which is most congruent with the members' approach to life. The members' customary methods of recognizing and handling problems may indicate the type of process which will facilitate their growth toward maturity. Members who have not developed their potential capacity for self-understanding and decision making in depth may need a different kind of process from those who have.

The best in all processes is the recognition of, and involvement in, the sublime. A common act may, through trust and caring, become sublime. Sublime acts are those which are healing and expanding. Tillich defines sublimation as "the act which transforms something not sublime into something sublime." [1] He describes the sublime as something qualitatively new.

For the sublime to come into being requires a creative act. This means the exercise of freedom in a special sense. The member reacts centrally to a stimulus by deliberation and decision. This is the decision of the "centered act of the centered self." The usual biological and sociological interpretations do not explain the drive toward the sublime. Without a personal center, sublimation leading to the centered act of decision is not fully possible, in which case the individual is almost completely reactive, not a creative person.

Reactive individuals need a stimulus to initiate reaction. If the reaction is going to push one into an attempt to know himself, the situation must be fraught with much emotion. Those individuals who lack a personal center, for whom a centered act is rare indeed, need a strong stimulus to direct them toward the sublime. This kind of stimulus is found in the ambiguous, frustrating experience of the

[1] Paul Tillich, "Existentialism, Psychotherapy and the Nature of Man," in Simon Doniger (ed.), *The Nature of Man,* Harper & Brothers, New York, 1962.

beginning T group and the basic encounter group. According to Riesman there may be many who are "outer-directed," resembling Eliot's "Hollow Men." These may derive benefit from analytic therapy, T groups, and basic encounter groups.

On the other hand those who have a personal center do not need the experience of frustration, of ambiguity, or of aggressive confrontation in order to discover who they are and in what direction they wish to move. They are not governed by the homeostasis principle of Freudian psychology, or the status drive of Adlerian psychology, or the more recent emphasis on self-actualization. Instead they are motivated by a will to meaning. The fulfillment they seek is not fulfillment of self, self-actualization, but the fulfillment of meaning. They do not obliterate or contradict the self-transcending quality of human existence; they actualize it in their striving toward this goal.

Man is pushed by drives but pulled by meaning. This implies that it is his responsibility to decide whether or not he wishes to fulfill it. "Meaning fulfillment always implies decision-making." [2] Those who have a personal center are pulled by meaning. Their striving leads to a vertical examination of the issues of life. Their motivation is intrinsic, part of the warp and woof of being. Their decision making does not require nor is it facilitated by an environment in which drives toward power or self-actualization are expressed even in the intense form of group experience. These are those who engage in genuine change on the basis of their own intrinsic motivation and in situations in which in the Lewinian sense they are free to do otherwise.

For these it would appear that the group-centered group provides the psychological climate most beneficial in their striving to fulfill meaning in their lives. Those who have a personal center and have developed "the inner choice" consistently engage in creative evaluation of the issues of life in terms of their striving to fulfill meaning.

### Is It Love?

The several types of groups depend upon the caring relationship among members as the necessary condition for positive be-

[2] Viktor E. Frankl, "Self-Transcendence as a Human Phenomenon," *Journal of Humanistic Psychology,* vol. 6, no. 2, p. 100, fall, 1966.

havioral change. This is the final phase that Rogers, in writing on the basic encounter group, refers to as "the love feast."

One does not question the efficacy of love as the chief means for bringing about healthy cooperative groups and changed individuals. The more urgent question becomes, Is this truly love which is described as "the love feast," or is it a form of egocentric behavior masquerading as love? And are the individuals really freed, loving persons, or are they simulating a condition because it is considered to be appropriate?

There may be, then, grave possibilities that an intensive group encounter, especially of short duration, does not attain the personality changes which have been accredited to it. These changes have been predicated upon an interpersonal relationship which has been described as one in which love is the chief dynamic catalyst.

Love has several appearances; what seems to be love may be something very different. To take one possibility briefly referred to earlier, it is quite possible that a feeling of societal guilt results from the personal attacks which in some form usually occur in the middle and later stages of the group. Assuming this possibility, the members may be moved by this uncomfortable feeling toward doing what is socially considered "good" or "correct." If so they begin to relate increasingly in a manner which may be interpreted as acts of caring, of union, of responsibility, of love. In this case the members are not really motivated by love but by the proper thing to do. They are being obedient to normative ethics previously accepted regarding what should be the conduct in such a framework. They are not really relating at a depth level or genuinely changing as appearances may indicate. This manner of behaving is viewed to be objectively and eternally valid. It is the assumption that there is a standard of conduct which should be unequivocally applied in such situations. This is the legalistic approach to decision making. "Love, legalistically understood, is not so much an attitude or relational category as it is an axiomatic description of correct and proper human behavior." [3]

A second possibility is disturbing also. Instead of asking, "What ought I to do?" the members may ask, "What am I to do?" Since the intensive group experience of the T group or encounter group focuses on the "here and now," emphasis is given to the category of

[3] Harmon L. Smith, "When Love Becomes Excarnate," in John Bennett et al., *Storm over Ethics,* Bethany Press, 1967, p. 91.

immediacy. Reflection is not encouraged; it is immediate response which is expected and favored. With the possible reduction or elimination of reflection, the process becomes one of a wholly psychic and subjective level of feeling. This procedure discounts both epistemologically and ontologically any continuity between existential movements. The members are then engaged to a large degree in an unconditioned and arbitrary response to unrelated stimuli.

The assumption in such processes is that the real and desirable are the self responding spontaneously and reflexively to the "here and now." The "here and now" environment is emphasized because only this environment developed by the members is considered by the leader and themselves as valuable for the purposes of the group.

The situation which develops in the middle and final phases appears as previously described. However, each member has become both creator and judge. Each participates with other members but perhaps as one who stands over against them. He is momentarily but not necessarily lastingly affected by mutual involvement. He may not take the risk of genuine love by giving himself in the actual and decisive moment of encounter. Such involvement has the appearance of the noble and humanitarian but may be only a form of egoism and informed only by its own moral precommitment.

There is at least one other possibility which should not go unnoticed. In this case in the same intensive experience the question is not "What ought I do?" or "What am I to do?" but instead "What do I want?" This position is that there are only hypothetical principles in the decision-making context. Their application makes them valid. Love in this context is not substantive or formal; it is only a predicate; it is doing. Such a way of explaining love avoids legalism on the one hand and existentialism on the other.

In this position there is no history or time except the present. The only world is the world of becoming. There is no connection between being and nonbeing. The member in his decisions is not part of the situation. The situation and the member are not in communion. The member is not embodied in the situation in the group; he is instead "up against" a situation. What he does *in* the situation is unrelated to what he becomes. The situation is out there; it is "the case," or "what is."

The members perform as if love which is outside and apart from the situation can be almost immediately introduced. It is introjected through the members' feeling of helping other members. If the result helps, it is good. Without any reference to principles of being and not on the basis of any substantive movement over time, the members engage in what they perceive as a helping relationship.

If love is to be considered the curative dynamic in group counseling, greater attention should be given to understanding its basic qualities. If it is considered a simple variable recognizable by its effects, confusion and misunderstanding may result. To assume that persons who last week were strangers and this week reveal to one another their limitations, societal guilts, and hostilities will next week as a result conclude by loving one another is in itself saying something about love and human nature which calls for study.

We have seen that love may take many forms. All three forms discussed indicate clearly that any personality change of a lasting and constructive nature would be unlikely to occur. Yet it is both possible and probable that an intensive group experience primed by ambiguity and frustrations may, following the venting of confusion, indictments, and hostilities, eventuate in interpersonal relationships which basically are answering one or more of the questions "What ought I to do?" "What am I to do?" or "What do I want to do?" To the degree that this takes place, the personality change is most probably phenotypical and its value of questionable consequence.

It should be recognized that such caricatures of love could and perhaps do occur in various kinds of groups. Relationships in all groups should be studied under the complete knowledge of the difficulty which exists in understanding the conditions of love and the meaning of the love relationship. The very dynamic of the intensive group experience which heightens and intensifies personal involvement in the immediacy of the group process may, because it moves too quickly and impulsively, prevent mediation of the more difficult relationship which makes love possible.

It may be that if love is to be genuine, taking the risk of the personal giving of oneself, a group process based on different assumptions is implicated.

In the essential examination of the crucial dynamic of love in counseling in all groups, it should be recognized that none of the three possibilities, legalism, extemporism, or situationism, is the basis for the changing of behavior to competent and satisfactory living. This is so because none of these includes the reality of risk within the decision-making act. Each one of these attitudes is absolute in its own way, removing any genuine risk and responsibility.

The place of risk in all three possibilities is extrinsic. The risk in these is not within the act, having its meaning within it, but is in consequence of the act of choice and has its meaning only in terms of results. In the act itself there is no risk as a constitutive part of the decision. The fact that risk is excluded from the act makes each of these basically a nonhuman way of relationship. Genuine love embodies genuine risk.

# 4

## DYNAMICS OF GROUP COUNSELING

*It is common practice to place the emphasis in group counseling on the method and functioning of the leader. But the leader works within a climate, uses structure, and depends upon communication for the quality of the experience. The leader, climate, structure, and communication are inextricably related, and each is separated from the others only for the purpose of description.*

*Each of these is a function of the interrelatedness of members and leader. However, the leader plays a more significant part in establishing the climate and structure. The members have an influential part in developing the communication aspects and indirectly influence both climate and structure.*

The leader initiates a method and in so doing uses structure, which in turn significantly influences the kind of climate which develops. The climate in turn encourages a particular pattern of communication. For example, a group-centered leader uses a minimal degree of structure and is accepting, permissive, and nonevaluative; this structure and climate are conducive to a three-way communication system of member to member, member to group, and leader to group. An authoritarian leader, in contrast, uses a maximum degree of structure and is evaluative and permissive regarding only that which conforms to his perceptions; this structure and the ensuing climate encourage only two-way communication—leader to member and member to leader.

The four chapters which follow explore the several aspects of the dynamics of group counseling. Each chapter considers one aspect and relates it to the others. The last chapter of the four shows the interrelationship of the various aspects in the total functioning of the group.

# 8

## A CLIMATE FOR GROUP COUNSELING

Some kind of psychological climate is an integral part of every group experience. It is developed through each member's perception of his own recognition of worth and the feeling that others have for him and that he has for others, together with a general attitude about what is taking place in the group environment. This climate is not totally the same for each member. The group climate for each is as he perceives it to be. It is a function of what is taking place but even more importantly the sum total of his expectations flowing from his past experiences.

### DETRIMENTAL INFLUENCES

One detrimental influence is the failure to take into account one's own past experiences and those of the group. James Plant, in *Emo-*

*tion and the Educative Process*, chided teachers for assuming that each child was born that morning on the doorstep of the school. Group leaders can easily fall into the same error by neglecting to take into consideration not only their own past but especially the differential conditioning influences of the background experiences of the members.

Another is the influence of the "marketplace" and the competitive structure of society. A member may believe that his place in the group is dependent upon what he produces, that is, how well he lives up to the expectancy of peers and authority figures. He may perceive it to be similar to other competitive societies in which he has had to make his way and which he has now come to accept. He has learned to rely on the word of authority with only minimal interest in thinking things out for himself. He has learned that a creative idea or action of higher quality than that presented by the leader is sometimes unwelcome and seldom accepted. He may have been conditioned to learning experiences which consist of only the intellectual assimilation of ideas which are frequently discarded after they have been presented back to the leader in the expected form. He has developed evaluative attitudes which have seemed necessary to him for the purpose of survival. Listening may have become an activity whose purpose is not to understand but to reduce, demolish, or discover logical weaknesses or lack of information. He tends not to be interested in other members of the group, giving concentrated attention only to the authority figure.

All these beliefs and attitudes as well as others are detrimental to perception of the meaning of a group and to the ability to be a member of a group. At times it seems that home, school, and society have not helped youth in developing an ability to be a functioning, helpful member of a group. And higher education apparently does little to alleviate or improve the situation. Therefore to help the members develop the attitudes and capacities for giving and receiving help in a group situation is an undertaking of no small proportions. To go further and develop a climate of caring and responsibility for one another often seems an ideal beyond grasp.

A third detrimental influence may be that a member of the group is so accustomed to thinking only pragmatically that he finds it exceedingly difficult to examine experience in depth. In the process of the members' moving from an aggregate of individuals to an organic group each is challenged to look into himself to discover who he is, what he is going to believe, and how he is going to relate to others. This is a difficult task and more so for some than for others. It may be that some never accomplish it; if they do not, this is due in part to the fact that such a journey inward is foreign to their way of life. They may be accustomed to reacting to life's demands on a strictly pragmatic basis. They try something, and if it works, they continue it; if not, they try something else. To ask the effect of these actions on others or themselves is not considered or is presumed to be irrelevant. They ask the questions of expediency or the legalistic question "Is it right?" meaning *right* in terms of societal expectancies. They lack a depth dimension, or personal center. These members may be quite active in a group, but they contribute little of satisfying meaning to themselves or to those in the group who may be challenged by searching instead of driven by drives.

## NECESSARY CONDITIONS

What, then, would characterize the relationships within the group which would result in an ideal climate for group counseling? To these conditions we now turn.

### *Unconditional Acceptance*

Many children and adults do not feel accepted unless they can prove that they are worthy. Frequently to be worthy means meeting satisfactorily the demands of others. It is a recognized fact that the child progressively loses his spontaneity as he advances through the grades. "The fear of evaluation invariably operates to reduce spontaneous participation of teachers in the administration of our schools and of students in the classroom learning situation." [1] It is unfortunate that evaluative procedures, instead of acting as incentives, foster dependence, conformity, and submission and drastically inhibit unique achievement.

[1] Thomas Gordon, *Group-centered Leadership,* Houghton Mifflin Company, Boston, 1955, p. 72.

In this technological revolution the sense of personhood becomes increasingly lost. We treat one another as objects, and others treat us in similar fashion. The fact that we deserve consideration and respect because we are persons fades into the background in the face of our competitive society. Since others by subtle and other means frequently decide our destinies, we lose touch with ourselves and surrender our abilities for knowing and self-evaluation to authority figures.

The influences which cause one to see himself and others as objects with utility value only are deep and pervasive. After many experiences of this it is exceedingly difficult to see oneself as a person and to accept others as persons. Members and leaders of groups alike have in this area a difficult task of reeducation which involves a wholistic becoming of some proportion.

Yet experience affirms and group leaders agree that for significant growth to take place each member must feel that he is accepted as a person regardless of his attributes. It is only gradually, however, that members develop the realization that they are accepted regardless of whether or not they conform or display those accomplishments which they believe to be necessary in other situations. Unconditional acceptance of one another develops only at the rate at which it is experienced. It has to be a part of the interaction in order to become a fact. Such a change does not take place immediately. It is hard for a person to recognize as unessential the crutches on which he has come to depend. It is equally difficult for him to believe that others accept him and include him when from his point of view he has contributed very little or has been a dead weight in the progress of the group.

When the ability evolves to accept such a fact, he begins to use psychic energy in self-examination. He becomes his own evaluator to see himself as he really is. He commences to accept his positive feelings, beliefs, behaviors. This despite the fact that he may, according to Loomis,[2] find this even more difficult than the acceptance of his failures.

As he gradually develops an inwardness, or personal center, he focuses upon group interaction more insightfully, and his contributions are of much more value to the group.

[2] Earl Loomis, *The Self in Pilgrimage*, Harper & Brothers, New York, 1960, chap. 1.

## Personal Adequacy

This is an individual's perception of himself in relation to those aspects of his life which he feels are important. Genuine personal adequacy cannot be conveyed or imposed by another; it develops by a slow process from within. As a group leader or as a member he can try to develop those conditions which could be expected to help him feel adequate. To feel that significant others accept him as he is, is considered one of the most helpful influences in becoming personally adequate.

A member develops personal adequacy by degrees. When he is able to feel adequate in a small group, he then can more readily succeed in a slightly larger group. In an anonymous self-report a member who, after being one of a seven-member group for seven 40-minute meetings, moved into a group of ten described what took place: "I have found myself more at ease than I thought I would since going into a larger group. The small group, which I felt might be the better experience, is now a thing of the past. I don't really seem to miss it. However, this is probably due to the fact that almost all of us in the smaller group are now in the larger one."

The member who succeeds in becoming personally adequate is one who recognizes that he is not and whose desire to become so is great enough that he will overcome obstacles. One of these obstacles is normal resistance. Each of us feels some resistance in moving from the tried and familiar to the new and unknown. When necessary we should help one another to recognize this as a fact of life. Sometimes this feeling of normal resistance is accentuated and unknowingly used to defend ourselves against the acceptance of the new. Of course any pressures upon us increase our resistance to change, causing us to speak and act defensively or aggressively.

However, increased acceptance and reduction of threat should reduce the need for defensiveness. When fully realized, unconditional acceptance does much to reduce defensiveness and to increase a feeling of personal adequacy in the members.

## An Open-minded View of Authority

Such a view is maximally possible only to a minority, that is, to those who are relatively open-minded. A person's belief-disbelief systems are considered open to "the extent to which the person can receive, evaluate, and act on relevant information, received from the outside on its own intrinsic merits unencumbered by irrelevant factors in the situation, arising from within the person or from the outside." [3] The relatively closed-minded person is a threatened person. He finds great difficulty in relating to authority figures in such a manner that he does not ignore his own abilities for discussion and decision making. His usual behaviors in relation to authority are those of conformity, or submissiveness, or reaction and hostility. Such attitudes and behaviors in part are an outcome of his early experiences in his home and school situations. Such members are not sufficiently free to present what might have been their unique creative contributions.

The closed-minded member who has been conditioned to see authority as virtually infallible is unable to evaluate the ideas of significant others. He is not able to distinguish between the source of the information and the information itself. Since he is threatened and insecure, he accepts ideas uncritically and also changes his position with each new authority. The group is a very different experience for those who are open-minded and those who are closed-minded. In the following anonymous self-report each is a member of the same group and reports on the incident, planned in advance, of moving from a group of seven to a group of ten members. The open-minded member writes: "In the group of ten persons, I found the experience very beneficial. I felt free to express my thoughts and react to others." The closed-minded member writes: "I felt very uneasy when we formed the larger group and I think it was because I was uncertain about what we were expected to do, how we were supposed to get started discussing when we had no leader or topics and were relatively strangers." The need of the latter person to depend upon, and to be directed by, an authority is quite evident, whereas the open-minded member is uninhibited by ambiguity and participates easily in the new, open, and unstructured situation.

### Other-centered Participation

The ability to think and perform for the good of others in the group develops slowly. Members differ in the rate at which each

[3] Milton Rokeach, *The Open and Closed Mind,* Basic Books, Inc., Publishers, New York, 1960, p. 57.

can and does become interested in what is happening to others in the group. Some members attain this other-centeredness fairly early in the group's existence; others attain it, if at all, very late. This is the experience of many group leaders. Gordon describes it in these terms: "One of the most difficult things for a group member to learn is how to achieve the delicate balance between satisfying his own needs and helping others to satisfy theirs. Those who successfully find this balance are the ones who ultimately contribute the most to the group's development." [4]

Although each member, being a unique person, changes at his own rate, there is a fairly predictable mode of change. This mode may be viewed as successive changes that overlap but nevertheless have some distinctiveness. The progressive movement could be characterized by the following stages:

First, there is a *willingness to be present.* A self-report of a student reads, "I enjoy the company and the remarks of the other people. I feel a sense of wanting to improve and an eagerness to get on with it."

The second stage may be described as *a desire to see and hear and to be seen and heard.* Illustrative of this stage are these anonymous self-reports: "A good, free discussion. I did not exactly open and vent all of my feelings, but others were on the way and this was good." Another member writes: "I feel that the people in this group listen and are willing to share their feelings with others."

The third stage is *an urge to understand and be understood.* One member writes: "All the people expressed some of their opinions as they believed them to be. Conclusions could not be determined, but everyone listened, thought, and spoke freely." Another writes: "This evening I felt there was more evident concern expressed for the feelings of other members of the group."

The fourth stage may be characterized as *an ongoing desire to care and to help.* A member writes: "I felt concerned for one member in particular. I found myself wanting to find a way of helping her become comfortable in the group." Another writes: "I felt uncomfortable. Perhaps it was caused by the fact that I wanted to be sure I was contributing something worthwhile for the group rather than for myself."

This brief analysis indicates that to become less egocentric

[4] Gordon, *op. cit.,* p. 76.

and to be able and desire to be helpful to others is a process in becoming which is quite difficult. It is virtually expecting members to receive satisfactions not from what happens to them but rather from what happens to others.

The climate, then, of group counseling develops. The time required for a group commencing as strangers to become able to relate meaningfully to one another varies with each group. Members who for various reasons have difficulty in thinking outside themselves deter others in their efforts to develop a climate of trust and caring.

To ignore the fact that ability to relate meaningfully is preceded by a feeling of "closeness" is to enter into a relationship which is too superficial and too precarious to be useful. Gendlin insists that closeness must precede unmasking. He considers it "useless and harmful to claw at another person, insultingly insisting that he is 'not being real,' 'not opening up,' as groups unfortunately try to do. Many of these desires to hear from the other person are highly artificial, throwing the difficulty of the process onto the other person." [5]

### Trust

Much of what is accomplished in a group depends upon a climate of trust. What members share with one another bears a direct relation to the amount of trust they feel they can place in one another. If they do not trust one another, they suppress the information needed for problem solving and for understanding one another.

Necessary as trust is, it cannot be attained by establishing it as a goal. Trust is a by-product of perception, attitudes, and experience. Learning how others respond in various situations does not necessarily raise the level of trust. Actually all that can be done is to encourage a climate conducive to trust.

This of course does not mean it is a climate of trust for everyone or to the same degree for any two members who perceive they can trust the other members or the leader. Each member perceives the situation differently. At the close of the first meeting of a group, one member wrote: "As a member I proceeded warily in my group. I found myself becoming shaky both when I met disagreement and

[5] Eugene T. Gendlin and John Beebe III, "An Experimental Approach to Group Therapy," *Journal of Research and Development in Education,* vol. 1, no. 2, p. 22, winter, 1968.

when I was not understood." Another member of the same group in the same session wrote: "I felt much more stimulated and willing to participate verbally than I have in most of the courses I have taken at this university."

How well any one member trusts others is a function of his perception of his past experiences. Authoritarian teachers, managers, and parents who have pretended to be democratic but are later recognized to be otherwise make it difficult for those whom they have deceived to trust in other situations. One member at the close of the first session wrote: "He seems to want us to make decisions and to be really interested in us, but I'm going to wait and see. He's really too good to be true."

A lack of trust does not often show itself in its true colors. It hides behind a demand for more structure, superficial and frequent verbalizing, and general aggressiveness. These forms of expression become the means of the person's defending himself against a possible situation in which he may be expected to trust. To attack and be attacked are much more tolerable to the insecure member than to find himself in a situation requiring that he risk his ideas and meanings to the consideration of others.

To trust requires a greater degree of risk taking than to attack, conform, or submit. The results in each of these latter are more predictable and receive an earlier feedback. To trust requires a great ability to tolerate ambiguity, uncertainty, and the risk of being misunderstood. One member wrote: "When I said that I thought we should talk more about our relationships now than about our teaching experiences, I felt I was taking a risk and I am still not sure how the others felt about the idea."

It is difficult to recognize trust among members of a group; it can be only inferred after the behavior has taken place. One person may conclude that a certain member's behavior is an expression of trust, whereas another may present reasons why the same behavior may be based upon other motives. This may be the reason why some members require more evidence than others before they are willing to trust. To trust means that you are willing to enlarge your world by sharing yourself with certain definite others. Some members may reach the place where trust in certain others or in all the members becomes reasonable and viewed as useful in making progress as a member of the group. Nevertheless they remain unable to take the necessary risk to make it an actuality. They apparently do not attempt to extend their life space and exercise only the "courage to be as a part" and may even be unaware of many of the stimuli which might have helped them to become more discriminating concerning interpersonal relationships.

It is not uncommon for leaders to assume that members come into a group ready, willing, and able to trust one another. This is of course unrealistic. Some leaders recognize that both those who are accustomed to trust every one and those who trust no one experience the greatest difficulty in this area. If a choice were granted, leaders might well prefer in the group those who had learned to discriminate between those they could trust and those they could not, on the basis of reliable objective evidence. In the competitive and manipulative world the members have learned that it is necessary to discriminate. This fact is a deterrent to their entrance into a relationship of trust in the group.

It is evident, then, that much becoming has to take place in the members of the group before they can have a climate of trust among them. This is of course more difficult to develop in an adult group than in a group of children. However, some children have experienced incidents in which someone, a child or adult, revealed their secrets and severely damaged their growing ability to trust. The counselor who explains the necessity for, and the condition of, confidentiality knows full well that trusting can become a true reality only after they have experienced that it is safe to trust. Trust built on pragmatic reasons, such as "You trust me and I'll trust you and no one will get hurt," is not a kind of trust which has the depth to function as a healing and truly constructive influence in the group.

Trust cannot be built on the injunction that one ought to trust or on intuition—"He looks like someone you can trust"—or on exaggerated needs for sympathy, or on power needs, or even on various kinds of subtle reinforcement from others. Trust conducive to constructive behavioral change is much more elusive and demanding than the results obtained by these methods.

### Development of Potential

A climate for group counseling is one in which the potentials of members develop and continue to develop. These are not only skills and critical thinking but the development as well of the member's potential to experience the depth dimension within himself in relation to the awesome realities of his world.

A depth dimension is not encouraged or expected by the modern situation. Reason, which was once used for the examination of all levels of experience and for the examination of the historical ways of society, is now used chiefly for technical advance and control. Society now capitalizes upon the exploitation of reason in the service of technological advancement. This has severely minimized the use of reason for the development of the individual's inner choice.

The threat of an atomic catastrophe has made us easy captives to submission "to the peaceful production of the means of destruction, to the perfection of waste, to being educated for a defense which deforms the defenders and that which they defend." [6]

It is in the interests of industrial society to perpetuate the danger of destruction, since this contributes to its success and development. Such a society offers more and more sensual fulfillment and ease based on materialism. It also extends man's conquest over nature and ego satisfaction. Mass media have become quite efficient in selling particular interests. The purchasers of these are always presented as men of good reason and judgment. Political needs of society become more indistinguishable from individual needs and aspirations and therefore receive less investigation and criticism.

Freedom from toil and increase in sensual and material satisfactions diminish the possibility of intelligent criticism. The lack of searching criticism and of the sustainment of discusson of industrial society is unfortunate. In terms of theory and practice, values and facts, needs and goals, this has led to an unprecedented lack of discrimination and to the acceptance of opposites in politics, human relations, and government. Marcuse describes the change in these words: "This containment of social change is perhaps the most singular achievement of advanced industrial society: the general acceptance of the National Purpose, bipartisan policy, the decline of pluralism, the collusion of Business and Labor within the strong State testify to the integration of opposites which is the result as well as the prerequisite of this achievement." [7]

[6] Herbert Marcuse, *One-dimensional Man,* Beacon Press, Boston, 1967, p. ix.
[7] *Ibid.,* p. xii.

At times it seems almost incredible that we live so unconcernedly in a society which at every level ignores or brazenly accepts wide inconsistencies. Consider the seeming compatibility of the growth of productivity and the growth of destruction, the continuance and increase of misery in the presence of unprecedented wealth, the militant striving for freedom of thought and opportunity, and the surrender of power, hope, and reason to the existent powers. Is this not an indication that there is an unmistakable trend toward living superficially, toward a failure to recognize the distinction between a one-dimensional and a two-dimensional way of life? Marcuse views our present society as irrational and reprehensive. He writes, "Men must come to see it and to find their way from false to true consciousness, from their immediate to their real interest." [8]

Everyone is affected to some degree. There are those who have developed the potential of the depth dimension and those who have developed it only partially. Those who live self-examined lives need little urging from without. They go beyond the question of utility in the consideration of any course of action. The members of our groups range along a continuum from those who are relatively one-dimensional to those who are relatively two-dimensional. Almost everyone to some degree actualizes both his horizontal and depth-dimension potentialities.

There is perhaps no one who has over a period of time lived completely by his one-dimensional possibility. Some have developed the potential of the depth dimension to such a degree that they may for descriptive purposes be considered as two-dimensional. This does not mean that they use only the depth dimension in making all decisions. When they perceive the decision to be one of utility, bearing no direct human-relations values, they decide on the basis of the one dimension. They may frequently decide on the basis of utility but reexamine the decision in terms of human values.

On the other hand those who have not developed the depth potential to the same degree have usually reached decisions using only the one dimension. Occasionally in unusual circumstances they have actualized the depth dimension in trying to reach a difficult decision in which the outcomes would seriously affect the lives of others. It may be said that to use the proper criteria, exercise, and concentration required for a depth-dimension decision is more diffi-

[8] *Ibid.,* p. xiii.

cult and likely to be avoided by these than by those who regularly recognize and use this dimension. For descriptive purposes this latter group is referred to as one-dimensional.

With the recognition, then, that it is not possible to categorize persons accurately as entirely one-dimensional or two-dimensional, the descriptions that follow are presented only for the purposes of clarifying the concepts.

If there were such persons as one-dimensional persons, they would in this schema be viewed as having the following characteristics: Such persons would be guided chiefly by the values of significant others with whom they relate. They would derive meaning from status, power, and possessions. They would be pragmatic in their approach to experience; that is, their approach would be that the value of something is judged by the results produced for the one using it. They would be impelled by drives, and their imagination, being chiefly reactive, would not be developed to extend meaning in depth. They would be motivated by forces extrinsic to themselves. Symbols would not readily influence them, since they would lack depth and a personal center. Lacking depth they would not profoundly experience joy, sorrow, or the pull toward the meaning of existence. They would misidentify their small world, in which they live with only the "courage to be as a part," as the whole universe. Only occasionally when some experience took them unawares would they be likely to sense that their lives are partial and deficient in a troublesome way. Even then they probably would be lulled back into accepting the status quo of their own lives, since society "delivers the goods," persuading as it does that these hold the key to a satisfying life accepted and acceptable by men of sound reason. As explained by Wilson, "Man has reached his present position on the evolutionary ladder because he is a tool-making animal, a machine-making animal . . . in fact, a robot-making animal. But his sheer cleverness is proving to be his downfall." [9]

The relatively two-dimensional person would know that this was not so. He would be contrastingly different in a number of important respects. He would not be driven by drives but pulled by meaning. His deep joy and satisfaction would not be derived from status,

[9] Colin Wilson, "Existential Psychology: A Novelist's Approach," in James F. T. Bugental (ed.), *Challenges of Humanistic Psychology,* McGraw-Hill Book Company, New York, 1967, p. 70.

power, or possessions but from his sense of discovery and participation in the meaning of life. His imagination would not be just reactive but also productive. He would create new forms and sense new meanings. Symbols would enrich his life and challenge him to engage in meditative search. His motivations would be chiefly intrinsic. He would confront issues in their interrelationship and bearing on his values. He would be the chief evaluator. Although he would use information from many sources, he would decide in the depth of his being their significance in terms of his inner choice. He would respect himself as a person and would have the attitude and intent of respecting others as persons. He would be self-motivating and in the sense just described self-evaluating. He would open himself to experiences of joy, beauty, sorrow, and love.

To the degree that a person varies from the middle of the continuum toward the extremes of one-dimensionality or two-dimensionality, he would perceive the climate and dynamics of the group differently. The more a person varies in either direction, the more his expectancies and needs as a group member will differ.

It is conceivable, then, that a process which is useful to the more one-dimensional person could be less useful to a more two-dimensional person. Relatively one-dimensional persons may be helped by direct confrontation of one another in relation to issues they choose to discuss. The "here and now" approach may uncover and reveal to each and every one the fears, doubts, loves, hostilities, resentments, strengths, and inadequacies of all the others. This may be the means of forcing each to accept and actualize for the time being and to the degree possible the depth dimension of inwardness and to initiate in some measure his inner choice.

On the other hand, the two-dimensional person may find such an overt and extrinsically motivated encounter unnecessary or even inhibitive; that is, the person who has developed to some degree his potential of inwardness does of his own accord and on his own initiative consider ideas, whether of the "there and then" or of the "here and now" experience. These are analyzed and examined in relation to his basic value structure and the judgment of his transmoral conscience. Allport emphasizes that this conscience is "functionally autonomous of its roots and the arbiter of adult values." [10]

[10] Gordon W. Allport, *The Individual and His Religion,* The Macmillan Company, New York, 1950, p. 89.

It is not uncommon for the relatively two-dimensional person, as Wilson would say, to transcend his everyday "human aspects" and become a kind of immortal [11] or, in Husserl's language, to place the "world in brackets and become aware of himself as a transcendental ego." [12] This person has much in common with Bonner's "proactive" individual who "has both the will and the capacity to resist external pressures toward conformity and to transform himself in the light of his personal goals and values,[13] or as the apostle Paul encouraged, "Be ye not conformed to this world but transformed by the renewing of your mind that you may prove what is the good and acceptable and perfect will of God." [14]

Counselors and psychotherapists agree that it is the exercise of this depth dimension, the transmoral conscience, which makes psychotherapy possible. Group counseling relies upon its actualization for significant behavioral change. It is evident when a member accepts his own conflicts, seeing them for what they are and suffering because of what he sees. In this inner experience he goes beyond what society considers moral, because he cannot integrate a sensitive and good conscience. Tillich writes that "those who have a sensitive conscience cannot escape the question of the transmoral conscience." [15] Thus we come back to the affirmation that a climate for group counseling is one which is conducive to encouraging the development of a sensitive conscience. Those who have a sensitive conscience are on the way to actualizing the depth dimension in which the transmoral conscience can be heard. It is a reasonable hypothesis that the necessary climate for group counseling differs directly with the dimensionality of the group members.

Such a hypothesis in effect suggests that the relatively one-dimensional person may need and profit from basic encounter and T groups and that the relatively two-dimensional person may need and profit from group-centered groups. Such a hypothesis may account in part for the fact that some claim to receive great help from a basic encounter group or a T group and others as strongly

---

[11] Wilson, op. cit., p. 76.
[12] E. Husserl, Ideas, George Allen & Unwin, Ltd., London, 1912.
[13] Hubert Bonner, "The Proactive Personality," in James F. T. Bugental (ed.), Challenges of Humanistic Psychology, McGraw-Hill Book Company, New York, 1967, p. 65.
[14] The Bible, King James Version, Rom. 12:2.
[15] Paul Tillich, Morality and Beyond, Harper & Row, Publishers, Incorporated, New York, 1963, p. 81.

claim and demonstrate that it was of no help. It would appear from conversations with those who were helped that they caught a glimpse of, had a fleeting encounter with, something which they want to experience again.

The climate for group counseling is one in which the members are involved in such a manner that they actualize the depth dimension in their search for the meaning of the "here and now" and of life in general, not only for themselves but for others.

### Understanding

The climate for group counseling is one of understanding. In such a group there is a high degree of self-understanding and understanding of others. Members who attain understanding feel an unconditional acceptance from the leader and one another and trust one another. They are open to authority, feel normally adequate, and have developed to some degree the depth dimension, or inner choice.

But to achieve understanding of one another is not easy. It is reached only gradually and through much effort. Most members discover that to understand another requires a risk that is a difficult challenge to meet. The perception that they will enter a new experience in relationship inhibits many from taking the first step. They hesitate to *will to understand.* There are several ways generally unrecognized by which they avoid "signing up" to understand. They do one or several of the following: They perform superficial acts such as pretending to listen, nodding their heads, and otherwise going through the motions, but they are not really interested; they are not willing to become involved. Lacking the will to understand they feel uneasy, since pretense is not satisfying. This causes them to find fault as a defense against taking the crucial step of entering into an agreement to understand, which includes allowing themselves to be understood.

When a member achieves the first step of willingness to understand, he discovers that this requires that he give himself, that he express himself. But to express oneself In any manner is a risk. Not only this, but if the expression is to lead to genuine understanding, one must express himself with increasing honesty and frankness. To learn how to do this tactfully and kindly yet clearly is a task in itself. Difficult as this is, the member realizes that in expressing his convictions to others he becomes really aware of them. He senses a new understanding of himself, a new freedom.

There may be those who feel that they can open themselves to others quite easily. If these persons carefully examined their endeavors, many would find that it is a superficial opening up. There may be a flow of words, but these may only disguise their deepest thoughts and feelings. Recognizing the great difficulty and hesitancy to let oneself be known, it has become the practice in some groups to manipulate one another by some form of aggressive action driven to frustration by an intolerable situation. Each is then impelled to accept an incisive judgment of another, only to return an equally judgmental statement. Such an attempt, whether masked or open, does not have the considered willingness of the member to express it. This condition alone may jeopardize its usefulness as a therapeutic act.

The will to understand and to express oneself genuinely and in depth requires courage. This courage cannot be forced. It comes only through the hours the members spend in a careful, unincited drawing together. It grows out of the seedbed of acceptance, trust, and the slow nurturing of a personal center. In its development at least two fears must be overcome, the fear of critical judgment and the fear of receiving advice. As the members grow in their experience with one another, they come to realize that they are accepted and that they can trust. The fact that they are not criticized or given strong advice diminishes their fears and assists them to have the courage necessary to try to understand and to be understood.

To understand we must accept one another's natural differences. These differences are various. Some members do not sense what another is saying and how he feels about it, because they cannot get past or suspend the sensory mannerisms or other differences. They have an established image, and when the speaker does not conform to it, they are unable to get beyond it and accept him.

Another natural difference is the variance in the ways members think about a problem. Some approach it on a strictly scientific, cause-and-effect relationship. Others may confront the same problem intuitively and artistically. The former may be interested in things exactly as they are. To the latter, the same things are symbols of other values which they intuitively sense and associate with them. These approaches complement each other and lead to a richer experience than is possible with only one of the approaches. Yet it is sometimes very difficult for each to appreciate the other's way of looking at the situation.

Another natural difference may be a member's accustomed way of expression. He may speak arrogantly, defensively, timidly, emphatically, or in a superior manner. He may create the impression that he is an authority not to be challenged or the impression that "I'm just a humble man," to use an expression from Charles Dickens. Mannerisms call forth feeling intrusions from members which make it very difficult for them to hear and appreciate what the member is saying. But these members greatly need to be understood. Members can become able to understand. This is most probable if the members really come to care and feel some responsibility for one another. Some find this possible even when others present strong interferences to their realization.

Those who have to a large degree succumbed to these nullifying influences require a group climate which will awaken them to the possibility and their capability of making an "inner choice." For these the initial phases of group experience may be those which induce them to confront the nonbeing episodes in their own lives. How strong this inducement should be and what form it should take await further examination and research.

Those who have with varying degrees of difficulty developed and maintained a depth of meaning in their lives need a somewhat different group climate. Since they have developed this potential of depth to some degree, they are accustomed to examining issues and life in general in terms of their own inner values of responsibility and caring. These then do not need the inducement needed by those who are strangers to the self-examined life and the use of the transmoral conscience.

It is generally agreed that a climate conducive to behavioral change is one of acceptance, trust, and caring leading to a sense of responsibility for, and helpfulness toward, one another. It is hypothesized that the impact of such a climate varies directly with the dimensionality of the members. Until members have begun to develop the potential of the depth dimension, changes in behavior of these members may remain at the superficial, phenotypical level. The recognition of this possibility may assist us in differentiating relationships in the group and individual change in depth in relationship with others. Changes realized in the group may be low in transfer value. It is informative to observe the number who listen with understanding and empathy to others on "the mainland" following their group experience.

The ideal group climate for any member is one which helps him to relate more openly and in depth with other members. This being the case it is possible that the character of the group climate should also differ in relation to these member characteristics. The relatively one-dimensional members may learn that confrontative interpersonal exploration of the basic encounter and T groups impels them to approach reality at a deeper level than that to which they have been accustomed. Such an experience aids them in their preparation for entrance into groups with a different orientation, whereas the relatively two-dimensional members may prefer the unconditional acceptance of the group-centered group, which encourages them to maximize their usual approach of examination of important issues at a depth level.

Despite past conditioning and varying approaches to life's problems certain conditions apparently facilitate change for most members, especially at certain points in their development. These are the conditions of acceptance, understanding, trust, caring, and a sense of responsibility for others. It should be noted, however, that these conditions only facilitate behavioral change; they do not bring it about. Change takes place only by interaction—verbal and nonverbal—at a level deep enough to unfreeze old patterns and start the person moving in a more creative direction. But which conditions will ensure this? As Shakespeare wrote, "Ah! there's the rub."

During the question period following a talk by a well-known behaviorist, he was asked this question: "You talk to us like a behaviorist, but in your response to us you are like a humanist. Why is this?" The speaker replied that he could not explain it. There is something indefinable about a person. This something, a mystery, may be quite significant in the influence he has on others.

The more precise we become in describing group process, the more we are likely to lose sight of these indefinable qualities of the person. Not only is this quite possible, but we become less able to make conflict creative. For each of us knows that what changes conflict to a creative, productive experience is not logic but the maximizing in each of us to the degree possible this indefinable quality, this mystery by which we know that we are not objects but persons. At this point we actualize for the time being the depth dimension. Values beyond utility and opportunism are assuming their rightful place. We have also prepared ourselves for the insight that we understand another only on our level of development.

Further, we know that we can be defeated but not overcome, victorious but not proud, and beaten but not broken. We have human freedom, a creative choice which can wield its influence against any odds.

# 9

## STRUCTURE IN
## GROUP COUNSELING

*Structure* is a term used to describe the relationship of forces, objects, and society. We speak of the organization of people, of authority, of various kinds of forces both in the natural and human world, of the status structure, the organic structure, and many others. "Structure is the arrangement or interrelationship of all the parts of a whole with respect to each other." [1] We use descriptive or explanatory aspects of observed process as evidence for understanding the relative positions of the parts and the relationship or lack of it among them.

The understanding of structure bears a direction relationship to

[1] Kenneth D. Benne and Bozidal Muntyan, *Human Relations in Curriculum Change,* The Dryden Press, Inc., New York, 1951, p. 90.

whatever progress we have made. The study of structure in the inorganic world received attention first, followed by the study of structure in the organic world, and last in the human world, which continues to be studied. Concepts developed in the inorganic and organic worlds have preceded understanding of the relationship of parts of a structure in the human world. Interpretation of relationships in the subhuman world as mechanistic was transferred to the human world, resulting in authoritarian relationships and aggregate groups.

Commencing in the nineteenth century another way of interpreting relationships gained recognition. Early protagonists of new relationships are generally considered to be Galileo, Newton, and Descartes. This new way of viewing parts saw them integrally related and received the name *organicism*. Nature and later man were explained by the concept of the "field" with emerging forces and needs satisfied by the integrated energy of the whole organism. This concept radically changed the structure of human relationships. "Distributive leadership, cooperative planning, and democratic action emerged with the development of this philosophy." [2]

But under the guidance of the scientific method structure may become an idol. When this occurs, the uniqueness of the individual ego is ignored, and then it is assumed that the corruptions of self-interest of the individual may disappear with the overcoming of the "cultural lag." The optimism of Dewey and Whitehead [3] that the overcoming of the cultural lag would lead to a society which would ultimately be governed purely by rational suasion rather than force now seems far removed. Dewey's faith in science [4] was based on the conviction that methods which were successful in the field of physical nature would succeed in human relations.


PURPOSE

Some structure is always present. Even a situation which is formally unstructured is still structured in its unstructuredness. Initially a study of structure was for the purpose of classification; that is, similarities

[2] C. Gratton Kemp, *Perspectives on the Group Process,* Houghton Mifflin Company, Boston, 1964, p. 4.
[3] Alfred North Whitehead, *Adventure of Ideas,* chap. 5, The Macmillan Company, New York, 1933.
[4] John Dewey, *Liberalism and Social Action,* G. P. Putnam's Sons, New York, 1935, p. 51.

and dissimilarities were noted, and this aided intelligent and ready reference. Second, structure was studied to understand its functioning. How did each part of the structure function, for what purpose, and with what result? Third, structure was studied to develop competence to change it. Attention was given to the relationship between parts, the nature and purpose of this relationship, and how and to what degree modification of a part would affect the whole.

The great time and effort given to the study of a single organism and of its functioning in relation to others have provided a model and rationale for the study of relationships both in the subhuman and in the human world. Frequently findings in the subhuman have aided in the understanding of human beings. Thus rats have been used to try to develop insights into how people learn or react under certain conditions. Sometimes grave errors have been made when it was forgotten that persons are unique, with special dimensions and characteristics which make the transference of certain assumptions from a subhuman to a human being questionable. This is the problem of those who apply insights gained from animal conditioning to human beings.

Nevertheless, the study of structure remains necessary and significant. Without it understanding in depth would be impossible. It is difficult, as well, to assess outcomes in a meaningful way. Improvement becomes increasingly difficult and uncertain without a basis for interpretation of the system of motivating tensions and "increments" from previous interactions.

Structure has been found to be one method of examining the complexity of group process. By varying the structure toward several foci results can be studied from different points of view. Such a method can provide more information in answer to such queries as the relationship between various structures, ranging from rigid to very flexible, and group productivity, the effect of structure on members' involvement, or the relationship between degrees of structure and change in behavior.

Group counselors vary widely in the attention given to structure. Some commence with theory, then consider structure in relation to it, and process in relation to structure. These see the evolution of structure from theory and of process from structure.

Others commence with process and then determine the structure, especially if they are dissatisfied with, or pleasantly surprised by, process outcomes. Occasionally they may try to determine the degree of "goodness of fit" between the process they used and a certain theory or theories. Three behaviorists counseled with groups and upon examination of the tapes decided that their counseling was group-centered.

Still other group counselors seem to be concerned only with process. They talk about incidents, have little to say about structure, and when asked about theory proclaim with an air of freedom and pride that they are eclectics. When pressed further, eclectic means to them doing what is natural in each situation. To be careless about structure and theory can limit the possibility of sound research. Replication becomes impossible in the sense of respectable research.

## KINDS OF STRUCTURE

Studies of structure in social systems indicate much variation. They vary in terms of the hierarchal level studied. Whyte concluded that variation could best be studied in relation to the observed processes of communication and particularly the criterion of who originates action for whom.[5]

Another approach to the study of structure has been through sociometry. One of the early studies by Bonney[6] revealed that choices of "work with" among sixth-grade children called forth greater differences in preference among children than the "play with" choices. This indicates that structuring for play may differ from structuring among the same population for work purposes. Jennings, through her work in sociometry, also discovered that in the informal leisure-time groups individuals chose those with whom they felt psychologically close but in work groups selected "individuals who can importantly create a milieu benefitting many members."[7]

Research supports the conclusion that structure is a complex concept. There exists in the group the formal structure (fairly fixed ends which may include rules, regulations, methods, outputs), the

[5] William F. Whyte, *Pattern for Industrial Peace,* Harper & Brothers, New York, 1951, p. 68.
[6] Merle E. Bonney, "A Study of the Sociometric Process among Sixth Grade Children," *Journal of Educational Psychology,* pp. 359–372, September, 1946.
[7] H. H. Jennings, "Sociometry of Leadership," *Sociometry Monograph 14,* Beacon House, Inc., New York, 1947, p. 28.

informal structure (free, social, open, permissive), and the resultant interplay of these two. If the formal structure is so rigid and fixed that the relationships of the informal are ruled out, individuals will try to create it within or outside the set group. Jennings concludes that the worker will live as a person whatever the official community says and will put this psyche-permissive behavior ahead of his work performance if he must.[8] Regardless of the objectives of the group, a proper balance of the formal and informal is necessary for best results. Every group has certain established and certain free conditions. Lack of this recognition by leader and members results in confusion and inefficiency. The method of determination of this proper balance and how and by whom more of the group's activities become unfixed are the crucial problems in the life of the group. Premature unfixing of ends and failure to realize the direct relationship between freedom and responsibility can lead to chaos. Leader and members should work together to establish and continuously modify the internal relationships of the group.

It has become an experienced fact that the growing numbers in an organization, whether it be educational, social, business, church, or industrial, have diminished the natural possibility for persons to be part of small groups in which they genuinely belong. These small groups provide a permissive climate in which each feels safe to indulge in more spontaneous, impulsive behavior. The importance of such groups has long been recognized, but balance requires having work to do which is related to, and makes an impact upon, the formal organization as a whole. Such groups function well only in a decentralized form of organization. Gibb [9] describes the significance of these when he writes:

> Growth-centered administration is mediated by healthy groups and management teams; the administrator committed to participative rather than defensive managing looks on his job as that of building healthy and vigorous groups and management teams rather than one of creating strong boss-subordinate pairs. . . . The healthy group does not ignore the goals of the large system, but its primary efforts are directed towards activities that are sustaining and fulfilling for individual members.

[8] *Ibid.*, p. 11.
[9] Jack Gibb, "Fear and Facade: Defensive Management," in Richard E. Farson (ed.), *Science and Human Relations,* Science and Behavior Books, Inc., Palo Alto, Calif., 1965, p. 211.

The group counselor can hardly escape being involved with structure. To understand the process he needs to study the structure. Both his failures and successes are to a significant degree an outcome of the interrelationships among the structural forces.

## CONSIDERATIONS FOR THE LEADER

Leaders, whether they be administrators, executives, managers, school principals, teachers, counselors, or among the many others, are confronted by at least three problems in their decisions regarding structure. These are expressed by a teacher in considering her work with fourth-grade children: "Is the problem one for which the children can be expected to have practical suggestions? Can I accept the ideas of the group and work with the children in putting their ideas into effect? Do the administrative conditions permit this freedom?" [10]

There are, then, three considerations which, in order of priority for consideration, can be stated as follows:

The leader commences with self-examination. This examination has two aspects: The first is concerned with his beliefs regarding learning and behavioral change; the second, with his ability in this particular situation to encourage and support the conclusions he reaches in consideration of the first aspect. A group counselor said, "After all these years of training if I do not know what is good for this group of young people, then something is wrong." For such a counselor to initiate and try to use a democratic or group-centered structure is too incongruent with his beliefs and personality to be successful.

The office manager or department head who finds that he feels uneasy unless he has a significant part in making each decision should recognize that, as much as he intellectually favors decentralized decision making, this is not for him until he himself has made a significant change. Many an organizational manager, teacher, and group counselor has with the best of intentions undertaken to work with a group democratically only to become so threatened and concerned that he has modified his approach In order to have more control and more certitude regarding the outcomes.

The second consideration is the determination concerning the

[10] C. Gratton Kemp, "The Democratic Classroom," *Elementary School Journal,* pp. 68–71, November, 1960.

capability of the members in the proper use of freedom and responsibility. Leaders find this too a very difficult decision to make. Some avoid a realistic appraisal by concluding either that the members are incapable of making decisions related to either means or ends or that they are generally capable of making all necessary decisions and require only the opportunity. Group counselors who take either position could improve their conclusions if they more effectively used their imagination to realize the implications of the situations which could be expected to ensue from their conclusion.

The decisions they reach bear a direct relationship to their beliefs regarding the functioning of groups and the abilities of the members. This is of course also a reflection of their own personalities. The authoritarian person is inclined, in relation to his needs to direct, control, and determine, to see members as less capable and responsible than is actually true for many. The democratic person respects their capabilities, but he assumes that he can help them to improve their decisions and to develop a sense of responsibility. The group-centered person not only respects their abilities but assumes that in a situation in which they are permitted to decide, their decisions will be constructive and of sufficiently high quality to lead to progress. He also assumes that they will be responsible for the decisions they make.

This demands that the leader have a high regard for their capabilities but also have a high degree of trust. Such a leader recognizes the integral relationships among trust, freedom, and responsibility. He is aware that for a sense of responsibility to be developed there must be freedom and that genuine freedom does not exist without trust. The Gibbs write: "To the degree that trust is present people can be truly interdependent. . . . Feedback is dependent upon trust. Goal formation is dependent upon feedback and trust. Interdependence is dependent upon goal formation, feedback, and trust." [11]

Whereas the group counselor with authoritarian tendencies decides who is capable and responsible, the democratic and, especially, the group-centered counselors rely on the members' own perception of their capabilities and judgment with reference to their responsibility.

[11] Jack R. Gibb and Lorraine M. Gibb, "Humanistic Elements in Group Growth," in James F. T. Bugental (ed.), *Challenges of Humanistic Psychology*, McGraw-Hill Book Company, New York, 1967, p. 163.

The third consideration of the leader, especially with reference to innovations, is the framework, administrative and/or traditional. Every situation has some fixed or nearly fixed ends. Many situations afford the counselor more freedom to use group process principles than he concludes is the case. It is convenient to free oneself from the responsibility of undertaking innovations by assuming that the administration or other conditions prohibit it. Frequently counselors find that if they consult and plan with the administration to proceed experimentally with proper controls and progress reports, an innovation is permitted on a trial basis. In any case the counselor working with groups must be cognizant of the framework within which he works and take it into account in his planning.

The most important consideration of the three described above is frequently the most neglected. Counselors are prone to conclude that a knowledge of theory and especially of skills is what is chiefly needed, whereas, useful as these might be, more important is the initial and continuous self-examination to determine what is the possible and most comfortable structuring for him or on the other hand to recognize what basic personality change he must gradually achieve in order to be congruent in using the method to which he aspires. Such introspection is a must and should have first priority in his considerations.

Also his initial decision with reference to himself and to the group needs careful scrutiny from time to time. Groups change, and the counselor aware of this uses a flexible structure which can easily yield to the developmental changes in the group.

## CONGRUENCE OF STRUCTURE AND GROUP

It is common practice to impose structure on the group regardless of its nature. Whether it is a T group, basic encounter group, or group-centered group, the leaders expect all the members to conform and adjust. Such a practice ignores the fact that members differ in their possibilities and needs. For groups which are authoritarian-based such procedure accords with the theory, but for others the procedure disregards the theory underlying the process. It is especially surprising that leaders who base their leadership on self theory also proceed to impose structure.

This situation has not received the attention commensurate

with its importance. This despite the fact that leaders know that some members benefit greatly from the group experience but some claim not to benefit at all, while others insist that the effect has been detrimental. What can be done to ensure that all members will receive some benefit and that possibly all will benefit more than they could under present procedures?

A self-theorist, believing that the members know themselves better than he can know them, may ask each one to indicate the kind of group he thinks would be most useful to him. But since the great majority of the members have not experienced any type of group, they have insufficient basis for judgment. Even reading about the groups would be of little help to them in making a valid decision. On the other hand each leader, to be congruent, sincere, and honest with himself, must conduct the group according to his beliefs. A leader who genuinely believes in the T group could hardly be expected to be interested or comfortable in conducting a group in accordance with group-centered principles, or willing or able to do so. Should leaders of various theoretical positions provide an opportunity for those who are not benefiting from the group experience to leave at some point in the total group experience? Should individual counseling be provided for those for whom the experience could be helpful if they had individual assistance with some of their personal hurdles?

Further, if an educational group experience precedes the experience in group counseling, this may well place members in a better position to know which kind of theoretical approach would be most beneficial to them personally. In university settings, the use of video tapes illustrating various group counseling approaches might serve to acquaint counselors-in-training with the methods used. Also they would be helped to decide which they felt was most congruent with their own present approach to self-understanding and problem solving.

## HOW MUCH STRUCTURE

Studies have shown that in situations in which structure is virtually absent the group is much less productive. Some structure is necessary and must provide sufficient security in order that members can feel safe enough to control their impulses. On the other hand, it must be amenable to modification in whatever ways are desirable to make possible constructive growth.

A group of three may after a time develop a sense of trust, freedom, and responsibility toward one another, but how and when should the group be enlarged? One leader commenced with groups of six which met for five consecutive times and then were enlarged to form groups of ten. In their self-reports regarding this change some said: "I wish the leader had left us in groups of six for a longer period of time. I was just beginning to be able to share some of my doubts about myself." But another wrote: "I wondered a little about what it would be like in a larger group, but after tonight I feel right at home and just as free as I was in the smaller group." Members vary in their readiness to move into larger group formations. The frequent occurrence of this variability in readiness suggests that the members themselves should make the final decision. With support in looking at the alternatives but with the expectancy that they will decide how and when, they are helped to use freedom in an atmosphere of trust which encourages responsibility. Any change in structure is not fully growth development unless the inner control of the member matures.

In other ways structure must be "tuned" to the immediate group. That is, it must be realistic in relation to the ego strength and impulse control of the members. This becomes clearly apparent when a leader conducts group counseling in an upper-middle-class suburban school and follows this with leading a lower economic group in a school in the inner city. Whereas in the former the children and adolescents have become more able to accept the organizational demands of living and have developed sublimated outlets for their impulses, this is not the case for the latter group. This group of underprivileged youth who have not developed these controls need opportunity for "impulse drainage," less frustration, with better spacing and budgeting of frustration experiences, and program planning which is close to their sociological framework.[12]

Not only children and youth need structures adapted to their present development, but adults as well. One counselor educator working with a group of graduate students, counselors-to-be, gave them this opportunity: They were offered the privilege of choosing

[12] Fritz Redl and David Wineman, The Aggressive Child, The Free Press of Glencoe, Inc., New York, 1957, vol. 2, pp. 330–340.

membership in either one of the following groups with the understanding that they could change later if any felt a strong need to do
so. Group 1 was a semistructured group, highly democratic in its
functioning. Group 2 was unstructured, without a leader most of the
time. When he did sit in the group, he did so as a member and on
the periphery. Two-thirds chose group 1, and one-third chose group
2. One person in each group left and joined the other group.

In their self-reports they gave indications of their basis of
choice. One who chose group 1 (semistructured) wrote: "I am glad I
chose a group with some structure. I seem to need some assurance
that there is a goal, even if it is tentative and changing." Another
wrote: "My choice turned out to be a good one for me. I could take
part and at times be spontaneous since I felt things would go along
all right." One who chose group 2 (unstructured) wrote: "I wondered
about my choice at first but soon was quite pleased with it. I liked the
freedom of working things out with the others, and the ambiguity
bothers me less as we go along." Another wrote: "We laugh and
disagree but get things done; it's free in a way, but we have planned,
too. I am finding it a good experience." The member who moved
from the unstructured to the semistructured group wrote: "I am
moving to the other group; it bothers me too much not to be sure of
where I am going, so to speak." The member who moved to the
unstructured group wrote: "This group is all right, but I just feel I
would like to be freer in planning with others what to do, and this is a
good chance for me to find out." To read the self-reports is to be
convinced of the differences in individual needs in relation to group
structure.

## CONCLUSIONS

A certain degree of structure is basic to all group activities. The
type and amount of structure are crucial considerations. In determining the kind of structure to be used the leader must be intelligent
regarding his own needs and skills. He must also consider the group,
not only their experience, but their organizational level and possible
impulse control. He also has to be reasonably certain that the kinds
of procedure he envisages are acceptable to those to whom he has
responsibility.

In determining how much structure is to be used it is necessary that he reach a balance between form and flexibility. He should examine his conclusions against the degree of possibility they present for the development of trust, freedom, and responsibility. A structure which encourages member growth is recognized to be one which encourages members to be open and accepting, trusting and responsible.

Since structure to many members is a main source of security and one on which they rely in order to understand their world, it should not be too incongruent with the members' perceptions and expectancies. To leaders who are comfortable in planning the structure cooperatively with the members or who support the members in developing their structure, the possibility of initiating a useful, workable structure is good.

Leaders who recognize structure in its proper perspective view it as a means rather than an end. They are alert to the possibilities of its relaxation in order to increase the possibility of members' growth. As the leader increases in ability to trust the members intelligently and as they grow in trust of one another, structure can become an asset rather than a dominant control.

# 10

## COMMUNICATION IN
## GROUP COUNSELING

Authorities agree that communication is necessary for behavioral change. They are not in agreement as to the form this communication should take. Some consider that it must have the following elements: personal awareness, particularly of one's positive aspects, encountering one another, and opening oneself to personal feedback from the encounters.[1] Others take issue with the idea that it requires "a kind of psychological nudity—a stripping away of one's defenses" and ask, Is there "no longer the privilege of private psychological catharsis?"[2] There is agreement that communication should be

[1] Marilyn C. Barrick, "Similarities and Differences of Marathon and Ongoing Strength Groups," unpublished paper presented at the American Personnel and Guidance Association Convention, 1968.
[2] Richard H. Cox, "The 'Being Real' Neurosis," *The Christian Century,* July 17, 1968, pp. 918–919.

authentic, honest, and "real" but disagreement as to whether it is obtained via "studies in comparative emotional pathology" or through a development in self-becoming.

All agree that involvement is inherently a part of communication. Lewin and Grabbe, writing in the 1940s, considered involvement on the cognitive, emotional, and motoric levels necessary to behavioral change.[3]

Current enquiry has shifted to the relative importance of the interrelated aspects in the communication process. Although Charles Sanders Peirce,[4] who in his interpretation of the psychology of the act placed first, feeling, second, the active response of the body, and third, thought, the concept, might today be somewhat dismayed by the emphasis placed on the first without a proportionate emphasis on the other two. The idealization of feeling and the increasing emphasis which it is receiving should be a matter of deep concern and study on the part of those engaged in group counseling. We need to distinguish between emotions as *one* component in knowing and as *the only* component in knowing.

Regardless of the disagreement as to the method and emphasis necessary for communication, it should lead to increasing freedom and openness toward living in an expanding world of ideologies. Frequently it does not. Numbers withdraw and are content to live apart in a small world of their own making. Others insist on maintaining their world as it is. Such reactions are indicative of the serious breakdown in communication. Many avoid the risk of doubt and threat of ambiguity by surrendering the right to question and doubt. By so doing they hope to retain some meaning in life. This retreat gains for them a false feeling of belonging and well-being. They thus escape loneliness, existential doubt, and despair. They have gained certitude but at tremendous cost, through the sacrifice of the freedom of the self. This sacrifice requires a self-assertiveness. The deep anxiety it engenders demonstrates itself in the disproportionate, almost fanatic need to defend their position and attack those who disagree. This is especially the case when the other plainly

[3] Kurt Lewin and Paul Grabbe, "Conduct Knowledge and Acceptance of New Values," *The Journal of Social Issues,* vol. 1, pp. 45–64, 1945.
[4] Charles Sanders Peirce, "The Psychology of the Act," in *The Collected Papers,* vol. 5, pp. 66ff.

shows that he has continued to question and doubt and seek meaning at the level of the depth dimension. Those who have resigned themselves to live only with "the courage to be a part" instead of with "the courage to be" (Tillich) are forced by their anxiety to challenge and persecute at their own one-dimensional level those who have retained and developed their freedom. Group counseling becomes increasingly dynamic as each member struggles with doubts and life's happenings which he does not and knows he cannot fully understand.

## THE NATURE OF COMMUNICATION

From the foregoing it is evident that communication has many aspects. It may have several forms, which take place at various levels of understanding and differ greatly in meaning.

Much that is generally considered communication is of little value for the purposes of group counseling. It is too mechanical, superficial, and only the converse of "things." It may be useful, however, in its own right and for the intended purpose. For example, you dial a telephone number to find out what time it is. You are not interested in the voice which comes over the tape, but merely in the time. The criterion is not understanding but correctness and efficiency. When this happens in so-called "communication with others," each is only a thing to the other and may thereby become only a thing to himself. This treatment of one another as things is where many people become lost in the search for themselves. When they fail to communicate with others, they fail to understand themselves.

Communication is frequently only token. This has definite maintenance value and helps each of us to move through the mechanics of the day. For instance, in taking the bus downtown we engage in somewhat automatic gestures and expressions which facilitate the process of reaching our destination. Intimate conversation on a person-to-person basis, even if possible, would play havoc with our accomplishment of the routine demands of life. Our graciousness and warmth, natural to those who view others as persons, falls far short of the communication necessary for helping another to discover who he is and how he may help others to find who they are and together build a meaningful community.

### Communication Beyond Token Form

Group counseling may commence with these token forms, but its usefulness is in large part dependent upon a deeper, more risk-taking, and genuine form of relationship. The key to fulfilling communication is to hear one another not as things to be pushed around, maneuvered, or used, but as persons. When the other becomes a subject, it means hearing him as a person.

This seeing and hearing of one another as persons is the first condition in becoming genuine, open selves. To attempt to become open in order to attain self-fulfillment is self-defeating. Buber contended that self-concern does not provide self-fulfillment. Indeed, we need to relate to others with as much sincerity as we find possible. It is through the reaction of others that our existence is confirmed and also denied.

Our existence is denied when we treat others in terms of some status price tag or as doormen or ushers. We also of course are unable to communicate at the depth or with the genuineness necessary for the evolvement of the meaningful relations which generate health. Communication, then, is meaningful and effective not only when it is between those who totally acknowledge one another for themselves but also when they truly care what they hear from others and say to others.

### The Need for Depth

Even when these difficult conditions are met, the quality of the possible communication differs from person to person. This is because we bring our values to each communication. These become apparent regardless of the topic and to some degree without words. It is also possible for a group to spend an enjoyable time with much interaction concerning the what, when, where, and how of a multitude of things such as automobiles, styles of clothing, vacation spots, and even political conventions but depart without having touched upon the related issues of why and the meaning of outcomes for people in general and for one another. Or they may spend time in discussing felt injustices, personal frustrations, intolerable personal relationships, dissatisfactions with one another, and appreciation for one another and also depart without having discussed the meaning of these for their personal lives. In other words the degree to which communication makes possible the examination of personal values and the setting and resetting of more healthy and helpful personal goals is a function of the degree and depth to which the members are involved in the issues and problems.

There was a time when considerable importance was placed upon this depth dimension, the developed potential of the person to engage in inner dialogue, to stand outside himself and critically to examine his actions in terms of his personal standards and beliefs. It is now well known that this developed potential may have determined the survival of Bruno Bettelheim and Viktor Frankl in the concentration camp. Frances Wickes, a Jungist psychologist, writes: "This undiscovered self, this 'isness' is always, even in childhood, trying to make itself manifest through the life of the individual. To discover and live out the meaning of the self through the choice of awareness of the hidden movement of non-ego forces is the journey into wholeness." [5]

Currently there are strong influences on the individual to take a pragmatic, utilitarian approach to problems. It is easy to neglect, ignore, or discount the existentialist approach of being, of meaning, and of depth. Herbert Marcuse insists that the political man, economic man, and any other man who silences the inmost self may be only half a man, a one-dimensional man.[6]

### Conflict

Current trends increasingly call for a fresh, incisive look at conflict as significantly basic in communication. Somewhat different from previous modes of thought, this requires that we become able to accept and use conflict creatively. There is growing evidence that this may help overcome alienation and bring the experiencing of growth.

So deeply do some believe this that they are dissatisfied in a group unless there is overt conflict and therefore do all they can to bring it about. Conflict encouraged for its own sake, simply because we are convinced it should take place, is not conflict that is likely

[5] Frances G. Wickes, *The Inner World of Choice,* Harper & Row Publishers, Incorporated, New York, 1963, p. 272.
[6] Herbert Marcuse, *One-dimensional Man,* Beacon Press, Boston, 1967.

to be therapeutic or lead to a higher quality of behavior. Real conflict, like dynamite, has power to change things but unless understood and oriented toward constructive ends can lead to disaster.

SOME CONSIDERATIONS  (1) Productive conflict arises because the members are so bound together that their actions affect one another; that is, they have accepted the fact that they have become interdependent. (2) Conflict occurs if we care. Often members who have very great creative differences share a very deep relationship. Because they care about one another and the group as a whole, they are willing to make, if necessary, a costly emotional response to help improve a situation. (3) Each member has different needs and values. Unless the group represses these needs and assigns the direction of the group to an authority figure, these differences become evident. Members sense this and sometimes, rather than accept the fact of their creative differences, allow themselves to be taken over by such a leader. They thus relinquish their birthright for a mess of pottage. Conflict emerges when the group faces decisions which are central to its ongoingness.

Occasionally members evade a situation by not confronting the true reasons for the conflict. They delay overt response to it until high temperature melts the evasions. More serious, however, is a situation in which members develop skills in uttering sweet pleasantries in the presence of subterranean conflict, which then may drain itself through unrealistic actions that obscure reality.

Two decades ago Lawrence Kubie emphasized in a speech to educators the psychologically unhealthful climate in which only a small part of the student's thinking and feeling was accepted in our classrooms. There was, and to a large degree is, no place for conflict or for the expression of the parameters of living, for love, hate, boredom, and feelings of emptiness. Kubie writes: "Instead of bringing up infants and children under a system of taboos which make it impossible for them to talk among themselves or to adults about their hates and fears, their jealousies, their bitterness against the adult world, their bodily shames and envies and lusts, all of this could be lived out, acted out, and talked out in groups from the nursery years on." [7] Instead we have asked them to repress it. We say, "Nice

[7] Lawrence S. Kubie, "The Psychiatrist Considers Curriculum Development," *Teachers College Record,* vol. 50, no. 4, p. 246, January, 1949.

little girls and boys don't do this." Such experiences are poor preparation for the recognition of, and participation in, conflict, honestly and creatively.

The outcomes of conflict are a function of the members' usual approach to life's issues. A conflictual topic in one group may lead to a deeper understanding of life and its meaning, but the same topic in another group may eventuate only in a consideration of ways and means of eliminating the apparent cause of the conflict and of avoiding it in the future. The usefulness of conflict in the deepening and enrichment of the personal lives of the members bears a direct relation to the depth at which the members are willing and able to consider it.

In almost every discussion in which conflict arises because of contrasting or contradictory feelings and ideas at least a minority of the members find it virtually impossible to become involved. The topic may focus directly on a similar conflict in the personal life of a member which he has avoided and to which he is now reluctant to give verbal expression. He may, however, be encouraged to examine it at some depth between group sessions. In fact there are members who may or may not of their own accord participate orally but who are able to use insights gained from the discussion to work through their own personal conflicts outside the group meetings.

It should not go unnoticed that there are those who apparently thrive on conflict. To them conflict is the mainspring of all group process. Without conflict they are uneasy and feel the whole endeavor lacks a purpose. Conflict for these may satisfy some drive for identity, for a sense of adequacy, for power. They overparticipate but are not changed. This may be a result of a lack of commitment to the members of the group and of intention to change personally. Without a commitment they are unable to permit themselves to be influenced by ideas and attitudes different from their own. Other members who in Viktor Frankl's phraseology are "pulled by meaning" rather than "driven by drives" are able to use creatively new ideas and understandings ensuing from conflict.

Others may be seized upon by the seeming vitality of conflict, since it affords them a means of releasing frustrations, or of escaping from boredom, or of avoiding demanding responsibilities. These have at least one characteristic in common: they are militantly negative. This is understandable when one considers that to be positive would require that they become committed to something and work to achieve their aims.

Still others know no other way. Their cultural conditioning has not helped them to develop a level of organizational ability which would enable them to perceive ways in which they could sublimate their negative impulses through constructive channeling. Their degree of impulse control is exceptionally weak, and they are easily caught up in imitative and often destructive behavior. They are deeply threatened by new experiences. It is therefore difficult to help them to become interested in cooperative behavior and to develop a sense of responsibility. Invariably they are unable to entertain any acceptance of responsibility for their behavior, and they blame others or circumstances. Lacking impulse control themselves, it is not surprising that they perceive punishment as the only means of control and regard aggression as the only way to control others.

Another group stands in severe contrast to the one just described. They have all the qualities this group lacks but take no part in conflict. They appear to take the position that the best and proper thing to do is not to expect too much, to adjust to the seemingly given conditions, and to be reconciled to, and in large degree content with, their lot. Harvey Cox views this as the result of the insistence upon the wrongness of human pride which results in a dependency which refuses to recognize and assume responsibility for decision making. Such a position is used to "excuse us from the frightful responsibility of renewing and reconstructing our moral tradition in the light of unprecedented issues our forebears never had to confront: the bomb, the computer, the pill." [8]

Cox and others now insist that we have overemphasized the sin of pride and have neglected to give place to apathy as one of the seven deadly sins listed by the early Christian theologians. By the nineteenth century the merging of faith and docility was so ingrained that to declare against it was to become an enemy of Christendom. Perceptive thinkers, Kierkegaard, Marx, and Nietzsche, each from his perception took strong issue against the docile, apathetic, passive acceptance of things as they are. Kierkegaard regarded this attitude as man's despairing refusal to be himself; Marx criticized severely

[8] Harvey G. Cox, *On Not Leaving It to the Snake,* The Macmillan Company, New York, 1967, p. ix.

those who looked upon society as a "given" rather than accept responsibility for its condition. Nietzsche concluded that the kind of God people of his time believed in must give way to belief in God who expected man to shape the symbols and meaning of his world in each ensuing generation.

Apathy has provided for many an uninvolved, one-dimensional, "floating with the tide" kind of existence, lacking a sense of responsibility, living with only the "courage to be as a part." These do not have "the courage to be" and are not truly human. Joseph Piefer, in *Leisure: The Basis of Culture* (p. 38), considers these as renouncing the claim implicit in their human dignity.

The number of these in any group is too many. Some have yielded too easily to the conditioning influences of so-called "education," in home, business, church, and school. But the alternative, although vastly worthwhile, is exceptionally difficult. It means the deepening of life and the acceptance of human dignity, which demands going against the tide when the situation demands. It views conflict as a transitional stage toward becoming truly human. For the individual it is deciding who he will be rather than living introjected platitudes; it is confronting with open eyes how power is distributed and used in each area of his experience; it is standing firm and giving assistance to any image of life that encourages criticism and espouses responsible human creativity. Such a person is a staunch friend of conflict, rightly used.

THE CREATIVE HANDLING OF CONFLICT One tremendous understanding that is difficult to attain is that change does not result without conflict. We have recognized this truth for a long time, but now perhaps as never before we are challenged to live it. What, then, may be some guides toward handling conflict creatively?

First, we must endeavor to recognize the fact that problems cannot be faced without conflict. We need to accept from the start that different feelings, different value structures, and different idea systems are going to collide.

Second, each party to the conflict must accept the right of others to their feelings, values, and ideas. In all conflict the members must retain their human dignity; each must be accepted as a person in his own right, regardless of his behavior and point of view. This is the kind of acceptance necessary for an open, honest confrontation of differences.

Third, if this confrontation is going to have depth, trust in each member by all the others must prevail. "Basic trust" (Erik Erikson) requires that each of us be honest not only about our ideas but about our feelings as well.

Fourth, we must not evade the primary source of conflict but proceed courageously to the realistic location and make a careful intelligent analysis of the parts. We must honestly and as openly as possible examine the issues and then, using our joint productive imaginations, project different solutions and make tentative decisions and plans in relation to them.

Finally, we must develop new ways of acting and being, subjecting these to ongoing evaluation.

CONCLUSIONS  Although conflict is inherent in communication, it may be positive in some instances, negative in some, and irrelevant in others. Change can and does take place without overt conflict. To use some method to stimulate conflict is to misunderstand its nature and function. This is the same kind of error as the injunction "Let us be democratic about this," or "Let us take an open-minded approach." It is the attempt to treat ourselves as objects, to manipulate ourselves, or to allow ourselves to be manipulated. It is a failure to recognize that in the expression of differences conflict arises just as water seeks its own level. It is just as bad judgment to perform acts to initiate conflict in the hope that better understanding and constructive outcomes will follow as to drink a quantity of water in order to initiate thirst in the hope that one will drink the proper quantities of water in the future.

Conflict is not a goal to be achieved in order to cause something to happen but a result of honest exploration of meaningful issues concerning which there are significant differences. Conflict is nonexistent when the members of the group do not care what results and irrelevant when they are so dominated that they dare not take action. Conflict is negative when it results from compounded hostile, impulsive drives to destroy. Conflict is positive when it results from compounded desire and will to heal, unite, and improve. Conflict aids man to become more human when it moves toward a higher quality of behavior in a healing community.

### Communication That Heals

Ordinarily groups provide two psychological certainties for an individual: first you are among us, as one of us; secondly, we receive you, we accept you, you share with us, and we share with you. But if the group reaches its full potential, its communication goes beyond these. It also extends healing.

This healing is the high calling. It is special since it has no conditions of performance attached, no ifs or buts; it is healing of an accepting, forgiving kind, the "in-spite-of" quality of love which is open-ended and complete. It is complete since it is physical, moral, psychological, and spiritual. Each person is seen as a whole being.

The group, now a community, enters into, suffers with, and rejoices with each member. The koinonia of the group—what the members now basically share—is that each member cares. Each comes to know this caring is present, even though a member may try to deny it, to separate himself from it, to ignore it, or even to erect barriers against it. For some members it is threatening to recognize that others care, that these others have their well-being at heart.

The givens of the healing community are hard to establish and the gifts difficult to accept. So often a method whose excellence becomes recognized begins to congeal; its adherents begin to expect certain outcomes at certain stages, to become intolerant, incapable of accepting criticism or of extending the usefulness of the method to those deviants who vary so much from the usual. Zealous to protect the pearl they have discovered, they set up the method as the *sine qua non* of what reeducation, group counseling, or group therapy should be. Their very certainty erodes in time the usefulness of the group and what it might have accomplished.

### Communication in Love

Although difficult and hazardous, communication in love is the goal toward which groups move. It is never fully attained but remains a direction. Nevertheless, the basicity of communication in love is recognized and accepted as the necessary condition for constructive change and development. This viewpoint is not, of course, uniquely that of individual or group counseling.

In fact the goal for man and society has for centuries had the same focus. For Sören Kierkegaard it is the loving life in which one is willing to suffer voluntarily for the truth. For Reinhold Niebuhr love is the norm and motive in relation to justice. For Buber it is love in the form of mutuality. Teilhard sees love as the ultimate "force" holding things together and making human self-realization in personhood. Freud writes of being able "to work and to love." Huxley wants to affirm the "unique importance of love in human life . . . indispensable for the full development of the human personality." [9]

How is such communication achieved? There are many questions and little consistency. Some questions that remain troublesome are the following: What are the sources of hate and aggression, and what releases love in human life? Are hate and hostility the result of lack of love? Does loving acceptance eventually beget loving acceptance? Must one energize his capacity to think and feel deeply (depth dimension) in order to love? Are some members prevented from loving by the kind of internal conflict they endure? Is love a static or moving goal? Does one experience an increasing capacity to love? Can the relationship of love ever be attained, or is it one of only becoming? And what conditions best create the context for the nurture of the fulfillment of the individual in love? [10]

Some of our assumptions of the ease with which we can develop communication in love require reexamination. Niebuhr claims that the law of love is not something extra to be added to our morality and social relations. Instead "it is the guiding principle of them." [11] Love is not a simple possibility; it is always subject to corruption. Even those who are most loving may abuse power, since in their love they may claim to be certain of what is best for others. As a guiding principle it can help us to evaluate the relative merits of one part of action rather than another. The members who love one another are sensitive to injustice and seek justice for one another. Knowing the law of love as the final goal and the law of self-love as a persistent force supplies a basis in which power and self-interest evident in groups can be beguiled, deflected, harnessed, and transmuted for the ultimate end of establishing the highest and most

[9] Julian Huxley, *Knowledge, Morality and Destiny,* Mentor Books, 1960, pp. 210–211.
[10] Perry Le Fevre, *Man: Six Modern Interpretations,* The Geneva Press, Philadelphia, 1968, p. 119.
[11] Reinhold Niebuhr, *The Nature and Destiny of Man,* Charles Scribner's Sons, New York, 1943, vol. 2, p. 107ff.

inclusive possible community of justice and order in the group.[12]

In the words of an anonymous self-report of a group member: "Many questions are in my mind. Am I concerned for the other members of the group and their well-being? Do I listen to what the other members are saying with the idea of learning something from each one as well as from the group in general? When I contribute to the group, am I receptive and perceptive to the reaction of others? Do I listen to their interpretations and thinking? Do I consider each member as a unique individual whom I respect and with whom I would like to get better acquainted? Can I become one of the group, helping each member to achieve his potential, thus achieving the goals of the group as a whole?"

Differences in theoretical assumptions and methods become clear in the consideration of the relationship of freedom and love on the one hand and on the other whether love includes responsible caring and if so to what degree. Certain groups assume that reduction of defenses, openness, and the expression of strong emotional feeling develop individual freedom, which ushers in the state of love. Communication in love is considered an outcome of the revealing of each individual self and the remaining open to the perceptions and feedback of other members. It is difficult to assess the degree to which this condition carries with it a deep sense of mutual caring and responsibility.

A dissimilar approach assumes not that love flows from openness to one another but rather that openness is one of the results of attaining an accepting, trusting, caring, and responsible relationship with others. In this method each member relates to others at the level at which he feels interested and safe. The acceptance and caring which are extended to him and which he extends to others provide the basis for a growing trust relationship and the development of a sense of responsibility. Freedom in this approach develops gradually and differentially for each member as he accepts others and feels accepted as he really is.

Leaders and members of groups who retain the humility that caring encourages become more capable of seeing human nature in a realistic way. They can encompass the opposites and contradictions in one another in every recurring realism and honesty. They

[12]John Hutchison (ed.), *Christian Faith and Social Action,* Charles Scribner's Sons, New York, 1953, p. 238.

do not succumb to an easy tendency of negating the intensity of negative feelings or of failing to recognize true efforts toward love and understanding. Indeed they gradually realize that the possibilities for constructive and destructive behavior to some degree reside in each. Therefore it becomes possible to accept one another as given, in spite of the inacceptable in each.

There is thus an openness to surprise, which is also a characteristic of the communication that heals. But here again it is possible to stereotype it, to describe it in signs as if it were or could be a totally accomplished fact. When we do so, we stop it or interfere with its fullest expression. If we do not leave the process open, it can become mechanical, and caring is dissipated. If the group becomes preoccupied with caring at the expense of discipline, it becomes ecstatic, sentimental, or lawless. Thus the group operates in a tension between discipline and caring which make for disciplined caring. In this climate of communication is the element of surprise. It comes as constructive healing, and growth becomes a fact.

Everett Stowe [13] views communication, as herein described, as one of the few means whereby man may grasp the meaning and purpose of the transcendent in life which goes beyond what can be heard, felt, and seen. This becomes possible when, as emphasized by Martin Buber in his book *I and Thou*, each is a "thou," or person, to the other rather than the too familiar "it." In philosophical terms Karl Jaspers writes: "One of man's supreme achievements is the genuine communication from person to person, when from out of their historical situation in their search for the ultimate meaning of existence, the Transcendent breaks into thought, revealing to each the authenticity of his Selfhood and their common ground in the Encompassing." [14] This is the essence of communication in group counseling.

[13] Everett M. Stowe, *Communicating Reality through Symbols,* The Westminster Press, Philadelphia, 1966, p. 40.
[14] Karl Jaspers, *Truth and Symbol,* Twayne Publishers, London, 1959, p. 17.

# 11

## DYNAMICS OF GROUP COUNSELING

Group dynamics is the result of the interaction of tangible and intangible variables. Group members behave as they do because of their needs, attitudes, patterns of interaction, and skills, on which they rely for communication. Although attitudes and skills are interrelated, they will be separated here for purposes of description.

Each group member brings his unique self to the group process. This he does whether he lives superficially (driven by drives) or in depth (pulled by meaning), whether he is open-minded or closed-minded, whether he lives an open humanism imbued with the self-affirmation of life and "the courage to be" or a closed humanism, passive and apathetic, with only the "courage to be a part." These and other attitudes to varying degrees enter into the dynamics of group counseling. Let us briefly examine these attitudes in order to clothe each with meaning.

## ATTITUDINAL FUNCTIONING

### Dimensionality

Some members look at life chiefly from a one-dimensional viewpoint. Others examine issues chiefly from a depth, or two-dimensional, perspective. One-dimensional members interact in a somewhat superficial, expedient, or utilitarian fashion. They are chiefly interested in means and ends and what each may secure from the situation for himself.

They may be ill-at-ease or irritated when the interaction moves to a consideration of personal involvement and responsibility. On the other hand those who are accustomed to look at situations in depth do not settle for superficial and partial understanding; they go deeper to examine possible causes and outcomes and their own responsibility related thereto.

Although all members respond from both dimensions, so many frequently respond, regardless of the topic, from one dimension or the other that it is useful to characterize them as generally one- or two-dimensional. Group counseling is most beneficial when the interaction exemplifies both dimensions.

### Humanistic Patterns

Some members look at situations from a narrow perspective. They accept conditions as they are and conform to the status quo. They have made their world comfortable by making it small and by not getting involved in the new, the untried, or the experimental. These are the members Tillich aptly describes as living only with the "courage to be as a part." More recently [1] they have been described as those with a closed humanism. Such a member supports human values because it makes sense, not because he is committed or even interested but because to be loyal to mankind means his own survival.

Other members are struggling to have "the courage to be."

[1] Roger L. Shinn, *Man: The New Humanism,* The Westminster Press, Philadelphia, 1968, p. 170.

They meet life as it comes and try to understand it. They view life from a wide and comprehensive perspective. They acclaim values which have no utilitarian advantage for them. They do not meet life as a test of survival or in a mood of conquest or plunder but instead experience some grateful appreciation of the sources of their own being and the nonhuman environment that nourishes their lives. Each has a place in his life for search, beauty, and wonder and is pulled by a sense of meaning beyond his understanding.

### Openness of Belief Systems

Members are influenced by both the thought and emotional components of the discussion. These components influence the process and condition the outcomes. Accordingly each individual is motivated by both rational and rationalizing forces. The approach known as the *open-closed belief systems*, developed on this premise, assumes that "all belief-disbelief systems serve two powerful and conflicting sets of motives at the same time: the need for a cognitive framework to know and to understand and the need to ward off the threatening aspects of reality." [2]

As the members become involved, they make decisions. The quality of their ongoing decisions bears a direct relation to their ability to disregard irrelevant factors and to use only relevant factors. Irrelevant factors are always present in such forms as anxiety and the need to be accepted. These are heightened by peer expectancy, authority figures, and cultural and institutional norms.

The use of relevant factors in decision making bears a direct relation to the openness of the belief system. Each member has an open belief system to "the extent to which he can receive, evaluate, and act on relevant information received from the outside on its own intrinsic merits unencumbered by irrelevant factors in the situation, arising from within the person or from the outside." [3]

Those members with a relatively open belief system tolerate ambiguity well; they do not overreact to threat; they distinguish between the authority figure and his ideas, and evaluate a situation on the basis of its intrinsic merits. They perceptively examine different aspects of the experience, try to clarify the ambiguity, and try to see

[2] Milton Rokeach, *The Open and Closed Mind,* Basic Books, Inc., Publishers, New York, 1960, p. 67.
[3] *Ibid.,* p. 57.

the relationship among parts. Little threat is experienced in the integration of ideas into a new system.

The members with more closed belief systems are hindered by a pervasive feeling of threat and dependence upon authority. They experience difficulty in examining ideas on the basis of their intrinsic worth and in the integrating of ideas into a new system.[4] They are more at ease in a structured, authoritarian situation than in one which allows for some freedom of choice.

In an unstructured, open situation they may do one of several things: they may withdraw, becoming negatively passive, or they may try to secure a more structured, orderly, predictable pattern in the group, or, failing this, they may join with other threatened members in an attempt to sabotage the group and/or the leadership in order to bring it more into accord with their beliefs. It has been found that as few as two highly closed-minded persons change the character of the whole group and its activities even when the group contains as many as eighteen members.[5]

To stimulate and encourage conflict in a group which has relatively closed-minded members is a doubtful procedure. These members either withdraw, becoming negatively aggressive when pressured, or become extremely and overtly aggressive beyond what is useful and a function of the situation.

There are, then, contrasting differences in the performance of members between those with open and those with closed belief systems. Such differences were found in a study of the number and kinds of responses of relatively open-minded and relatively closed-minded members. When the topic was ideational with little personal implication, there were no significant differences between the two groups, except that the leaders and members of the open-minded group reflected and clarified ideas more frequently. But when the focus was on the emotional content, the closed-minded felt the need for more structure. They also listened less frequently to get the covert meaning of responses and much less frequently accepted strong expressions of the personal feelings of other members.[6]

[4] C. Gratton Kemp, "Critical Thinking: Open and Closed Minds," *The American Behavioral Scientist,* vol. 5, no. 5, p. 14, January, 1962.
[5] Based on the author's experience over several years.
[6] C. Gratton Kemp, "Behaviors in Group Guidance (Socio Process) and Group Counseling (Psyche Process)," *Journal of Counseling Psychology,* vol. 10, pp. 373–377, 1963.

### Security Needs

Those members who idealize security and live their lives in terms of increasing it for themselves are a depressive factor in the group. Shakespeare warned the playgoers of his time that security was man's greatest enemy. In this day, which Paul Tillich described as one in which many feel an emptiness in life leading to a loss of meaning, security becomes for many the goal of living.

Writing in the *National Observer* (January 29, 1968) on welfarism in Britain, Anthony LeJeune emphasizes that people prefer security to freedom and warns the United States of the growing acceptance of the ideology in this country. A random sample of thirty-three graduate students was given the choice between a structured course with preplanned methods, goals, and requirements and one in which they could have help in planning according to their wishes. Two-thirds chose the traditional security-giving pattern and only one-third the unstructured pattern, which offered much more freedom.

The need for structure and established goals varies widely among members. Only gradually do they become able to use and profit from an unstructured, freedom-giving situation. It is not unusual for leaders who accept the principle of individual differences to ignore this completely in setting up a framework for the group or, if they do recognize it, to assume they know better than the members how much structure is most useful. All need help to some degree in releasing themselves from security needs which inhibit and minimize their development as group members and as persons.

### Involvement

The foregoing attitudes and needs are reflected in the involvement of each member. Each involves himself according to his needs, which in turn influence his perception of the situation. Members attempt to satisfy their needs by both nonverbal and verbal participation. All use both methods; the extent to which each member uses one or the other influences the interaction and outcomes.

Upon analysis we recognize that any new, creative act does not receive from us a unanimous vote. All members experience some resistance. There is an evident risk in a creative act of participation which results in feelings of ambivalence, hesitancy, and some silence.

Some may react to the resulting ambiguity by oververbalization; others, by prolonged silence.

Resistance in group members may appear at any stage in the life of the group. It makes itself felt as (1) hindering or disturbing the initial developing unity and rapport, (2) impeding the achievement of insight, especially concerning the "here and now" problems of the group, and (3) obstructing the developmental changes in the process of occurring within themselves and others in the group.

Such resistances take two forms, the resistance to insight and the resistance to behavioral change after the insight is attained. Insight, though necessary, is not enough and does not of itself assure change. There is a troublesome intervening variable between insight and change. McClelland, in each of his twelve propositions concerning how to increase motive acquisition, uses the words *most likely.* He recognizes that despite the use of all methods of conditioning and reinforcement in the most conducive psychological climate, the person may not act.[7] There is a too easy willingness to ignore this variable and to assume that when insight is gained the victory is won.

Noy warns against the assumption "that the newly gained insight will automatically give rise to reintegration, which will produce the expected changes . . ." and emphasizes that "resistances may crop up, resistances directed against the second stage of the therapeutic process, the stage of application and exploitation of insight in the service of reintegration resulting in change."[8] When the second stage is lacking or only partially completed, the resulting change may appear to be genotypical but in actuality is only phenotypical, or superficial.

Leaders can help members to recognize that some resistance is a fact of life and to distinguish between resistance which may prevent one from understanding and resistance which appears as rationalizations for disregarding insight. Members can be helped in the use of productive imagination to diminish or eliminate the underlying fear. The group will eventually perceive that basic to various forms of resistance is the fear of change. The leader hopes to develop a psychological climate in which resistance is accepted and understood and the fear of change reduced.

[7] David C. McClelland, "Toward a Theory of Motive Acquisition," *American Psychologist,* vol. 20, pp. 321–333, 1965.
[8] Pinchos Noy, "Resistance to Change," *International Journal of Group Psychotherapy,* vol. 17, pp. 375–376, 1967.

Silence may indicate resistance but as well serves many other needs of the group and the individual member. It can be useful and constructive but not necessarily so. As the members' sense of interdependence, unity, trust, and caring becomes an accepted fact, silence becomes increasingly more useful.

Hughes, who takes a positive position, maintains that in the silent period "a free atmosphere prevails and that this very freedom to speak, to be the one to resume the discussion, is self-enhancing to each group member: possible statements are fashioned and refashioned, clarified and reclarified, though they go unspoken . . . their very completeness increases the eventual chance for a core of agreement throughout the thinking of the group members." [9]

Verbal involvement differs from member to member. Some focus on the issue, make useful contributions, and receive help from the interaction. Others try to meet their needs through verbal conflict. They may engage in conflict for its own sake. For these the use of reason has a special purpose aptly described by Alfred North Whitehead. He considers human reason to include the reason that Ulysses shares with the foxes and the reason that Plato shares with the gods. [10]

It may be that for these members the former use of reason is compellingly attractive. If so, they may not yet have become able to see others as persons. To them group members may be only things, impersonal, without a mysterious freedom as Reinhold Niebuhr would describe them, or "just a part of the world of things; since the experience of the human eludes them." [11]

Verbal conflict may be a function of neurotic patterns of behavior. One form is the "help-rejecting complainer." Such a person is object-related; he tries to manipulate people as objects on a giant chessboard. He supplies a multitude of reasons why the help is useless and unworkable and complains that the members do not understand him. They become frustrated and annoyed, since his compulsive neurotic needs affront, directly and powerfully, the *raison d'être* of the counselor and group. Berger and Rosenbaum suggest

[9] D. Patrick Hughes, "The Silent Period in Group Process," *The Clearing House,* vol. 32, pp. 230–231, December, 1957.
[10] Alfred North Whitehead, *The Function of Reason,* Princeton University Press, Princeton, N.J., 1929, p. 7.
[11] Dietrich Bonhoeffer, *Prisoner for God,* trans. by Reginald H. Fuller, The Macmillan Company, New York, 1954, p. 183.

that the counselor and the members help him to feel that he can still be unique without maintaining his need to fail to live successfully.[12]

Involvement which requires only intellectual assent is common. However, this seldom leads to action and behavioral change. When change in behavior is desired, total involvement is necessary. Such involvement is on the cognitive, conative, and motoric levels; that is, the member's involvement consists of his perception, feeling, thinking, meaning, and the action implied in the accomplishment of his decisions.

Charles Sanders Peirce, writing on the psychology of the act in his *Collected Papers,* places feeling first, action second, and thought third. Samuel Beck concludes that "We cannot know without the intellect; we do not know until we experience with the emotions." [13] There is an increasing emphasis on emotion as the prime mover in the process of total involvement.

Emotion is now considered to operate on all levels up and down the scale of sensory-cognitive processes. Becoming involved is a function of perceptual processes, and representational processes are seen as perceptions. What this does, in effect, is to establish a perceptual involvement theory of emotion.[14]

The theoretical implications strongly emphasize that effective group counseling depends upon emotion as one of its chief constituents in the process of change. The acceptance of this position focuses attention on the method or methods which hold the best promise of encouraging the total involvement of members. This necessitates the continuing study of contrasting theories of learning and motivation.

To perceive and maintain the degree of involvement most useful in helping one another in the group needs consideration. Members and leader may be less effective because of either overinvolvement or underinvolvement. Overinvolvement takes place when emotion is so strong and pervasive that listening, clarification, analysis, and

[12] Milton M. Berger and Max Rosenbaum, "Notes on Help-rejecting Complainers," *Journal of International Group Psychotherapy,* vol. 17, pp. 357–370, 1967.
[13] Samuel Beck, "Emotional Experience as a Necessary Constituent in Knowing," in Martin L. Reymert (ed.), *Feelings and Emotions,* McGraw-Hill Book Company, New York, 1950, pp. 59–108.
[14] C. Gratton Kemp, *Intangibles in Counseling,* Houghton Mifflin Company, Boston, pp. 145–146.

other useful means of working through a problem are so hampered or relinquished that little or no progress in understanding and planning is made. Overinvolvement frequently occurs when a member or group counselor has suffered a similar experience as the one related in the group. Unable to understand and accept his own experience, it is difficult to be as objective as the situation demands.

Underinvolvement takes place when the member or leader has suppressed or repressed an experience similar to the one under discussion. He then is reluctant and fearful of allowing himself to recognize the similarity. To do this would cause him to suffer both within himself and with the member or members involved. He is unwilling and perhaps unable to become sufficiently involved to be facilitative.

Both the members and the counselor become unable to cope with problems to the degree that they lack self-awareness. Counselor and members need to improve continuously their understanding of both the values and motives which they can affirm and those which for them are negative, questionable, and fearful. Those who through effort develop a personal center and an "inner choice" may become genuine and perceive the degree of their over- or underinvolvement in their relationship with others.

## SKILLS

Regardless of the attitudes of the members, the quality and breadth of communication depend in a large measure on the skills which each brings to the group process. These skills vary greatly from member to member, and exceptionally few members appear to have the requisite skills for effective functioning. Many lack such skills as listening, clarifying, linking, synthesizing, and summarizing.

The frequent assumption that skills develop without any particular attention is as inaccurate as would be the assumption that the group counselor does not require training. One has only to observe an inexperienced group to be convinced of the lack of facility in the use of needed skills to maximize the meaningfulness of the interaction. To expect such skills to develop without intelligent examination and effort is unrealistic. A consideration of those most frequently required emphasizes their complexity and need for development.

## Listening

One of the most important skills to be developed is that of listening. Unfortunately it is assumed that listening develops in the course of communication. However, listening for the purpose of trying to help another to understand himself and his situation becomes possible only through much intelligent effort.

The approach to listening bears a direct relationship to the counselor's theoretical position. It is to be expected, then, that a group counselor with a self theory orientation will listen with purposes different from those of one whose counseling is based upon a different theory. An examination of the aims of counselors from different orientations will illustrate some of the salient differences.

Consider the group-centered leader whose approach is based upon the concepts of self theory. The quality of his listening flows from the assumption that the group member needs to improve communication within himself, which in turn will lead to better interpersonal relations. This assumption becomes operative in the counselor's efforts to understand. He sincerely desires to see the world as far as he is able to from the other's viewpoint.

This is not easy and requires dedication to the principle and continued effort. The source of difficulty is extensive conditioning in listening for quite different purposes. These purposes vary from evaluation to discerning omissions, illogical statements, or lack of information. In this framework one may listen in order to be able to present his own ideas, suggestions, and alternatives more effectively. Such a leader may listen with the concern that a member should view reality differently, whereas the group-centered leader is intent upon trying to understand how the member himself is perceiving ideas and situations.

Since usefulness to the members depends upon the accuracy of his listening, it is important that he make reasonably certain that he understands. This he does especially in the early stages of the group's development through his reflection of feelings or meanings. He tries to mirror the member's expression with sufficient accuracy that the member feels satisfied that he is understood.

This kind of listening makes unique demands on the leader and poses some threat. The chief demand is the necessity that the leader become able to accept the members as persons regardless of their behaviors and ideas. Such unconditional acceptance is a developmental process, the result in part of the leader's dedication to this ideal.

The threat is present because of the risk involved. To understand another's point of view means becoming that person to a significant degree. Since he has suspended judgment and withheld evaluation, he runs the risk of having his view altered by another or possibly of adopting it. For the leader to enter into this kind of relationship requires a good measure of personal security and courage, knowing that he himself may be changed in the process.

Such listening has far-reaching effects which deepen as the number of sessions increases. The member develops a new feeling of adequacy. This results from his experience of being listened to and understood. When members no longer experience devaluation, there is a helpful reduction of threat. Reduction of threat initiates the possibility that members will drop their defensiveness. A lowering of defenses leads to more flexible thinking and better problem solving, and prepares the way for new understandings. When a member is heard with interest and understanding by the other members and the leader, he makes an effort to express his feelings, ideas, and opinions clearly. Group members observing that the leader is listening with understanding begin to listen to one another with increasing attention and a growing desire to understand.

As genuineness and interest in understanding develop, members can expect, accept, and encourage in one another the expression of their creative differences. This they do in relation to the "there and then" and later the "here and now" of the members' thoughts and feelings.

Differences in the function of listening develop as each leader experiments, becomes convinced, and finally accepts a theoretical position. For example, those who have moved to experiential psychotherapy (the third phase in the evolution of client-centered therapy) have additional purposes and aims in their listening activity. They focus their attention on the "here and now" depth experiencing of the member. Such experiencing refers to subjective processes not always conscious in the sense that they can be verbalized. The data of these processes of experiencing are the individual's sense of personal meanings. It is a personal sensing which the listening counselor tries to understand and to assist the member in bringing to consciousness and expression.

Therefore these group counselors add another dimension to their listening. They not only listen to hear the ideas, their meaning per se, and their possible meaning to the member but, as well, they listen and respond to what they interpret to be his nonexpressed or vaguely expressed preconceptual feelings. To do this they focus their listening on the member's experiencing processes.

Members gradually improve their listening ability. Early in the process they experience difficulty in following the trend of thought and in assimilating the ideas expressed. As they improve their concentration, they are able to relax and sense the meaning of what a member is saying. Each senses how he feels in relation to what is being said. They then become able to respond more meaningfully to one another. Members come to realize that continuous improvement in listening is basic to their development as group members and to the usefulness of the process to everyone.

### Clarification

The counselor who listens fulfills one of the prerequisites for skill in clarification. It is difficult to grasp among the incompletely formed ideas the basic meaning which the member hopes to convey. It is, however, a necessity if clarity and understanding are to prevail. Clarification makes possible a creative searching and expansion of meanings.

In a small group which is discussing relationships with parents, John, a high school student, is describing his father.

*John:* My dad is tops in anything to do with sports. We have a good time at football games and at bowling. But when I tell him that I haven't time to be good in sports, that I have to put it in getting grades, he is plainly dissatisfied and once in a while lets me know.

*Counselor:* It is hard for your dad to see that sports should not be a main interest in your life.

*Bill:* My dad is just the same in an opposite way.

*Counselor:* You mean he has the same attitude, but it is about something different.

*Bill:* That's it. He considers studying and making good grades just about all I should do and is unhappy if I mention anything about participation in sports.

The counselor who clarifies will encourage the members to express their creative ideas in the formative stage. They become interested in emulating him and through discussion of their efforts improve their understanding and capabilities.

As they improve in their recognition of what needs clarification and become increasingly able to say briefly what another has attempted to express, the discussion moves ahead. The sense of purpose and direction which ensues leads to more ideas and clearer insights.

### Reflection

The purpose of reflection is to express the meaning of an idea. It is important to have ideas as clearly expressed as possible, but it is from the meaning of these ideas that insights develop. The more accurate the reflection of the meaning, the more self-understanding the member attains. As well, the understanding of other members and the leader is enlarged. This results in an increased breadth and depth of relatedness.

When someone says, "I don't understand you," it should not always be inferred that the idea as stated is beyond his grasp but rather that he senses a meaning in what you say that he does not comprehend. The deeper meaning which you intended eludes him. He may not be accustomed to think in the depth which your statement or question demands. Your meaning has symbolic overtones which are foreign to his usual approach to meaning.

The high school student discussing vocations in a small group says, "Well, then, I might as well be a dentist like my father; you have to go on living, don't you?"

When group counselors were asked to indicate the kind of reflection they would make, their replies had wide variation. Some counselors indicated that they would respond in this fashion: "Yes, that's right, Bill; maybe dentistry is the vocation for you."

Others indicated a different kind of response. "It seems to me you are not really satisfied about becoming a dentist."

A third group suggested, "You are wondering if life is really worth living."

The counselor reflects only the meaning the idea has for him. Counselors unaccustomed to think about the meaning of life may not readily capture the depth of meaning underlying the apparently unimportant prefix or suffix.

Group-centered counselors believe that reflection provides a means for the counselee to gain insight in accordance with his own framework. Therefore they rely on this method of response. Counselors who believe in the necessity and usefulness of reflection use discretion and proceed cautiously, especially until they have gained considerable experience.

The member whose meaning has been accurately reflected by another has an encouraging sense of being understood. He feels more part of the group and accepted as a member in his own right. The way is prepared for his further participation in self-understanding and understanding of others.

Members find this skill difficult to develop. In part this results from the fact that it requires putting oneself fully at the service of the task. It is born of a commitment to aid another to gain understanding and direction.

### Interpretation

Beginning counselors find it difficult to distinguish between a reflection and an interpretation. Of course in some instances there is only a thin wall of separation. The following guideline is found useful: A reflection remains within the meaning of the member's response; an interpretation goes beyond it, presenting ideas which are not included in what the member says.

There is wide variance in the use of interpretation. Counselors differ in their use of interpretation, since they differ in their beliefs about the capabilities of members. As a result they differ in their theoretical assumptions regarding the usefulness of interpretations. The counselor who believes that in a climate of genuine acceptance the member is capable of examining himself in depth and will do so considers his interpretation unnecessary and possibly detrimental. On the other hand the counselor who perceives the members and their possibilities differently may consider interpretation necessary and one of his important responsibilities.

One point of difference focuses on the meaning of acceptance. Group counselors agree on the significance of acceptance, but they disagree on its meaning. Those who use interpretation consider acceptance within a framework of normal expectancy. It is a broad conditional acceptance, having limits which are marked off by what is acceptable to the particular counselor. Others, especially group-centered counselors, believe in unconditional acceptance and view the making of interpretations a contradiction to their basic belief and detrimental in its effects. Following are some of the effects as viewed by these counselors: Members perceive interpretations as an indication of lack of acceptance. They often react defensively or even with hostility to the attempts to interpret their thoughts, motives, or intentions. This takes place regardless of the accuracy of the interpretation. Any interpretation may have the effect of conveying an evaluation, or a disbelief in the validity of what is said, or an intention to influence another's thoughts or behavior.

Such viewpoints of group-centered counselors are reinforced by such studies as those of Bergman [15] and Porter.[16] These clearly indicate that interpretations are followed by "abandonment of self-exploration" and by "resistance" more frequently than could be expected by chance.

Group-centered counselors who believe in experiential psychotherapy have become less concerned with the "what to do" and "when to do it." Instead they focus upon the process of inner experiencing. This means that the counselor uses whatever kinds of responses he believes most useful in aiding the group member to confront his present experiencing, to grapple with it, and to work it through. His aim is to help the group member to put his personal meanings into concepts which accurately state them.[17]

Recently group counselors have used variations of what may be broadly considered interpretations but from a different point of

[15] D. V. Bergman, "Counseling Method and Client Responses," *Journal of Consulting Psychology,* vol. 15, pp. 216–224, 1951.
[16] E. H. Porter, Jr., "On the Nature of Psychotherapeutic Interpretation," *Journal of Consulting Psychology,* vol. 16, pp. 343–346, 1952.
[17] E. T. Gendlin, "Experiencing: A Variable in the Process of Therapeutic Change." *American Journal of Psychotherapy,* vol. 15, pp. 233–245, 1961.

view. One of these is the counselor's explanation and interpretation of his own experiencing. In so doing it is quite possible that the counselor may introduce for the members' consideration an attitude, a belief, a behavior, or information which causes them to examine themselves from a different perspective. Some counselors [18] consider this method useful in stimulating introspection. It may influence some members to respond verbally by describing their attitudes and feelings to other members of the group. Also it focuses attention on the acceptability and safety of this kind of searching in the group environment.

Another variation is a member's decision to explain and interpret his present and/or past behavior, beliefs, and goals to the group. When the decision to do so is freely the member's choice, it proves helpful both to the member and the whole group. If he can be truthful and feel safe in doing so, it appears "to facilitate the counselee's self-directed change through publicly committing him to change." [19] Mowrer emphasizes that the possibilities of change and stability in the new pattern are greatly enhanced if he explains and communicates his new attitudes and intentions to those whom his actions may have harmed.[20]

### The "Linking" Function

In the discussion of a topic the comments may be related to the topic, but their internal relatedness may not be evident. There are at least two reasons for this: The meaning of each comment may be clear but their relatedness to one another obscure, or the comments may be involved, lengthy, and unclear and therefore their relatedness more difficult to grasp. In these situations the thought of each member remains independent or unlinked to the expressed ideas of other members. This causes the group to feel at a standstill, lacking a sense of continuity and direction.

As the leader listens, he may decide, if the comments are clear and not involved, only to indicate their interrelatedness. If they are

[18] G. Roy Mayer and John J. Cody, "Festinger's Theory of Cognitive Dissonance Applied to School Counseling," *The Personnel and Guidance Journal*, vol. 47, p. 236, November, 1968.
[19] D. J. Benn, "Self-perception: An Alternative Interpretation of Cognitive Dissonance Phenomena," *Psychological Review,* vol. 74, pp. 183–200, 1967.
[20] Hobart W. Mowrer, *The New Group Therapy,* D. Van Nostrand Company, Inc., Princeton, N.J., 1964, p. 8.

involved, he searches for the meaning of each comment and how these meanings are related. By penetrating the content to its meaning the leader can recognize the relationship of each new comment to the old. He is then able to show the strand of meaning running throughout the separate comments and to convey this to the group; the discussion becomes clear, and each succeeding comment bears a useful relationship to what has gone before. The following excerpt may help to illustrate the function of linking ideas:

*Roger:* I don't see this talk about trust. I think I trust the rest of you. I don't mind talking about activities I am interested in, and that's all I want to do.

*Janet:* Trust, I think, is something that you develop when you are a child. If you miss it then, it is more difficult later.

*Mary:* I am worried about this whole idea of trust. What if you trust someone and they let you down? That happened to me, and I find it hard to trust.

*Bob:* I go along with Janet's idea. Trusting is not easy to develop. It takes some doing.

*Counselor:* We have some questions about this idea of trust. We wonder about its value: Can you and should you trust?

*Jean:* But you have to trust people, or you will never get along with them.

*Bill:* I think you trust people as you get to know them. I feel we trust each other now much more than we did a few weeks ago.

*Freida:* You only get to know someone as you come to trust. Because until you trust each other, you are afraid to say anything with much meaning in it.

*Betty:* Isn't that what's holding us up—some of us are not yet willing to take the risk of letting others know us?

*Roger:* But what's the point in all this? Why should I want to let others know me?

*Eric:* I would like to know how some others feel about all this struggle to get a degree to get a job to—well, if we could trust one another, I could tell you how I feel, and maybe what you could tell me would help me and all of us.

*Counselor:* Are you saying that to trust is a risk but necessary if we are to give and receive understanding and help from one another?

The leader on two occasions has tried to link and focus the thinking of the group. In the first case his response was chiefly a feedback of what the members had said. Since this was early in the discussion, it served the purpose of letting the group decide in what direction they wished to continue the discussion. In the second instance the leader searched out the thread of meaning basic to the various comments and responded in a manner that placed the central idea before the group. If he can do this well, the members have a sense that they are understood, a certainty concerning what they have said, and a realization of progress. Involved in the development of this ability to link ideas is a carefully evaluated ongoing experience in listening, clarifying, and reflecting the meaning of members' comments.

### Summarization

There is common agreement that summarization is the most difficult skill. Yet a good summary plays a unique and important function in helping the group to recognize the basic ideas they have discussed. Also it provides the members with a sense of direction and aids them in planning next steps. When continuity of ideas is important to the purposes of the group, a summary proves invaluable.

A summary may take several forms. An orderly presentation of key ideas discussed is useful and a necessity in educational groups. A summary which presents the various approaches in the consideration of problems is facilitative in a counseling group. It focuses for the members possible ways in which each may try to understand himself and his interpersonal functioning.

A summary may be offered at different times in the group discussion. The leader or member summarizes when he considers it to be helpful to the group. This may be during the discussion, especially if the group is trying to explore its own interpersonal relationships and progress, and also at the close if the aims of the group are educational.

All age groups regardless of their formal education experience difficulty in summarizing. Educational experiences such as note taking and responding with single ideas related to one aspect of discussion are not conducive to the development of this ability. Frequently it is assumed that it develops as a concomitant of participation in the group, but experience indicates that it cannot be left to chance. Such a necessary and difficult skill warrants intelligent and concentrated attention for satisfactory development.

A question often asked is, "What method can you use?" An analysis of the process indicates that a summarizer performs three operations: he encodes the information (ideas which members present), he stores it, and later he retrieves it. This process is described by Melton [21] and Broadbent [22] as a "flow" of information. Melton describes the three stages in this manner: The information, or "trace," is formed at the time of initial presentation. Next, it is stored as it was subjectively formed, or it is encoded as belonging to the same item of information preceding it or different. Third, it is recalled in the form in which it was stored.

The most important and difficult stage is the first, the encoding stage. What the summarizer is able to present to the group depends upon the act of encoding. Theorists have used various models to describe the encoding process. Miller [23] uses the idea of memory slots. He considers the memory system to be able to accommodate from five to nine different kinds of material. The summarizer develops the ability to recognize similarities and differences between the encoded ideas and those which are currently being expressed. This enables him to encode incoming ideas as having the same meaning as those already encoded or several different meanings. The ideas which follow are then subsumed under one of the established categories or placed in a new one.

One encoding difficulty results when several pieces of information are placed in the same category. There may be interference among them and therefore difficulty in retrieval. This may be diminished by making sure that similar pieces of information are encoded as one. But although this may facilitate retrieval, important shades of meaning may be lost.

Retrieval is made easier and more accurate when it is possible to place ideas in distinct categories. This keeps each frame of refer-

[21] A. W. Melton, "Implications of Short-term Memory for a General Theory of Memory," *Journal of Verbal Learning and Verbal Behavior,* vol. 2, pp. 1–21, 1963.
[22] D. E. Broadbent, "Flow of Information within the Organism," *Journal of Verbal Learning and Verbal Behavior,* vol. 2, pp. 34–39, 1963.
[23] A. G. Miller, "The Magical Number Seven, Plus or Minus Two: Some Limits on Our Capacity for Processing Information," *Psychological Review,* vol. 63, pp. 81–97, 1956.

ence or significant idea discrete and enhances the recall facility. Each new piece of information acts as a buffer to protect any generation of interference which could cause it to dissipate.

Does the mental review of the points during the discussion facilitate recall? This problem has been a source of study and controversy. Postman [24] and Underwood and Keppel [25] take the affirmative position, while Rock [26] and Estes [27] take a different view. The former group considers repetition helpful if the number of repetitions is sufficient to place associative strength above threshold. Silent recall is useful to the degree that it focuses the ideas quite clearly and with some force in the summarizer's mind. Rock and Estes take the position that repetition merely increases the probability that a particular item will be sampled and learned on that trial. Thus an important question remains unanswered: Does repetition act to strengthen an item, or does it cause it to become distinctive and form a new class, that of repeated versus nonrepeated items?

The summarizer, then, is involved in a task that requires concentration and practice. First, he must be able to hear and organize ideas, often not in accord with his own point of view. Suspending his own evaluative process, he listens to hear the import of what each member says. Second, he encodes the items; that is, he penetrates to the meaning of each item and determines which items can be contained under one basic idea. Third, as he proceeds, he sets up categories. This requires recognition of a different subject or of a different focus on the same subject and a decision on the category and the meaning it will convey. Fourth, as he clearly differentiates and encodes the items, he stores them under their descriptions and proceeds to concentrate on current inputs. Fifth, as opportunity presents itself, he reviews the encoded information in each category. Sixth, he retrieves it in the order and in the form in which he stored it.

Discussion with those who are dissatisfied concerning their ability to summarize reveals that the chief difficulty is in hearing

[24] L. Postman, "Repetition and Paired Associate Learning," *American Journal of Psychology,* vol. 75, pp. 372–389, 1962.
[25] B. J. Underwood and G. Keppel, "Proactive Inhibition in Short-term Retention of Single Items," *Journal of Verbal Learning and Verbal Behavior,* vol. 1, pp. 153–161, 1962.
[26] I. Rock, "The Role of Repetition in Associative Learning," *American Journal of Psychology,* vol. 70, pp. 186–193, 1957.
[27] W. K. Estes, "Learning Theory and the New Mental Chemistry," *Psychological Review,* vol. 67, pp. 207–223, 1960.

various items and then encoding them in distinct categories. Part of this difficulty is an inability to state briefly for oneself the meaning of each contribution.

### *Conclusions*

The leader should involve the members in diagnosing and improving present skills and in increasing the range of skills each is able to use. Attention should be given to the development of insight with reference to those skills which are appropriate at various times in the group's progress. The leader can assist members to recognize and understand the relationships between their personality structures and the range of skills each supports and develops. Such understanding may prove a strong motivation toward the expansion of skills in accordance with development of self-understanding.

Students of group process recognize the great complexity of the interaction even in small groups. This complexity serves the group to the degree that each has the insight and skills to assist in bringing order and clarity to the members' expressions.

Although it is accepted that these skills do not develop without intelligent effort, little attention has been given to the diagnosis of skill needs and practices.

# PREPARATION OF THE GROUP COUNSELOR

*The current model for the preparation of counselors leaves much to be desired. The present experience is too narrow, too brief, and too shallow. The new age places more difficult responsibilities on counselors. In this age, in contrast to other times, an increasing number of counselees have existential concerns and are asking different questions. Formerly, the many concerns could be subsumed under the question "What is man?" Now concerns have a different dimension and are at a greater depth. The counselees now are asking, "Who is man? Who am I?" The Deweyan naturalistic environmentalist–based questions are giving ground to what some consider more basic. The primary questions now emerge from an existentialist premise regarding being. Martin Heidegger's view expressed in his*

*Time and Being is closer to the members' concerns than the experimentalist viewpoint of yesterday.*

*This necessitates broadening the perspective of preparation experiences. The counselor needs training in other disciplines besides those of the behavioral scientist. Experiences in philosophy, religion, and art are needed to equip him to ask of himself, "Who am I?" If he asks this question and ponders upon it, he will more easily perceive the true nature of the counselees' questions and perhaps be able to respond to them with greater sensitivity.*

*The chapters in this part describe and illustrate the nature of such a training program, which seeks to prepare the counselor for the present world, in which there exists a deepening search for meaning. These chapters depict, as well, the stages of development in the counselor's becoming by the differential use of protocol of contrasting groups.*

12

# THE GROUP-COUNSELOR
# EDUCATOR

## INADEQUACY OF ACADEMIC PREPARATION

Far too many counselor educators with responsibility for training group counselors have insufficient academic preparation and experience. They secured their training at a time when the values of group process were only dimly recognized. In many institutions only one course was offered, generally labeled *group guidance.* It was frequently a lecture course focused on methods of giving vocational and other information to small groups. Some may have had courses on groups from a sociological viewpoint or group discussion from the perspective of adult education.

All, of course, have had some experience in groups—the majority, no doubt, in only one kind: authoritarian, or aggregate, groups.

Groups of this type are oriented toward planning and problem solving. The successful group was the one whose planned strategy resulted in satisfactory outcomes. How members felt toward one another, how well they listened, and what happened to each as a person was generally considered irrelevant. The internal dynamics of the group was a refined pragmatism, competitive and product-oriented. Such experiences were of little value in learning the reality of a true organic group.

The method of aggregate groups was acceptable because it was congruent with the educational experiences and thinking to which the counselor was accustomed. It required no difficult personality change—only greater knowledge of human behavior and skill facility. It is not surprising that the leaders usually perceived groups only as a means of improving the quality of thought and only seldom as a means of developing self-awareness and understanding of self and others. When they did, it was largely an intellectual matter, making use of some method of association learning.

A minority became interested in the ideas of group-centered leadership as described by Nicholas Hobbs [1] and others. Fewer still experienced membership in, or leadership of, a group. Those who were fortunate enough to have such experiences became more aware of the functional rationale and the demands it made on the leader. For the majority the theoretical bases of group-centered groups were foreign to their thinking and practice. These tended to distort some of the principles, since they felt more comfortable with an authoritarian method of conducting a group. Research in individual counseling indicated that success was as much a function of the quality of the counseling as of the particular theory the counselor used. Such a conclusion minimized the importance of theory and increased that of performance. With a decreasing emphasis on theory the counselor became less well informed. Knowing less and less concerning the assumptions of learning and behavioral change he gradually relinquished his interest in the theoretical assumptions of counseling practices.

Other counselors who received careful instruction in the theory of counseling were also disadvantaged. These were trainees who were unable or did not endeavor to transfer theoretical assump-

[1] Nicholas Hobbs, "Group Psychotherapy in Preventive Mental Hygiene," *Teachers College Record,* vol. 50, no. 3, pp. 170–178, December, 1948.

tions to practical situations. It was assumed that the trainee could and would transfer psychological and other theories to his practice. This, we now understand, rarely takes place. It is increasingly recognized that each trainee needs specific help in order to understand and apply theory to practice.

Theory became decreasingly important, and planning in a pragmatic framework received more attention. Trainees and group counselors emphasized experimentation with techniques. The effectiveness of the techniques was judged on the basis of results, using the criterion of efficiency.

## PROCESS OF BECOMING

### The Problem of Congruence

Examination of counseling methods leads to the recognition that some do not have a unified theoretical base. For example, Rogers describes the basic encounter group based on Lewinian, psychoanalytic, and other theories. Since these present, in part, diverse positions regarding behavioral change, the counselor educator is in a dilemma with reference to which position he will embrace.

One aspect of this dilemma is the problem of congruence. Can he accept contrasting and contradictory points of view? If he accepts the theory that genuine change takes place when the individual is free to do otherwise, can he accept as well that genuine change takes place through reinforcement? Or can he believe in operant conditioning and accept the individual's use of his human freedom as partial explanation of times of failure? Recognizing that individuals differ widely in the conditions which initiate, increase, and deepen involvement, can he subscribe to only one method? Does he avoid this issue by assuming that if it works, it is good and further examination is unnecessary? If so, can he justify such a completely pragmatic approach?

He should also consider the fact that congruence is not gained by an intellectual exercise alone. It is a total integral intentionality. Man struggles to be congruent often subconsciously. To attain this congruence he engages in "party line" thinking; that is, he compartmentalizes, limiting conscious communication among incongruent theoretical ideas. On the other hand he may maintain communication but in doing so may ignore or distort certain aspects of one theory which irreconcilably challenge aspects of another. This kind of difficulty becomes apparent in the widely used term *permissiveness*. All theorists claim to be operating according to this theory, but their meanings of the term vary so widely both theoretically and operationally that they differ not only in degree but also in kind.

Some group-counselor educators are incongruent in a different sense. Since they do not know what they believe, they are incongruent in their performance in the group. They may usually be analytic, interpretative, and accepting in a very limited sense, but at some time they may reflect, clarify, and accept unconditionally. They are inconsistent, because they have no standards by which to appraise their behavior. This incongruence from one group meeting to the next is difficult for the members. They may finally conclude that the counselor educator is basically consistent in satisfying the same psychological needs each time but in different ways. If and when the members understand the counselor educator, he may be at a disadvantage, for he has no satisfactory basis by which to explain his action.

The counselor educator who retains incongruence in his theoretical foundation decreases his possibility of genuineness in his relationships with group members. To be genuine he needs to know what he believes and to be willing to express it when doing so would be useful to the group. If he does not recognize the incongruence of the theories on which his action is based, he is unlikely to recognize the problems of the trainees.

On the other hand he may give little thought to the theoretical assumptions underlying his procedures. He may be quite content to justify them on the basis of their efficiency. Difficulty arises when the trainees require foundation principles as a means of understanding the process and then have to accept contradictions or theoretical inadequacies.

The knowledgeable counselor educator will integrate his thinking and action. He will keep them related and not adopt a method only because he finds it satisfactory. He will carefully analyze the process and determine to the degree possible the theory or theories on which it is based. Knowledge is necessary, but he must also determine whether his intellectual conclusions are congruent with what he believes about human nature and how change takes place.

It is not enough to consider the psychological and sociological bases of the assumptions; he should also ask if they agree with his beliefs concerning the possibility of human freedom, self-transcendence, or the "inner choice," and his conception of the interrelationship of form (critical thought), vitality (feeling, imagination, and will), and spirit (the numinous depth potential).

He not only will give attention to clarifying the nature of the theory he accepts but will also examine the degree to which his method exemplifies the theory. If he finds that his method is not in accordance with the basic tenets of the theory he accepts, he should reexamine both in order to attain more congruence between his beliefs and action. To the degree that he can resolve this, the trainees will also see the relationship between theory and practice.

### Openness toward Self

The dedicated trainer strives for openness in his belief systems. He heeds the indications that he may be minimizing his own and the trainees' possibilities for more useful experience. When he is inclined to view a situation in terms of a dichotomy, he stops and asks himself, Why? What threatens me?

When he has a problem, he recognizes that to remain open to the use of all information is crucial, whether it is his own or that of one or more trainees. He reminds himself of the possibility that he may reject or distort data which will adversely affect the quality of his decision. He knows that as he integrates information he may try to alter the outcomes to fit his preformed attitudes and value systems. Allport and Postman [2] observed in their study of rumor that what leads to obliteration of some details and falsification of others is that the force of the intellectual and emotional content existing in the individual's mind leads to the assimilation of ideas in accordance with the values resident in the individual. This, Maslow concludes,[3] wards off threatening aspects of reality and at the same time provides the individual with a compensatory feeling that he understands it.

He will become aware of his inclination to become a "party line" thinker. Rokeach describes such a person as one "who not only re-

[2] Gordon W. Allport and Leo Postman, *The Psychology of Rumor,* Henry Holt and Company, Inc., New York, 1947, chap. 6.
[3] A. H. Maslow, *Motivation and Personality,* Harper & Brothers, New York, 1954.

sists change but can change only too easily. What he does depends on what his authorities do, and his changes and refusals to change conform with authority." [4] Who has not known at least one group counselor who has attended a weekend marathon group, or a two-week basic encounter group, or a three-week T group and returned fully decided to conduct such a group without any further hesitancy or consideration! Why are some persons swayed by an authority or an experience beyond the degree of prudence?

The reason is found in the compartmentalization and isolation of ideas which derive from an exaggerated reliance upon authority. The cognitive system may be conceived to have three regions: the central region, which contains the earlier-formed beliefs; the intermediate region, the beliefs concerning authority and authority figures; and the peripheral region. The peripheral beliefs may be intrinsically related to each other as well as to beliefs about authority. In those too easily swayed, the peripheral beliefs are isolated, or segregated, from each other but are interconnected via the authority region; that is, they seem to be arbitrarily interrelated, because they all seem to emanate together from the same authority. Thus instead of interrelating and integrating all pertinent evidence and withstanding the ambiguity of search and indecision, the "party-liner" accepts with little criticism the authority figure or authoritative experience. His thinking has its origin in authority rather than in intrinsic logical connections.

It is much easier to accept a current method receiving popular approval than to work through with care and patience a true understanding of it. The group counselor who is forewarned can be forearmed and ready to analyze the basis of his conclusion.

### Openness to Each Member

The group-counselor educator gives serious consideration to the meaning of individual differences. However, such a consideration is incomplete if it takes into account only the descriptive facts of personality characteristics, mental abilities, and vocational and leisure-time activities. These are significant and helpful, but in trying to understand and assist the trainee further there is another consid-

[4] Milton Rokeach, *The Open and Closed Mind,* Basic Books, Inc., Publishers, New York, 1960, pp. 225–242.

eration that is equally important and more difficult: he should also include an analysis of his approach to life. Is it generally on a pragmatic, utilitarian, horizontal examination of issues, or does he also include a depth dimension of responsibility, integrity, and moral rightness? Does he reflect deeply on the meaning of life and ways in which he can use his potentialities more constructively? Indications that the trainee does may be reflected in his attitudinal position regarding one or more of the following: to what degree does he put others before self, place people above things, dispel fear with faith, refute falsehood with truth, view violence with understanding, judge with compassion, supplant indifference with concern, offer justice instead of sympathy, seek to serve rather than to "succeed"?

The counselor educator's attempts to understand the uniqueness of each member will improve the quality of his communication with him. This quality is in part a function of his respect for the trainee and the demands of his own need structure. It is difficult for some to believe that trainees are capable of the quality of thinking necessary for the kind of decision making and performance which the situation requires. In fact the counselor educator's ego needs may be so great that he assumes as a matter of course that it is necessary to "guide" trainees into certain experiences. Unfortunately many are threatened when the trainees indicate that their understanding and insights are superior. On the other hand some react differently. They recognize the inadequacy of the traditional role of "counselor knows." They are encouraged when trainees know more, have better insights, or think more accurately than they themselves. They delight in the challenge of their function as resource persons. They perceive their work as the improvement of trainee behaviors in the direction of maturity and counseling efficiency.[5]

### Openness toward Methods

The adequate counselor educator is open to the possibility of the fruitfulness of methods unlike his own. This openness is more than passive acceptance. It is expectant, inquisitive, and disciplined. He studies and reflects upon other methods and as opportunity permits participates in training groups. Such activity gives him a basis

---

[5] C. Gratton Kemp, "Educational Dilemmas," *College of Education Quarterly, Michigan State University,* Winter, 1961, p. 10.

for understanding his preferred method and for evaluation of the differences among methods.

Of course he concentrates also on securing more knowledge and understanding of the theory or theories on which the various methods are based. He endeavors to be open to the theoretical as well as to the experiential aspects of these. However, he is prepared to accept the reality of the ambiguity and impossibility of knowing as much as he deems necessary to warrant certainty. The sobering reality is that present theories in the social and behavioral sciences together with philosophical and religious insights do not explain completely either member or group behavior.

Perhaps even more difficult than openness to other methods is the exercise of a critical attitude toward his own. He may proceed with his method of training group counselors without seriously questioning it on either a theoretical or experiential basis. He may justify this closedness by the rationalization that the members are interested, learning, and changing.

It is hoped that he will experiment with methods to test his personal reaction and those of the members. In so doing he clarifies his purposes: are they congruent with those expressed by the members? He evaluates his behavior in the group in relation to his theoretical assumptions. He appraises his methods: is he doing what he plans and believes he should do in the group? Are there areas in his performance which have not been critically examined?

He proceeds to go beyond a descriptive to an interpretative analysis. He asks, What psychological needs am I satisfying in my relationship with the group as a whole and with the individual members? Are these needs justified in terms of group purposes and member needs? Are any of the needs I attempt to satisfy detrimental to the developmental progress of any member? Am I becoming more congruent, more able to be genuine, more willing and capable of expressing clearly and objectively what I really am and think? Do I engage in the same openness myself as that upon which I depend in members to aid them in resolving conflicts and in becoming whole? Within the framework of the I-Thou relationship, is each member a unique person in his own right? To what extent is this conveyed to him by my behavior? Am I interested in each member's making his personal decision regarding the usefulness of any method in relation to his beliefs and understanding?

It is difficult, however, for some members to decide what method and assumptions to accept and use. This is due in part to the counselor educator's enthusiasm for his own method and his lack of emphasis on the importance of self-determination. Some trainees focus on learning and using the method demonstrated by the counselor educator. If they arrive at this position without a critical analysis of the assumptions and requirements of the method, they are engaged in imitation; understanding and becoming are minimal.

Two groups of trainees, one group relatively open-minded and the second relatively closed-minded, were compared with reference to the kinds of responses each group made in two situations. In the first each individual chose the kind of response he would make in each of ten situations. In the second each responded in a "live" situation. The results gave significant evidence that the closed-minded in the first "pencil and paper" situation chose responses in accordance with their perception of the viewpoints of their counselor educator. They were client-centered in the first but directive in the "live" situation. The open-minded responded similarly in each situation.[6] Members who are insecure and threatened experience greater difficulty in exercising their own powers of judgment.

### Individualizing Preparation

Since the counselor educator is interested in each member as a unique person, he does not try to fit the student to the course but rather the course to the student. He recognizes that each member has some needs in common with others but also some which are uniquely his own. The length and kind of preparation required by each member are considered to be in part a function of his academic preparation, his experience in groups, and his mode of examination of issues. Through interviews, self-reports, opinionnaires, and other means he attempts to know each member and to be able to plan with him the most useful kind of preparation.

In order to do this effectively there must be available a variety of experiences. Each is helped to consider and choose among these in relation to their usefulness and compatibility with his life style. The counselor educator must be thoroughly familiar with the assump-

[6] C. Gratton Kemp, "Influence of Dogmatism on the Training of Counselors," *Journal of Counseling Psychology*, vol. 9, pp. 155–157, 1962.

tions and methods of the courses in the group sequence. He must, as well, be able to relinquish sufficiently his biases in order that the member may feel the freedom necessary for making an independent choice. The counselor educator needs to function well as a resource person and be able to maintain a genuinely permissive relationship conducive to the member's free expression of likes and dislikes, certainties and uncertainties.

During the first course in group process the counselor educator will attempt to determine the manner in which each member examines important issues. Does he consider problems by weighing only alternatives regarding their practicality, workability, and feasibility? Or does he further consider them according to the justice and moral rightness of the implications for those affected by them?

The counselor educator assumes that a member who generally gives full consideration to all aspects of decision making may wish to choose a group-centered experience or some variation of it, in which it is assumed that he will consider problems in depth without pressure. On the other hand if these depth insights are foreign to his considerations, he may wish to choose a basic encounter or T group experience or some variation of it in which he will be pressured to consider problems from a depth dimension as well. Information and cooperative planning are necessary in order that the member may have knowledge and insights to assist him. The final decision regarding the sequence and kinds of group experiences is the responsibility of the member.

### Accepting His Freedom

The counselor educator must endeavor to accept the anxiety of freedom. It is comfortable to view ourselves as master mechanisms programmed to do what we were built to do, no more, no less; but we know this is false. Man, as Niebuhr [7] explains, is caught in the interaction of finitude and freedom. He is therefore aware of his potentialities and not content to be a machine. He does not accept the limitations of nature and history; he transforms them.

His anxiety is generated by his objective uncertainty of the proper use of his freedom. He tries to alleviate it by using his freedom

[7] Reinhold Niebuhr, *Nature and Destiny of Man,* Charles Scribner's Sons, New York, 1951, vol. 1, p. 182ff.

to bring some new reality into being, to project new affirmations, and to bring a fresh creativeness to his work and life. Or he may choose to live with only the "courage to be as a part" and thus attempt to ignore his freedom. His experience may convince him that the two forms of anxiety, the destructive, deteriorative, and the constructive, creative, are inextricably intertwined.

He will accept his freedom and not try to escape it through routine activities, unexamined methods, or repression of inconsistencies and incongruences between what he would like to be and do and what he is and does. "The man who has learned to be responsive only to his senses and to be deaf to the voice of memory and conscience has made his exit from history and become prehuman." [8]

However, he finds the acceptance of his freedom difficult, and he may resort to one or more protective devices. He may think and act as if his ideas and methods are what others would do well to imitate; or he may conclude that certain principles, ideas, and/or methods are too radical to warrant serious consideration; or he may erect rationalizations which justify the continuance of what he has found comfortable and which give him ego satisfaction. Any one of these serves as an escape from freedom and from a measure of tension, but in so doing he forfeits the source of creativity.

The counselor educator wisely accepts his own freedom, endures the anxiety, and uses the tension creatively. He endeavors to be a creative person daring to look to that which does not yet appear. In 1962 John W. Gardner in his annual report as president of the Carnegie Corporation of New York wrote in "Renewal in Societies and Man" that it should now be possible to develop a society capable of renewing itself. Such a society needs creative persons in large numbers. He describes the creative man as "quite conventional with respect to all the trivial customs and niceties of life. But in the area of his creative work he must be free to believe or doubt, agree or disagree. He must be free to ask the unsettling questions and free to come up with disturbing answers." The counselor educator with a proper focus will cherish and support this in himself and for the trainees.

He will consider and accept the fact that he lives and works with young people whose values and purposes are not those of their

[8] Roy J. Enquist, "On Creativity," *The Christian Century,* vol. 18, p. 9, January, 1969.

fathers or even similar to his own. He will not reject the conclusion that this is an age of lost identity. The nation has lost it, the trainees do not have it, and his own is in transition. He may thus be saved from rash acts, rigid attitudes, and smallness of vision. He will enter the realities of time and people and share with the trainees in their own searching pilgrimage.

### Process of Becoming

Many group-counselor educators favor the lecture method of teaching. Most teach other courses in which they use this method as a matter of course. Even in classes with small enrollments and using a circle formation the method and interpersonal relationships are basically the same. The result is a collection of students without organic relationship. There is a difficult process of *becoming* for many who undertake to prepare others to work with groups.

The counselor educator may sense this early in the undertaking and react in one of several ways: he may ignore or repress the fact that group process is basically different, or he may recognize basic differences but consider these to be only matters of adjustment, the use of different methods and approaches. If these are his conclusions, the process of becoming is one of improvement of perception and refinement of skills. His personality structure remains unchanged. He gravitates toward those methods in which he feels most congruent and comfortable.

His observations may suggest to him that superficial adjustments are not accomplishing his objectives and that aggregate relationships remain. He perceives the attitudes and feelings of members toward one another and the group to be the same and the sense of responsibility to and for one another undeveloped. As he becomes convinced of these conclusions, he confronts the fact that as a leader of the group and as a trainer of leaders, he must himself change. He realizes that he is involved in a process of becoming.

This process he perceives requires him not only to improve his perceptions and refine his skills but to change his beliefs regarding the capacities of the members, to shift radically the source of his ego satisfactions, to become increasingly more congruent, and to clarify his basic assumptions regarding behavioral change. Group members ask how long a time is necessary for this process of becoming to be reasonably attained. They are surprised at first to learn that it is a long-range developmental undertaking.

One of the trainer's first steps in this process is to accept what he sees and experiences. For years he has been conditioned to assume that the leader earns his status by virtue of the fact that he knows more than the members. He accepts the tradition that the teacher knows more than the students. Assuming this he perceives his function to be that of imparting information in an efficient and interesting manner. It is difficult to change from this to the comprehensive goal of improving the quality of behavior.

However, once he can calmly entertain this purpose, he is ready to become actually aware of the capacities of the members. When he does, he listens better; he moves toward trying to view the idea, problem, or situation from each member's frame of reference. He becomes aware of the quality of the members' thinking, how well they analyze, synthesize, and evaluate, and with so little help from him. He is at times surprised and a little threatened when he is confronted with the fact that a member has a superior idea. He finds that his ideas and attitudes concerning their capacity are being modified. He begins to entertain the notion that many are dependable thinkers, good listeners, and an asset to the group in its process of becoming.

He recognizes that he himself no longer feels that he has to be the directing influence and the chief source of information. He relaxes when he sees evidence that the variety and quality of the members' ideas are adequate and useful. Now he is less perturbed when they do not look to him for the final word. To sense that he is on the periphery even when the interaction is dynamic and meaningful no longer makes him feel uncomfortable.

Although he accepted long ago the organismic concept of behavior, he discovers that he actually was an idealist placing chief significance on the capacity for reasoning. As he examines his own involvement and that of the members, he is convinced of the interrelationship of thought and feeling together with the deep sensing of the members' value system. He perceives that when genuine change in behavior is desirable, ideas are useful and necessary but operate within the context of motivation, feeling, will, and conscience. Content is gradually viewed in a new perspective as not separate from, or superior to, all other aspects in the learning process but important in its own right in supplying the basis for decision making and behavioral change. Placing content in this framework emphasizes its new meaning, not content for knowing but content used as an aid to becoming. Content becomes significant to the degree to which and in the manner in which it is conducive to the gaining of new insights and understanding prerequisite for total development.

On further introspection, he realizes that his sources of satisfaction from the group experience have changed and broadened. What was once his chief ego satisfaction is now minor or nonexistent. He smiles when he thinks of occasions when he thought he could teach group leadership and membership through the use of the lecture method. He senses that he continued thus so long because a well-planned lecture, carefully and forcefully presented, gave him great satisfaction. A deep sense of adequacy, sufficiency, and accomplishment came to him as the rapt attention of the students was everywhere apparent.

But now this is all changed. He has a sense of satisfaction but for a different reason. The source of this satisfaction is not in what he accomplishes but in what each member and the group as a whole accomplish. Since this is the case, he becomes increasingly more interested in the changes which are taking place in each person. He is able to assess with some accuracy his function and performance, especially since these are now divested of the pride which made them difficult to analyze. He discovers that he is relaxed, that he thinks clearly and understands to an increasing degree the dynamics taking place. In fact at times he concedes to himself that it is no longer a course to teach, a task to accomplish, but instead an interesting part of life; he enjoys it.

The environment of living together in search of meaning becomes a creative atmosphere of giving and receiving. Defenses are relaxed and fade away. Each one begins to prize genuineness and to move in the direction of congruence in himself and with others. The marketplace orientation and the competition that defeat so much endeavor disappear. These are foreign to the whole situation and strangely irrelevant. There is a feeling of respect for one another as persons, and a sense of responsibility develops very slowly but surely. Members who for years were afraid to express themselves because of feelings of inadequacy and inferiority sense that there is safety in doing so and venture forth, at first very timidly but with growing assurance.

As the counselor educator reflects upon it, he concludes that this is quite different from a lecture course or some simulation of groupness. It is like learning to live in a new world. Each attempt presents new relationships, new possibilities, and new challenges. Although he knows he will never arrive, the journey toward communion with others beckons him, for is this not one of the meanings of life itself?

# 13

# PREPARATION OF THE GROUP COUNSELOR

## CONCEPTUAL EXPANSION AND FUNCTIONING

In the early sixties the counselor educator gave little attention to group process and counseling. It was one of the least desirable and desired courses to be taught in the counselor preparation program. His preparation for teaching such courses was quite minimal. Also the place of importance such an endeavor received in his thinking and interest often agreed with his degree of preparation. This condition has gradually changed and continues to do so at an accelerated rate. Skilled teachers of group process are now much in demand, and the training of students in group process is required or considered desirable in a wide range of disciplines.

Formerly group counseling was viewed as an extension of one-to-one counseling. Its chief *raison d'être* was that more counselees could be helped in a shorter time, and the training received in individual counseling practicums was considered adequate for group counseling. Group counseling was perceived as more difficult only in degree of required concentration. Change in behavior was expected to take place outside the group session. There was only limited understanding of the possibilities of members helping one another. Skills were assumed to develop without any special attention or consideration.

Group guidance was conceived as apart from, and as having little relationship to, group counseling. It was used chiefly for the informal presentation and discussion of vocational, social, and educational information. The aim of group guidance was to provide needed information for students in this area, whereas in group counseling the concern was the understanding and working through of personal problems. Although these were viewed for some time as quite distinct, some understanding of the group per se in its interpersonal dynamic relationships has developed. Until recently, however, most groups in the school setting could be described as an aggregate collection of individuals without any understanding of, or interest in, becoming an organic group.

Many influences combined to develop a new understanding of the meaning and functioning of an organic group. Such influences have resulted from insights in many disciplines. The organismic functioning of man and the potentials of democratic planning have provided a necessary framework. Recognition of the importance of listening, together with developed skill, has increased the acceptance of the potential of the group for initiating change. And not least the great wave of felt depersonalization and loneliness has moved us to seek in small groups more meaningful relationships with others.

Such developments have greatly extended the concept of the group and its possibilities. The counselor training program commenced with the offering of a course in group guidance which for the most part was a lecture course and offered only minimal if any opportunity for a laboratory experience as a member and leader of the group. From this initial step attention turned to the literature on groups, especially to that which contained insights into the meaning of the group and its interpersonal patterns of dynamics. Group process came to be recognized as a method for the improvement of decision making, for the solving of problems, and for self-understanding and understanding of others.

As knowledge and appreciation of group process developed, it moved from an inconsequential aspect of counselor preparation to one of the major emphases. It was perceived as an area requiring special preparation, skills, and some personal becoming. From a course assigned to someone to complete his teaching requirements the area has become one of signal importance. Group process is now supported by a body of theory and practice, divided into several topics such as membership, leadership, process, and evaluation. Different group methods based on contrasting theoretical approaches have developed. These have different uses and lead to different outcomes. The study and use of various methods and their outcomes have led to the differentiation of groups into educational groups, group counseling, and group psychotherapy. These several methods have their origin in the basic concept of the group and group process.

The group counselor may now choose a large number of courses in the general "group" field. Instead of the single course of a few years ago there are now several avenues he may take in preparation for the use of group process in many settings for a variety of purposes.

## PREPARATION PROBLEMS

Problems in preparation in group counseling mirror three concerns of the trainees: (1) his own identity (What kind of method is best for me?), (2) the problem of choice (How do I learn what I need to know in order to choose? Can I be congruent if I use two or more contrasting methods? Should I begin with how well a method functions and then consider theory? How do I relate function and theory in my choice?), (3) the problem of performance (How much laboratory experience do I need to perform efficiently?).

The trainee has the problem of remaining open to contrasting theories and methods. He must be able to examine them with as little prejudice as possible and to reach conclusions regarding their personal usefulness. This he attempts on the basis of their intrinsic worth and their congruence in relation to his own manner of interpersonal functioning.

He succeeds to the degree that he is able to accept and consider creative differences. The possibility of expression and discussion of many viewpoints may properly be facilitated by all the faculty in counselor education. The danger is that his training experience may be too narrow and not provide him with a basis for intelligent decision.

Trainees who would like to make group counseling the chief emphasis in their professional work often find that the counselor training program provides for only one or two courses. It is not sufficiently intensive and extensive to prepare them for the responsibilities in which they are interested. In many institutions they are at present unable to gain the preparation that they need or that employers assume that they should have either to teach or to counsel in the small-group area.

There is no easy agreement concerning those experiences which are superior in the preparation of group counselors. Counselor educators tend to favor those with which they are familiar. The majority of training programs emphasize academic preparation in only the behavioral sciences, and as a result group counseling has merely this orientation.

Counselors are confronted with problems which their training equips them neither to recognize nor to work with effectively. Since the majority have only minimal training and experience in philosophy, literature, and the arts, they are unable to broaden their perspective to include the recognition and functioning in the struggles of the counselees of such intangibles as imagination, symbols, the will, and conscience.

## NEEDED PREPARATION EXPERIENCES

There is a growing realization that the counselor's preparation should be broadened and deepened. However, any discussion of necessary experiences at this time should be considered tentative and hypothetical. Present trends include not only academic experiences, emphasizing values and conditions, but also experiences oriented toward the understanding of human behavior.

Some of these trends are exemplified in the following insights, which may well be considered for incorporation in thinking about and planning for the preparation of group counselors:

1. There is a developing awareness that information about John, however well organized and sophisticated, does not assist us in understanding "the Johnian in John." [1]

2. Attention is now directed toward a different kind of truth. The assumption that the truth is an object to which the member is related is recognized as only one kind of truth. There is a growing acceptance concerning a kind of truth which may be false for everyone except him who expresses it. The result is that instead of emphasizing the subject-object relationship, reflection is directed to the relationship between the individual and his belief. Although the member's criteria and referents are objectively false, it is considered true if what he says follows logically from his perception of the matter.[2] Kierkegaard was convinced that the very increase of truth (subject-object relationship) may increase insecurity unless we are committed to relating to the truth in our experience.[3] This implies that the group counselor should, in his preparation and practice, commit himself to becoming a genuine participant in the relationship with each member of the group. This means in part that he must be willing and able both to rejoice and to suffer with the members as the occasion may demand.

3. It has long been accepted that the group counselor needs to be sensitive. It is now becoming evident that he must be imaginative and at home in the world of symbols.

4. As well, he must be able to accept ambiguity as a basic constituent of life. He must not be threatened, confused, or alarmed when members express this ambiguity and its effects upon them. Instead of accepting change as an academic concept he must be willing and able to recognize and work with change in its serious dimensions and bewildering unpredictability.

It is not an easy task to plan experiences which will provide with certainty the opportunity for counselors to engage in such becoming. Each individual derives from his experience something which is unique. We can, however, provide the kinds of experiences

[1] Gordon W. Allport, *Becoming: Basic Considerations for a Psychology of Personality,* Yale University Press, New Haven, Conn., 1955, p. 18.
[2] Soren Kierkegaard. "Concluding Unscientific Postscript," in Robert Bretall (ed.), *A Kierkegaard Anthology,* Princeton University Press, Princeton, N.J., 1951, pp. 210–211.
[3] *Ibid.*

which logically could be expected to hold the best possibilities for such creative development.

The balance of this chapter presents suggestions as to the direction needed experiences might take.

### Experiences in Literature and Drama

The study of noble characters in literature encourages the counselor to consider joy, tragedy, and ambiguity in depth, to relate to myths and symbols, to be open to the intuitive searching of the artist concerning the meaning of life. He should read, study, and discuss in small groups great prose and poetry in Greek, Shakespearean, and modern plays. The discussion should focus on what the characters experienced, possible reasons for their reactions, and how each counselor's perception of these situations would affect him. Consider possibilities for insight in a small-group discussion of such symbols as Hamlet's "To be or not to be. . . ."

The counselor could also participate as a member of the cast in several plays. These may be theater productions, if his interest and talent tend in this direction, or productions planned only for the educational experience. The purpose would be twofold: (1) to experience participation in an interdependent relationship to attain a common goal and (2) to be involved vicariously in the perception and feeling of love, joy, tragedy, and despair.

### Experiences in Philosophical and Religious Thinking

These could provide him with the understanding that man's deepest communication is through symbols. Viewpoints concerning man and human freedom would help him to expect and accept the unpredictability of members in his group. Knowledge of the past and present philosophical shifts in man's search for meaning would broaden his perspective, helping him to recognize the deep uncertainties of group members.

Think of the gain to the counselor who makes a study of Kierkegaard's *Diary of the Seducer* and analysis of Mozart's *Don Giovanni* and secures understanding of his three levels, or stages, of life, the aesthetic, ethical, and religious. He may recognize that we live within all of them but that the significance of this for him and the members of the group is the manner in which these levels are related to one another and the degree of predominance of each for individuals. Such understanding establishes a framework for the group counselor which substantially improves the possibility of his gaining useful insights.

Few counselors have given much thought to the place and function of symbols in day-to-day living. Some may have grown up in homes and schools in which symbolic language was rarely used. Help is needed through reading and discussion to explore the presence and use of symbolic thought by those who, in great need to understand and be understood, probe the unfathomable depths of living through the use of symbols. The counselor who thinks in symbols will be more perceptive and able to assist the member who engages in symbolic thinking.

Many counselors are so conditioned in trying to understand members in only a cause-and-effect framework that they experience difficulty and a sense of futility when the counselee ignores reason, or chooses to live by some obvious distortions, or fails to do anything. They have not been helped to recognize and accept the fact that although a member generally performs in accordance with some reasonable pattern, he can and may act otherwise. The group counselor has to reckon with human freedom, not as some remote philosophical concept, but as an essential possibility for each member. The member who on occasion exerts his freedom of choice by refusing to act or by acting in an unexpected positive or negative manner becomes a discouraging puzzle to the counselor. The counselor needs to accept the fact of history that man's freedom is his freedom to destroy himself or on the other hand to assert his powers against overwhelming odds.

### Experiences through Art

Counseling at its best is an art. Facts and relationships developed scientifically are helpful, but they do not encompass the whole of counseling. Although man transmits his thoughts by words, it is by art that he transmits his feelings. Effective counseling depends on the evocation of feeling. This is the function of art which is based on "the capacity of man to receive another man's expression of feeling and to experience those feelings himself." [4]

The member expresses a feeling which he has one time experienced. He may use movements, lines, colors, sounds, or forms expressed in words, and he transmits it in such a manner that others experience the same feeling.[5] Group counseling, then, considered as an art is an activity in which one member communicates feelings through which he has lived and the others, infected by these feelings, also experience and respond. Every work of art causes the receiver to enter into a certain kind of relationship both with him who is producing the art and with others who simultaneously, previously, or subsequently receive the same impression.[6]

The counselor is asked to consider art a basic ingredient in interaction, in growth and development, and in life itself. "We are accustomed to understand art to be only what we hear and see in theatres, concerts, and exhibitions; together with buildings, statues, poems, and novels. . . . But this is but the smallest part of the art by which we communicate with one another in life." [7] Ordinarily and in a limited sense we select from human activity some part to which we attach special importance.

Art in its true comprehensive setting has the following distinguishing qualities: (1) the intentional infection of others by an artist's feeling and (2) form, which determines its genuineness as art and has two ramifications: (a) that the quality of the feelings engendered are important to community living and communion and (b) that art is of equal importance with science for the life and progress of the race.[8]

The significant components of art are form and feeling. Whether counseling becomes an art depends on its form. The form must be adequate in order to have a work of art to consider. It is the form which can be taught and learned by practice. The counselor is taught such skills as listening, clarification, and reflection. However, regardless of his learning and skill he may not be able to counsel because he may lack imagination, intuition, and feeling. These two aspects of

[4] Leo Tolstoy, *What is Art? and Essays on Art,* trans. by Aylmer Maude, Oxford University Press, London, 1929, p. 121.
[5] *Ibid.,* p. 123.
[6] *Ibid.,* p. 120.
[7] *Ibid.,* p. 122.
[8] *Ibid.,* p. xiii.

counseling, science (knowledge and skills) and art (imagination, intuition, and feeling), are bound together in an integral unity.

The capacity of the counselor to share in the feeling of the counselees and to respond out of this experiencing cannot be taught but may be developed. This feeling is more than sensitivity. The counselor may be sensitive to the feeling of a member but not experience within himself sufficiently the same feeling to be able to commune with him. Counseling of the kind desired takes place when the distinction between member and counselor disappears. It is as if the counselor expressed what the member had been longing to express. The member is freed from his own separation and isolation and feels united with others.

This response of the counselor is meaningful to the member to the degree that it contains three qualities: (1) the uniqueness of the feeling the counselor expresses, (2) the clarity of its expression, (3) the sincerity of the counselor, that is, the greater or lesser degree to which the counselor is genuine or feels the emotion which he transmits. The greater the degree to which the response is uniquely the counselor's, growing out of what he has been and is experiencing, the more readily does the member become involved. If the counselor is clear, the member is enabled to mingle in consciousness with the counselor, and the feeling communicated to him seems to be what he has long known and felt and what is now expressed.

Most important of these qualities is sincerity. When the member feels the counselor is speaking out of his own genuine feeling and not merely engaged in a professional act, the member is helped. But if he feels that the counselor does not feel what he is saying but is doing it to help him, resistance springs up within him. Then regardless of how well the counselor puts his learning and skills to use, he not only fails to help the member but actually repels him. If the counselor is sincere, he will express feeling as he experiences it. And just as each one of us is unique, his feeling will be individual for all others. The more individual it is, the more he has drawn it from the depths of his nature, and thus the more sincere it will be.

The basic constituent of counseling, then, cannot be taught However, the conditions conducive to its development grow out of experiences which are meaningful and understood. They are the common experiences of joy, tragedy, doubt, and despair which he shares with all men. Art quickens his perception and understanding of them and opens doors to awareness of self. This it can do since it makes accessible to him both the feelings experienced by predecessors and those expressed by contemporaries. Especially significant are the feelings that our well-being, material and spiritual, individual and collective, temporal and eternal, lies in the growth of brotherhood among men in their loving harmony with one another.

Not all art enhances the possibility of communion of the counselor with his inner self and with others, but only the art which causes him to feel. Whatever form the art may take, the feeling it initiates and intensifies determines its usefulness. No two counselors can be expected to be equally and similarly helped by any art form.

The degree to which the counselor experiences a feeling of union with all men concerning the exigencies of life depends in large measure on the depth to which he is accustomed to examine life. I am looking at an oil painting of a rugged coastline. A few rocky islets near the shore, a small river running into the ocean, and a great expanse of water beyond. The tide is going out and the painting is appropriately named *The Ebb Tide.* One counselor may be caught up by the proportions, the shades of color, the sense of distance, the naturalness of the scene. It may cause another to reflect upon a pleasant vacation along such a coast. But to another it may suggest the temporality of life, and how it ebbs away. He may even be drawn to recall that Swinburne once wrote, ". . . and every weary river winds somehow safe to sea." For this last counselor it is a feeling experience in depth, a dipping into the meaning of life.

For the counselor who seldom reflects on the meaning and purpose of life, art in any mode may not deepen his sensibilities or attune his understanding to the mystery of life. For the counselor who deeply reflects upon his existence, art in some form can engender understanding of his basic feeling, a prerequisite for participation with others in the same quest. Counselors need the confrontation which good art, regardless of subject matter, makes possible. Such an experience deepens the counselor's understanding, preparing him to participate in the members' search for meaning, confidence, and hope.

For example, consider briefly the possible influence of one form of art: music. Music may provide for the counselor an avenue by which he senses the relationship between the struggles of man in each historical period and his creative forms of expression. As he increasingly recognizes that these forms mirror man's search for purpose and meaning, his possibilities of understanding can develop.

Music has the power to stir the emotions and to bring comfort. It has a mysterious quality. Was it not Plato who said, "Music is to the mind what air is to the body"? As the counselor's musical experience matures, he has a greater awareness of the infinite possibilities of man to see his mystical and profound relationships to the Source of all being. Great music can help the counselor himself to be uplifted and to grasp with new awareness that within the recesses of each of us are the soul's loneliness and longings related to thwarted or unattainable aspirations.

Thus a study of the meaning of music may assist him to glimpse its significance in the lives of counselees. Study and reflection will lead him to examine several viewpoints including that of Schopenhauer, who said that when we hear music we are able to come to rest in time and space. Perhaps for members in the group, music, for the time being, becomes the salvation of the restless will.

### Conclusions

The counselor with this breadth and depth of preparation sees himself more realistically. He accepts the evidence of his experience that he works in relation to, and in accordance with, processes some of which may not necessarily follow empirically developed scientific laws. He develops a growing respect for each member with reference to what he can explain and as well concerning that which he can never quite fathom or predict. He has a deepening respect for himself, for what he can observe, evaluate, and change, and for the part of himself which is influential, all-purposeful, and not explained completely within the bounds of rational thought or the wisdom of the organism.[9]

To offer such possible preparation experiences for counselors is a challenge to those who are cognizant of, and dissatisfied with, existing programs. Its interdisciplinary nature and counselor-oriented viewpoint require an approach which uses insights from disciplines not generally studied by the counselor. Moreover, these insights

[9] C. Gratton Kemp. "Another Note on Counseling and the Nature of Man," *Journal of Counseling Psychology,* vol. 8, pp. 187–188, April, 1961.

must be so presented and discussed that the counselor-in-training can perceive how they may assist him in his counseling.

The counselor's present preparation enables him to work with only a few aspects of personality. The dynamic "isness" of each member may escape him. When he recognizes something foreign to his pattern of approach, he may yield to the temptation to disregard it or at least minimize its importance. Such counseling is fragmented, partial, and unrealistic. In the words of Wrenn, the counselor "deals with a person as an indivisible whole—self perceptions, feelings of limitations, conscience, anxieties, search for purpose, and all." [10] If we accept this, we accept the challenge and responsibility to venture the planning of programs with new added dimensions.


SUGGESTED DIRECTIONS IN GROUP–COUNSELOR
PREPARATION

The current practices in the preparation of group counselors are inadequate. This situation is in part a function of the perception of its nature and a lack of understanding of the needed preparation. Present preparation tends to be too shallow, too narrow, and too dogmatic.

It is too shallow since it takes its direction almost solely from the thinking of the technological age. It slips into the world of thought that applies to objects but ignores the I-Thou relationship of persons. It attempts to derive its theory and understanding both of methods and of human life only from the behavioral sciences. It is "thing-oriented" and thought-oriented and is not balanced by a "person" and feeling orientation.

Thus there is an underlying assumption that *adjustment* is the touchstone of the goal of counseling. With such an orientation counselors are ill-prepared to work with groups and individuals who face the depths of life and must find meaning only indirectly related to the common goals of socialization. Our preparation must be oriented to the whole person and all of life. In order to move in this direction it is necessary that insights derived from other disciplines as art, philosophy, religion, and literature should be focused on the consideration of life's meaning and value.

[10] C. Gilbert Wrenn, in C. Gratton Kemp, *Intangibles in Counseling,* Houghton Mifflin Company, Boston, 1967, p. x.

Preparation experiences are too narrow, since group counseling is perceived chiefly as a skill based on the theory of the behavioral sciences. But a skillful counselor may not help the members in self-understanding and the discovery of purpose and meaning. He may not have developed his potential for entering into another's framework and for being able and willing to suffer or be glad with others who feel the need to commune with him.

Group counseling deals with the whole of life. The whole of life is not just contained in science but also in art; both are integrally related in the pursuit of meaning. Therefore the trainee needs experiences not only within the scope of science but also in the field of art. Art looks at an experience with different questions, different perceptions, and different expectancies. A comprehensive approach to reality is a religious experience, since it integrates the utilitarian (science) and the aesthetic (art). This the psalmist knew, for he could write that God, whom we worship in the beauty of holiness, is also a very present help in time of trouble.

Such an approach to understanding is continuously in the process of development. The counselor needs to study in the various fields of art, literature, philosophy, and religion. In each of these disciplines he should try to confront its meaning for life and for him. He must endeavor to relate the insights he gains to the problems of the members of the group. He will gain little if he attains only knowledge about each; he needs to have knowledge of it, to experience it, to be gripped by what it can tell him about the struggles of persons with destiny. The study of these disciplines could be expected to assist him to experience his own feeling and the feelings of the members, and to grasp meaning in both, and in his counseling to maintain a sense of direction and to be a significant catalyst in each member's search to know.

The desire to assist members to find a richer, more open and satisfying life may lead to certain dangers. One is to anticipate greater, more pervasive change than should be expected within the limitations of any method of group process. Such anticipation can easily lead to perceptual distortion of what takes place. Members themselves, sensing the expectations of the group counselor, may reach erroneous conclusions of the value of the experience to them.

When these conditions exist, they inhibit a more exact and reasonable evaluation. Instead of the recognition of the inherent strengths and weaknesses of each method, there is a strong tendency to view the experience as either a most helpful one or one which should not be repeated. Such approaches lead to dogmatic assumptions and hinder an experimental and open-minded approach which is so necessary in the knowledge and practice of group methods.

It is unfortunate that some group counselors assume that the particular method which they favor is superior to others and the only one which trainees need to experience. Such an attitude leads to a closed-minded and unexamined acceptance of a particular method and an unwillingness to entertain and understand other possibilities. The serious acceptance of individual differences should at least suggest that a method which may be useful to some members would not necessarily be useful to others.

Frequently theory is taught apart from practice. Sometimes it is assumed that practice is not very necessary and that given an adequate theoretical background, skills and insights are learned incidentally. Or on the other hand it is assumed that the laboratory experience alone is sufficient without special attention given to theory. Neither of these approaches leads to the provision of adequate preparation.

Many counselor educators are ill at ease in any form of instruction except the lecture method and therefore do not provide the necessary laboratory experience for trainees. When they proceed to lead the group, their participation is a modified short-form lecture which minimizes the possibilities of member participation and growth in group process. Some who do not consider an understanding of theory necessary to functioning as a group counselor give it little attention and concentrate upon the laboratory experience. Some, however, do not plan for leadership experiences for the members but conduct the group themselves and aim to provide an experience in self-understanding for each of the members.

Thus regardless of whether the counselor trainer emphasizes a knowledge of theory or laboratory experience or some combination of these, too little opportunity for leadership is given the trainee. The number of counselor educators who do not offer regular and continuous experience for each member In leading the group and in member participation is unfortunate.

There are those, however, who conduct all courses in the sequence on group process as a laboratory experience. Lectures are nonexistent, and the theory is learned through discussion of the various principles as they become necessary in practice. Improvement of the climate and the interaction of the members and of the needed skills are a matter of ongoing discussion, analysis, and evaluation. Not only is theory learned in its application to the development of a true group, but also members participate in learning the necessary skills of membership and leadership. These counselor educators find a growing demand for more sections, and college advisers in other areas make it a requirement for their advisees.

Since group counseling focuses on the meanings and issues of life, counselors depend on their understanding not only of the related behavioral sciences but also of philosophy, literature, art, and religion. Counselors not only are scientists in the sense that they use the insights and methods of science, but they also are artists making use of basic feeling and intuition. Since group counseling is both a science and an art, skills are involved. Outcomes depend not only upon the counselor's knowledge and understanding but also upon his performance. Since each counselor is unique, the method which he uses and the intuitive understanding which he develops is and should remain a function of his uniqueness. Each counselor must decide finally who he is, what he believes, and what method best expresses his beliefs in relation to his group-counseling endeavors.

To accomplish this the psychological climate pervading his preparation should be one of unconditional acceptance. In such a climate he is able to examine various approaches, evaluate theories, and in the process discover what he believes in relation to them. In freedom he can choose which preparation experiences are most congruent with his view of learning, behavioral change, and search for meaning.

The acceptance of the foregoing suggestions would require a change in point of view and expansion in breadth and depth of preparation opportunities. More specifically group counselors-in-training would recently have had or would engage in those experiences or courses in art, literature, philosophy, and religion that were individually deemed useful and necessary in the development of imagination, feeling, and intuition. Each would take the usual core of courses in guidance, psychology, sociology, and anthropology to provide the theoretical foundations of his counseling with groups.

He would participate in several seminars designed to integrate his knowledge and understandings gained from art and science.

His specific preparation in group counseling would be characterized by courses in group process in which he would learn the theory through discussion and use in the group setting. He would also experience the meaning of a group, group leadership, and group membership. He would learn through participation the skills necessary for involvement as a group member and a group leader. These educational group experiences would provide a basis for understanding group process and for some development of the necessary skills. They would assist him in his decision regarding his interest and aptitude in group counseling. Also he would be in a position to make a tentative decision regarding his preference for group-centered theory and method and for T groups, basic encounter groups, and similarly oriented groups.

In making this tentative decision he should have the help of the counselor trainers in group process and the opportunity to observe through one-way-vision screens or the use of video tapes the various kinds of groups in action. Having made this tentative decision he should be permitted to remove himself from the group if he finds that he is unsuited to the expectancies and method. In the group whose theoretical approach and method commend themselves to him he should have membership and leadership experiences over several quarters or semesters.

Following this he should have internship experience. This should provide for complete responsibility of a group under supervision. This internship experience should extend at least for two quarters or semesters. Each intern should be helped to select those kinds of internship experiences which approximate the age and sociocultural groups with which he anticipates counseling in his professional work.

# 14

# BECOMING A
# GROUP COUNSELOR

## THE GROUP EXPERIENCE

Many trainees enter a new world in their first group experience. They have previously been in groups but not in a group in which the usual aggregate relationships are nonexistent. An illustration will be used to describe and clarify the becoming which is experienced in an organic group. Although other groups vary in specific ways, this illustration will indicate one set of experiences and outcomes valid in this group setting.

The kind of group which will be used for illustrative purposes is composed of not more than eighteen graduate students. It is quite heterogeneous. The members range in age from twenty-five to approximately forty-five and come from several disciplines. The following are usually represented: counselor education, student personnel, counseling psychology, child psychology, nursing, medicine, dentistry, and home economics. The course is listed under *education*, as *group process.* It extends over one college quarter and carries a three-hour credit, repeatable to a maximum of nine hours. The students meet once a week in the evening or three times a week during the day.

The aims of the course are those decided by the students. With slight variation from time to time, they are three: (1) to become acquainted with the literature in the field, (2) to develop skills in membership and leadership, and (3) to gain self-understanding. The method to be used in the attainment of these goals is discussed. The consensus reached is that skills are developed through practice. In order to gain this practice each indicates his preferences for leadership and observer experiences in each of a small group (approximately six) and large group (eighteen).

The content is determined jointly through discussion. The general pattern is the use of one-third to one-half the time for planned topics and the remainder for unplanned experiences. The planned topics are those which are perceived as most useful in understanding: the nature of an organic group, group process, interaction, membership and leadership, and the underlying principles of contrasting group methods.

The member's understanding of himself is assisted in four ways: (1) through readings, (2) through the results of the Dogmatism Scale Form E (each member remains anonymous), (3) through the group's evaluation of its own activity, and (4) through anonymous self-reports. The self-reports are written at the conclusion of each meeting of the group under a self-selected number. All the reports are returned anonymously by number near the close of the group's experience for the purpose of review. The use of the opinionnaire (Dogmatism Scale Form E) [1] provides insights regarding the phenomena of open- and closed-mindedness and the means for recognizing tendencies in either direction. In addition it supplies informa-

---

[1] A standardized instrument for the measurement of openness of belief systems. See Milton Rokeach, *The Open and Closed Mind,* Basic Books, New York, 1960.

tion for the purpose of dividing the large group into three heterogeneous groups.

Most of the significant elements of the experience are chosen by the members. These include aims; choice of content; general method; leadership, observer, and membership functions; the use of small and large groups; and the need for evaluation. Grade requirements, the apportionment of time, and the evaluation period are partly structured.

The counselor educator functions as a member on the periphery. He reflects, clarifies, and accepts. Acceptance is unconditional, and his attitude encourages trust and a feeling of adequacy in individual members. He provides resources to assist the members in reaching their goals and assists in the evaluation which follows each period of interaction. The method is based on group-centered principles. The members in their discussion grow to recognize the underlying principles and rationale.

## TRAINEES' PERCEPTIONS OF THEIR BECOMING

There is a wide variation in perceptions, which may be explained in part by variation in degree of open- or closed-mindedness. The trainee's perception of his experience is written in the anonymous self-report. Excerpts from self-reports will be used to illustrate variations in perception. In order to present the perceptions from different foci, comments of the open- and closed-minded will be separated. Steps in the process will be elucidated from an analysis of the reports. Also the psychological movement of each group over time will be given.

The course in group process from which comments are randomly selected was a quarter's length, distributed over ten evening meetings for a total of approximately twenty-five hours. With reference to the first meeting open-minded members wrote such comments as the following:

"I didn't feel rigid and defensive as I often do in new groups."

"The thing that impressed me most was that it seemed all right to be what you are."

"I guess I just feel that I can be secure in the knowledge that I don't really have to have a preformed idea. I can weigh the information as it comes."

The relatively closed-minded responded in their self-reports with the following kinds of comments at the close of the first meeting:

"I felt our group discussion tonight was good."

"I like the topics we selected for discussion. Hope we can conduct the meetings in the same spirit as tonight."

"There were many new ideas introduced and many more that I felt we could have brought out. Very interesting."

This random sampling of responses from the two groups illustrates the differences in perception. The open group had a greater readiness to examine their feelings and apparently more insight into their personal needs. The closed group was more content-oriented; there was less introspection and a tendency to project repressed feeling onto the group. The counselor educator hopes, of course, that the experience will increase the open-mindedness of all members.

A random selection of comments from the next few meetings provides further ideas on the differences in perception. The open-minded wrote in the following vein:

"I am aware this evening that I was being more observant of verbal and nonverbal behavior of a greater number of group members. I also found myself trying to direct my comments more to the group and not just to one or two persons."

"I did contribute this evening. I felt strange in doing so. I often wish when I feel more anxious I would contribute more instead of less, but I understand why I don't. The understanding seems to take the pressure off, and this makes it easier to contribute. My major feeling for the evening was 'Aha, so this is how it goes. Definitely not painful, so let's give it a try.'"

"I felt more relaxed by the end of the second discussion. A number of us were able to interact on our observations of, and feelings about, the group."

The relatively closed-minded group over the same period made comments such as the following:

"I felt that the sessions this evening were both interesting and challenging. There seemed to be a good sense of openness, and many things were brought out that I feel will draw us closer together. I felt it was good to discuss these together."

At the close of the fourth meeting: "I said that I wished members of the group would document more of their statements and try to distinguish between facts and their opinions."

At the close of the fifth meeting: "Tonight I became quite involved in the second half. The first half was interesting, too, but I found it ended with too many unanswered questions."

"I did not think I knew enough about the subject to add anything. Moreover, I found myself thinking that there were others equally uninformed, but they were participating. For three meetings this brought about a degree of inner conflict in me. At times I objected to their taking up my time, which I feel is precious, and I resented having to listen to them. Later, it dawned on me that this was the purpose, not just to study the group process, but to exercise it and experience it."

"Each time I find I have more respect for those members of the group whom I held in such low esteem at the first few sessions."

As the length of time together increases, there are varying degrees of change. Behavioral change flows in one direction, but its characteristics and rate differ widely between the two groups. The more open-minded relax more easily and gain a feeling of adequacy and belongingness earlier in the process. The more closed-minded continue longer to feel a need for clarity and answers, become involved more slowly, and proceed with greater difficulty in their self-understanding.

Differences in perception continue in the latter part of the experience. Each moves along the process of becoming in a slightly different manner and at a different rate. Perceptions of the open-minded tended to be like the following:

"I felt as though I should take hold of things and help M. [the leader]. The feeling was a motivating one, and I became involved, especially so in the second discussion."

"As I looked at the group before we began, it really seemed that they weren't so very different from me. I was different from what I had felt before, because I not only thought it, but I felt it too."

"Things were much better tonight. If I had come up with a plan and tried it out, I would have been sure that what I had consciously done had made the difference, but I didn't try to do anything special. I guess I had decided to just play it by ear. I felt more comfortable and more willing to say how I felt than I did last week."

"It seemed to me we couldn't go any farther if we didn't clear the air. When the opportunity came to do so, I felt I was among those who kept us focused on the problems. At first I was afraid I was pushing the group someplace it wasn't ready to go, but we did seem to get some honest talking done. I hope this really was helpful to the group and not just to me. I guess what I'm saying is I hope I was filling a group role and not just meeting an individual need of my own."

"Toward the end of the discussion D. seemed under stress, so I decided to do something. She probably was coming up for coffee anyway, but I made an extra effort to see to it that she came with us and that we all kind of chatted together. D. did seem more relaxed when we started discussion again. Anyway I guess the important thing isn't really for D. to feel more comfortable and therefore act more the way I want her to act; maybe the important thing is for her to feel more comfortable, period."

The closed-minded members wrote the following reports and others similar to them:

"We discussed my role in the group, and the consensus seemed to be that I was a synthesizer of ideas both for myself and in turn for the group. Perhaps I constantly try to structure my thoughts and remove ambiguity from them by tying them together."

"We had a lively discussion of socio and psyche process. I have never given much thought to psyche groups. Certainly they are very important. I am beginning to unbend a little in some of my attitudes."

"There are those who feel there can be no true caring during a group relationship of such short duration as this. I believe there is concern for the group as such. I believe it is growing stronger. Wish I could get more free of self-concerns and become a larger part of it."

"I am at last beginning to trust myself to the group. Things are a little clearer to me. It's time I got myself off my hands and did something for the group."

"For too long I guess I have been thinking, What could what we said mean to the group? Now I am asking, What does this mean to me? What do I feel and believe about myself and group process?"

The relatively closed-minded have a continuing difficulty with the natural ambiguity of group process and accept it very gradually. Insights concerning the group and themselves come more slowly, since self-concern, fear, and insecurity inhibit them. Self-concern hinders them from putting into action their sense of responsibility, which is slow in developing. They move toward the same goals of becomingness but at a slower rate of development than do the open-minded.

## DEGREES IN THE BECOMING PROCESS

There are progressive degrees in becoming a group member and leader. The process is different for each individual, since he brings to the experience a past, uniquely his own. This becomes more evident as we review the psychological movement of two contrasting subgroups participating in the same general experience. The progressive and overlapping degree of progress of those who are relatively open-minded appear to be the following: (1) an interest in interpersonal relationships, an openness of positive expectancy; (2) some personal looking inward in relation to ideas and feelings, a willingness to examine what takes place in the group in relation to themselves; (3) an increasing feeling of adequacy and a sense of relaxation, an acceptance of the fact that it is all right to be oneself; (4) an interest in individuals and the group and a willingness to become involved; (5) a decrease in the need for clarity both ideationally and psychologically, a readiness to withstand ambiguity, and an attitude of positive expectancy; (6) an appreciation of the depth of interpersonal relationships and the beginning of a genuine sense of caring; (7) a sense of responsibility as an integral part of the ongoingness of the group.

Those who because of their past experiences are relatively closed-minded bring a different set of expectancies which influence their perceptions and rate of progress. The psychological movement of this group may be summarized as follows: (1) They are content-oriented: significance of an experience is a function of the knowledge gained. (2) They look at the group in terms of how they examine ideas: their introspection is in terms of the group's performance rather than their own. (3) They feel a need for clarity and answers; ideas give meaning: examination of their functions and feelings are difficult to separate from those of the group. (4) They become involved slowly, usually with one or two and only later with others. (5) They have difficulty with the ambiguity of the situation: their progress is adversely affected by self concerns. (6) They experience some apprehension, which inhibits a full commitment to personal goals and to optimum performance in the group. (7) They have some appreciation of others and a tendency toward openness in relationships resulting in a sense of caring and of responsibility.

## PROGRESSIVE DEVELOPMENTAL INDICES

Another method of analysis of the process of becoming a group counselor is through an examination of the general movement. Using self-reports and recordings of sessions, the process may be analyzed, for the purpose of description, into indices that may be summarized as follows: (1) wonderings and questionings about the group experiences; (2) tentative beginnings of involvement and some feeling of relaxation; (3) trying to listen, feeling a little more adequate, with less self-concern; (4) becoming accustomed to ambiguity and to the lack of answers and intellectual certitude, the recognition of individual differences, and the commencement of a positive attitude toward conflict; (5) realization of the importance of skills and the intention of developing these; (6) improved observation, greater use of introspection and growth in self-understanding, less uneasiness with conflict and the expression of creative differences; (7) growing appreciation of content and interpersonal relationships; (8) beginning of actualized sense of responsibility and caring; (9) increasing openness and willingness to be known, some feeling of adequacy, and understanding of others; (10) a sense of greater self-knowledge, an increase in sensitivity, interest in the process, a feeling of need of more experience to improve skills.

All trainees commence the experience with some feeling of uneasiness and inadequacy. Each has some fear regarding the possibility of a competitive structure and lack of acceptance. Each comes to the group concerned about himself with little readiness for cooperation with others. In varying degrees each is a product of the process of conditioning in the competitive structure of education.

From this position the trainee begins to experience a different situation. The atmosphere he senses is unusual. Human relations seem more tolerant and considerate. The others in the group begin to relax; the absence of evaluation engenders a safety which encourages him to listen. He is attracted by the careful listening of the counselor educator and through identification with him begins to listen also. At first he listens only to those who he hopes have ideas he can use. As one expressed it, "Tonight I listened more to others with a real desire to hear what they had to say. I noticed, though, that I don't listen to everyone with the same amount of interest or even respect. It's as if I am saying, 'You are an important person if you say something I find meaningful. Your worth lies not in the fact that you are a human being but in the worth of your statement.' "

The trainee is a little surprised that the counselor educator is on the periphery and that the discussion is progressing without his direction. He notices that the other members apparently accept this and are not especially interested in or desirous of having his support or encouragement. He begins to feel that he can let himself be involved, that he can learn from others, and that he really is one of the group. He ventures ideas and experiences satisfaction when the members listen and accept his comments.

As various conflicting points of view are expressed on an issue, he recognizes that there is a place for creative differences. He realizes that a new criterion is in operation, namely, "If it's genuine, it is welcome." He feels the relationship among the members in changing; each is becoming a person in his own right. He senses a responsibility to the leader and feels responsible himself for the progress and welfare of the others in the group relationship. One member wrote it this way: "I realize that it's as much my responsibility as it is for others to set the group climate." Another wrote: "I feel that as the weeks progress, I am becoming more sensitive to the thoughts and feelings of others. I am better able to accept the person as he is, regardless of what he says."

It becomes evident to him that members no longer seem to censure their thoughts and feelings. They are speaking spontaneously with enthusiasm. They are making self-revelatory statements which are being accepted as truth for the individual and worthy of consideration. On reflection he realizes that he too is involved and responding from his convictions. He remembers saying: "It doesn't help much to be stewing inside and playing it cool on the outside."

The topic of the evening continues in his thinking throughout the week. He discusses ideas with other group members and sometimes with friends. He feels more adequate and is able to listen and to function with some skill in reflection, clarification, analysis, and summarization. He is aware that he has difficulty in following the thread of thought and in the mental organization of the sequence of ideas.

He is no longer apprehensive when the members commence talking about personal problems. He feels that involvement, regardless of its intensity, can have constructive outcomes. He recognizes that others like himself have strengths and weaknesses of various kinds and degrees and that these are accepted with the understanding that each is searching in his own way to make a better life for himself and others.

He finds that he has feelings of satisfaction and of usefulness as he contributes and helps to provide information about, and clarification of, the issues discussed. He is aware that his responsibility has developed into a sense of interest in, and caring for, the members in the group.


## NECESSARY CONSIDERATIONS

Aided by the experiences in his first course, educational group process, the trainee will develop several questions to guide his thinking in charting his future. One of the first might well be, Am I able with reasonable effort to become a group leader, or are the demands of this aspect of my profession such that I shall have to devote an unusual amount of energy, time, and effort in order to become an adequate group counselor? He may at this point decide that he does not believe in the possibilities of groups or that he would like to work with small groups in an educational setting but not in group-counseling situations.

If he is highly motivated to become a group counselor and accepts the challenge, he will then proceed in his self-study. A second question would follow: Since I shall be engaged in inducing behavioral change, what theory or theories of change in behavior do I believe and accept? Are there contradictions in what I believe? How congruent am I or could I become in demonstrating what I believe and have accepted?

A third question could be, What is my chief source of ego satisfaction in my relationships with group members? Do I experience satisfaction in imparting information, in giving directions and advice, or in making interpretations and diagnoses? Do I enjoy the respect and expectancy that I shall provide the final word regarding a situation? Is there a certain ecstasy in formulating questions which cause the member to pursue his thinking at deeper levels?

Or is the chief source of my ego satisfaction observing a member venturing to present his thought and feeling to the group, or observing that another is relaxed, looks comfortable, and participates with apparent interest, or that another by his remarks indicates he has gained an insight which has much meaning for him, or that another clarifies an idea suggestive of good listening and careful thought? Although each of these contrasting types has proved useful, the group counselor-to-be will need to recognize that he tends in one or the other of these directions: he receives greater satisfaction either through influencing the members by use of his status, ideas, or direction or in their observed development toward maturity because of the freedom and acceptance of the climate he encourages and their involvement in it. This recognition will help him to decide in what kind of leadership function he would feel most comfortable.

A fourth question may follow when he reflects upon his leadership of the group in his first group experience: How did I actually feel about the members in the group? That is, did I assume and expect that they were capable of thinking through situations without my critical analysis, and did I have the expectancy that they would do so? Did I experience a compulsive need to direct, interpret, and to a degree control the interaction? Was I uncomfortable when the direction and usefulness of interaction were confused? Or did I feel willing and sufficiently at ease to depend upon the members and their involvement with one another and the topic to relegate myself to the periphery? If so, did I enjoy my function on the periphery as a resource member, a catalyst, and by my listening and observing attitude also an energizer?

A fifth question is, What do I consider to be the possibilities of group process? Do I perceive it as a method of improving the quality of thought and of reaching adequate solutions to problems? Or do I believe also that it has possibilities of improving the personality adjustment of members? Do I entertain as well expectations that modifications in the meanings, values, and goals may take place, or do I reserve personality change in depth for individual counseling only?

What he perceives to be the possibilities of group process is directly related to what he believes about people and human nature.

He may find it difficult to determine to a useful degree what he believes. He may proceed by studying his interpersonal relationships as a basis for inferences to be examined. He may to his chagrin be forced to accept the fact that in most situations others are objects. He perceives that he has a much higher respect for, and a different attitude toward, those who achieve, and at times he may manipulate others to gain some satisfaction or advantage. It is disturbing to him that he has given only lip service to such concepts as the person-to-person or the I-Thou relationships. He will wisely avoid trying to rationalize these concerns and instead will recognize that they are the result of a conditioning process which he can only hope gradually to change.

He may on the other hand conclude that he is making progress in living as if people were more important than all else. He will discern under what conditions he tends to retrogress to relating to others as objects. He will try to understand what in the environment and within himself predisposes him to be less than helpful.

He will seriously consider the matter of trust. He will try to understand its basic functioning in the group process and in the helping relationship. He will avoid the either-or position and thereby confront the complexity of this relationship. He will continue to try to analyze under what conditions he trusts and whether these are justifiable, and also those conditions in which he distrusts and why he does so.

Recognizing the importance of caring, he will examine his relationships with the members in the group. He will endeavor to seek out in his behavior evidences in his feeling and action of genuine caring or its absence. He will try to discern the superficialities of appearance or behavior which prevent him from coming to understand the personhood of a member. He will seek out within his experience the roots of these psychological walls of separation in order that he may understand them and deal with them.

He will recognize that his involvement or noninvolvement with others is a function of what he believes about people. They are of course inherent in the degree of caring and trust which he shares with others. He will try to understand why his involvement differs so widely from one situation to the next. He may be forced to conclude that his involvement is not with the person but only with ideas and that when the member's ideas are unusual, radical, old, or boring, he is not involved. Or he may discover that his involvement accelerates rapidly as the member expresses more emotion and determination. He may wish to examine why it is that he becomes unduly involved.

Of great importance also is what he believes about human nature. It may first be necessary for him to accept the fact that his performance illustrates not only that he does believe but also what he believes. Although he may not have clarified for himself what he believes, he nevertheless relates to others in terms of it. As he ponders this, he may conclude that he is inconsistent, that what he proclaims and thinks he believes differs from his actual beliefs as evidenced in his interpersonal relationships.

Does he rest his confidence for behavioral change on the critical thinking of the members? What meaning does he attach to critical thinking? Is it only perceiving relationships among ideas or the more inclusive organismic conception as expressed in the well-known phrases "The heart has its reasons which the mind knoweth not" and "As a man thinketh in his heart, so is he." If he accepts the less inclusive meaning, his counseling will reflect dependence upon rational analysis of situations and conclusions based upon their results. He places great importance on insight and assumes that when a member understands he will change. He may confront situations in which, regardless of the quality of the conclusions reached, the member may delay, or take no action, or proceed in a different direction.

The analysis of his beliefs as illustrated in his behavior may convince him that although he assumes critical thinking to be necessary, he relies upon vitality, that is, the member's use of his feeling, imagination, and will. He perceives that he places reliance upon "the wisdom of the organism," believing in the integrated functioning of these three to initiate and carry through behavioral change.

His introspection may lead to an awareness that neither critical thinking nor vitality alone, nor both together, explains completely what is involved in the process of becoming. He recognizes that some members consider issues from an added dimension. They ask questions concerning justice, moral rightness, and integrity. Such questions assume that each member has the potentiality of inwardness, an "inner choice." To what degree, if at all, does he expect this potential to function in interpersonal relationships and in the solutions of problems? Does he really believe that there is this potential, and what is his expectancy regarding it and reliance upon it?

He may be ready now to draw some conclusions. He may conclude that his belief regarding human nature suggests that he place his confidence in critical thinking, that reason best explains man's essence. He therefore emphasizes in his group membership and leadership the use of reasoning as the chief means of improving the quality of interpersonal relationships.

He may decide that although reasoning has a place, it is imagination, feeling, and will which initiate and promote behavioral change. Arriving at the decision, he plans to increase the emotional involvement and the use of the imagination. He concludes that these, together with the will, initiate action and induce personality change.

Or it may appear to him that emphasis cannot be justifiably placed on any part of man's essence, that to do so minimizes too greatly the importance of the functioning of other integrally related essences. The idealist, he concludes, is forced to subsume vitality and the potential of "inner choice" and human freedom under reason. He concludes also that the romanticist subsumes reasoning and man's capacity for inwardness under vitality (his feeling, imagination, and will). He is compelled to accept the organismic concept that all parts of the essence of man are functioning integrally in any significant behavioral change, each to the degree that the situation demands. In this case he remains open to all possibilities of change both in himself and in others, without placing undue emphasis upon one aspect of nature or encouraging more reliance upon one than upon another.

Regardless of his conclusion it is difficult accurately to analyze his beliefs and to assess the congruence between what he thinks he believes and what his performance indicates. Unless he does, however, he lacks a basis for self-understanding and the understanding and improvement of his performance.


SUMMARY

From the commencement of his preparation the trainee should fully realize that the training process is exploratory. He should be confident that his own decision regarding whether or not he continues to work with groups will be respected. He should of course recognize that one of the chief purposes of the initial experience in group process is to assist him in making a competent decision. It should not, therefore, be assumed that all trainees will as a matter of course become group counselors.

The trainee has several considerations to explore in determining whether or not he becomes a group counselor. These considerations can best have their bases in experience. It is hoped that his experience in educational group process will place him in a position to ask useful questions and to reach some conclusions regarding his future.

His questions will take certain forms. One set of questions may focus on his conclusions regarding the adequacy of the group process as a constructive experience in helping members toward a more meaningful and fulfilling life. Another set of questions will focus on what he believes constitutes the essence of man and how his understanding of man influences his counseling effort. A third set will be used to clarify his unique method of confronting important issues in his life. Is his life style one that resembles that of the one-dimensional man, or does he also use a depth dimension in trying to reach a conclusion? Does he make use of thought, memory, and imagination to relate himself to the past, present, and future and to what is ultimate, with the intentionality of self-observation and criticism? Another set of questions will explore his interest and anticipatory fulfillment in group counseling. Is this an activity in which he would be interested and willing to expend himself because he believes in its fruitfulness and in his own capacity to become?

Having pondered these questions and discussed them with other counselors he may arrive at one of the following positions: He may decide that he does not believe in the usefulness of group process and that he will give himself to working only with individuals. He may reach this decision for one or more reasons. Some of these conceivably might be lack of interest, inability to feel comfortable and to participate well in a group setting, or lack of belief in what may be accomplished through the use of group process.

He may decide that he would not be interested or comfortable in group counseling but would like to conduct groups in an educational setting in which the chief emphasis would be on educational planning, gaining information, and solving educational problems. If this is his conclusion, he will turn his attention to gaining further experience in a more advanced course in educational group process.

Or he may decide he would like to become a group counselor. He then has a second related decision to make, that is, what theory and method of group counseling would be most congruent with what he is or would like to become. He will recognize that there are several considerations. Some of these are, What is the source of his satisfaction in working with groups? What is his conviction regarding behavioral change? With what theory of learning and of motivation does he most agree? What is his conclusion regarding the necessity, possibility, and probability of members' considering problems in depth? Does he believe that the majority of members give in-depth consideration to problems with little urging and pressure, or is he more inclined toward the assumption that intense interpersonal emotional confrontation and conflict are necessary to induce change?

These important decisions should not be hastily made, and discussion of them with group-counselor educators and others affected by the outcomes will be recognized as a wise procedure.


CONCLUSIONS

Becoming a group counselor is a much more comprehensive undertaking than the gaining of knowledge and skills. It demands of the counselor-to-be a critical appraisal, difficult and painful, concerning who he really is. Only when he arrives at some measure of understanding is he able to be fully useful to those whom he would help. Congruence, or "purity of heart," is a necessary attribute for constructive therapeutic relationships.

The group counselor cannot afford to be tossed about by every wind of counseling doctrine. He needs to have a theoretical basis for his work. He may change or modify his theoretical position but only following careful examination and commitment to the new. He does not float along on some quasi-theoretical, quasi-pragmatic considerations. He takes depth soundings and readings and thus avoids the shoals of theoretical contradictions and inconsistency.

He endeavors to keep a proper balance between the tangible and intangible elements in behavioral change. He does not discount the use of such means as are available for the gaining of measurable insights but does not allow himself to become blind to the significant and influential intangibles which he can sense only in a limited fashion through intuition and productive imagination.

He does not capitulate to the assumption that group counseling is a matter of skill development. On the other hand he endeavors to assess and improve his skills. He realizes that what he is and what he believes require skills in order that they may bear fruit.

His respect for skill development should not entice him to fall prey to the assumption that his beliefs concerning human nature have no direct bearing on his influence as a group counselor. He may like to think that he swims on the ocean of relativity and can shift from one conception to another as a swimmer changes his stroke. Part of the price of such pragmatic behavior is a lack of needed stability and diminution of self-knowledge.

Unless he abdicates the human race by living in accordance with the sensual and one-dimensional superficialities, he must avail himself of his potentiality for "inner choice," the use of memory, intuition, and productive imagination. Unless he is open to the signals of inwardness, he remains immersed in trivialities.

Unknowingly his counseling behavior illustrates what he believes about the members in the group. He therefore wrestles with the age-old problem of "What is man?" To counsel is to have some response. His problem is to know what is uniquely his own and why he holds this belief instead of some other.

He may wistfully like to conclude that his skill performance encompasses the whole of group counseling and that his personal method of confronting life's issues is foreign to the outcomes of his efforts. But this approach limits his perception of the potentialities and possibilities of the members and removes him from the means of deepening and enriching his personal life. His outlook and efforts mirror a shallowness, and his relationships with group members leave much to be desired.

He is too wise to assume that he can escape the deep tensions of life. He is in the same position as that of Reinhold Niebuhr, who wrote in a letter of reply to Richard Roberts: "You are quite right in declaring that it is my business to keep alive the tension within me between the very relative good that I at best achieve and the ideal good that I profess." He will join reflecting men of all ages who have known the necessity of remaining open to reality in order to achieve some measure of self-fulfillment. He will progress from a one-dimensional person with only the "courage to be as a part" and will strive to have the "courage to be."

# 6

## FUNCTIONING OF THE GROUP COUNSELOR

*Regardless of the preparation and convictions of the group counselor he serves in a particular setting. He has to integrate his beliefs, training, and the present possibilities or those capable of development in the environment. He is engaged in establishing priorities and to do so must have a workable and satisfactory rationale. He uses his productive imagination to foresee creatively and plan in what direction and in what situations his beliefs, energy, and skill may have the most constructive results.*

*He needs valid data to guide his planning with others who have kindred interests, especially his colleagues and the members of the guidance committee. This necessitates that he engage himself in ongoing study and evaluation of his methods and activities. Some of*

259

this research he will conduct himself. He will gain insights from published studies. These sources cannot provide him with the certitude he would like but will eliminate a high degree of guessing. However, some ambiguity will always remain.

The two chapters in this part explore the difficulties of, and possibilities for, the counselor both within and outside the school setting. They also provide ideas and methods for the study and evaluation of his professional procedures.

# 15

## THE GROUP COUNSELOR
## AT WORK

Not long ago the counselor was engaged almost exclusively in individual counseling. Now he is giving more thought and attention to the possibilities of working with groups. In part this is the result of a growing expectancy regarding the usefulness of group process in many settings and for a variety of purposes. The inherent basicity of group life is receiving increasing recognition. The organismic approach to the understanding of groups has emphasized the existence, in any group, of possibilities not only of problem solving but also of behavioral change. The complexity of interpersonal relationships and the probability of diverse solutions to critical problems have focused attention on the need for genuine interaction. In industry, research, education, and medicine the value of a group approach is appreciated. It is recognized that searching within the group encourages intuitive hunches as precursors to better understanding of the means of improving interpersonal relationships and the solving of urgent problems.

The importance of the small group as a committee of the whole is now taken seriously. It is more frequently viewed as a dynamic task force and as such is expected to promote those working relationships which make possible the development of creative responses to situations. Small groups extending across hierarchal organizations are considered by industry as conducive to positive work attitudes, increased output, and more personal satisfaction.

The trend toward decentralization in many organizational settings is receiving careful attention. The grass roots approach to the solving of problems is now perceived as more than a fanciful idea. Many see it as a practical necessity. Gibb writes: "The healthy group does not ignore the goals of the large system, but its primary efforts are directed toward activities that are sustaining and fulfilling for individual members. If the group is not in tune with goals of the organization, it works toward creating new goals in both the group and in the larger organization." [1]

Such developments prepare the way for the group counselor's endeavors. It is a time when he is challenged to try to extend the application and usefulness of group counseling to several aspects of school and community living.

## HIS ROLE CONCEPT

The counselor's role is becoming more complex. At times it is difficult for him to distinguish precisely his uniqueness. There are some aspects of school functioning with which he is only tangentially related, but there are others for which he assumes chief responsibility. He has to differentiate among these and finds that the establishment of priorities is a necessity. High in this list of priorities he now places his work with groups. This is to be expected, since he has emphasized group counseling in his preparation and believes strongly in

[1] Jack R. Gibb. "Fear and Facade: Defensive Management," in Richard E. Farson (ed.), *Science and Human Affairs,* Science and Behavior Books, Inc., Palo Alto, Calif., 1965, p. 211.

its possibilities. This area of responsibility has several aspects. The chief purpose of his work with some groups is educational; with others it is group counseling. Some groups commence as educational and become more involved with personal concerns.

He accepts the conclusion that no group experience is purely and solely educational or therapeutic. He agrees with the differentiation of groups as socio process groups and psyche process groups elaborated by Coffey.[2] In the socio group aspects of the problem-solving group he includes the rich store of potential involvement, motivation, and ego fulfillment characteristic of the psyche process; in the psyche process group, concerned with such matters as projections, perception of self and others, aggression and submission, he includes such socio process dynamics as problem solving, decision making, and goal setting.

He also finds useful the following descriptive indices of each as developed by the author.[3] Listed as socio process behavior indices are (1) establishing the goal, (2) supplying relevant information, (3) stimulating thought related to goal, (4) listening to understand expressed ideas, (5) encouraging expression of problem-solving ideas, (6) linking together ideas associated with goal, (7) reflecting and clarifying ideas when necessary, (8) summarizing as required, and (9) endeavoring to reach a consensus. Pyche process behavior indices are listed as the following: (1) leaving the situation unstructured, (2) listening to understand the meaning to each individual of his expression, (3) linking together expressions of feeling for further consideration, (4) reflecting and clarifying feeling expressed, as necessary, (5) avoiding any attempt to reach a consensus, (6) endeavoring to further feeling-oriented responses rather than idea-oriented responses, (7) proceeding at members' rate without encouragement or rewards for verbalization, (8) expecting differences on both the ideational and feeling levels, and (9) accepting strong expressions of personal feeling as material useful in the process.

On the other hand he assumes the educational group to be sufficiently different as to be engaged in a different activity with

[2] Hubert Stanley Coffey, "Socio and Psyche Group Process: Integrative Concepts," *The Journal of Social Issues,* vol. 8, pp. 65–74, 1952.
[3] C. Gratton Kemp, "Behaviors in Group Guidance (Socio Process) and Group Counseling (Psyche Process)," *Journal of Counseling Psychology,* vol. 10, pp. 373–377, 1963.

different goals. The clarification by Boy and Pine [4] illustrates the extreme parameters of each of group guidance and group counseling. Thus he needs to be clear regarding the focus of his endeavor.

Even so, he can expect difficulty in defining his role. He will avoid a stereotyped function which someone may attempt to impose. Pierson writes, "The adequately trained school counselor develops his own role, a role which tends to be unique with him and unique to the situation in which the role is developed." [5] But to insist on working in those capacities in which he can make his special contribution will necessitate that he educate, insist, and persist. Needless to say he needs convictions based on a rationale which provide guidelines for his courageous undertaking.

Desired changes, however, must be viewed within the perspective of the best possibilities of the total school functioning. What is needed and what can be accomplished will vary from school to school. Nevertheless changes and improvements should be expected It is to everyone's advantage that the counselor be engaged in those activities for which he has special training and ability. Progress in the right direction may demand that the time given to group counseling be extended.

## NEED FOR KNOWLEDGE OF PROCESS

Although there is an increasing tolerance for group activities in the school, there is need for much more knowledge and understanding. The group counselor could well consider what may be some areas in which clarification and information will be needed. Let us consider a few for purposes of illustration.

First, some confusion of group discussion with group process can be expected. This takes place chiefly because no distinction is made between an aggregate and organic group. Group discussion as frequently conducted in and out of the school situation is chiefly two-way, leader to member and member to leader. Interpersonal communication among the members and interrelatedness in which each is working for the good of all and in accordance with group

[4] Angelo V. Boy and Gerald J. Pine, *The Counselor in the Schools: A Reconceptualization,* Houghton Mifflin Company, Boston, 1968, p. 51.
[5] George A. Pierson, *Counselor Education in Regular Session Institutes,* U.S. Department of Health, Education, and Welfare, Office of Education, 1965, p. 39.

purposes are lacking. Expression of creative differences and the encouragement of an individual search are missing. There is, then, both an operational and qualitative difference between aggregate groups, such as the usual classroom groups, faculty groups, and committees, and the organic group. In the latter there is a tangible qualitative interdependence of each upon others which operates three ways: individual to individual, individual to whole, and whole to individual.

Through his own example in groups the group counselor will help teachers, administrators, and students to "work together to release an emergent quality called psychological climate or cooperative unity through which each develops his inner capacities, releases better the nature of his self, releases more of his past experience and learns how to create this emergent quality." [6]

A second idea inhibitive to progress in the use of group process is the assumption that conflict is detrimental and out of place. In the school and the community there is a hesitancy to express one's true feelings, to "tell it as it is." Committee meetings, classroom groups, faculty meetings are expected to run smoothly and sometimes in accordance with Robert's Rules of Order. There is little acceptance of dissenting, divergent, and creatively different ideas, and conclusions arrived at through consensus. Through his attitude, his encouragement, and the creative use of his skills the counselor will try to make conflict natural, acceptable, and useful as a means of reaching honest and high-quality decisions. As the Overstreets have suggested, this is difficult. They would view the counselor as "the person who is spontaneously able, where the stage is set for conflict, to keep his perspective, see his adversary as a human being, and conceive of possibilities other than those of winning or losing." [7]

A third inhibitive factor in the development of group process at any level for any purpose is the poor quality of listening. Although many have an intellectual, few have an operational understanding and experience in listening for the purpose of understanding another from his frame of reference. Many will need help in recognizing and refraining from the injurious habit of evaluation of others' comments.

[6] L. Thomas Hopkins, *The Emerging Self in School and Home,* Harper & Row, Publishers, Incorporated, New York, 1954, pp. 186–189.
[7] Harry Overstreet and Bonarro Overstreet, "Creative Handling of Conflict," *The Saturday Review,* February 20, 1954, p. 59.

The group counselor can commence to help improve listening by his own example of good listening. He can indicate by his comments a readiness to dispense with an evaluative attitude and examine an issue from the various viewpoints of other members.

Fourth, some teachers may have a negative view regarding groups. Instinctively they may withdraw from having to associate with students in the closeness of relationship demanded by organic group functioning. They may still feel the need to use security or other interbehavioral qualities as rewards for those who do their bidding. They may hesitate to reveal themselves to the degree demanded by true group functioning.

Another source of negative attitudes may be the difficulty teachers experience in working with what are falsely called "small groups" but in actuality are cliques. It has been found that in an authoritarian situation insecure students will form small groups which band themselves together and act as one. Their ties are psychological and their purpose is protection against "the system." Such cliques unfortunately are confused with small groups in the thinking of some school faculty and community leaders. The group counselor will need to be aware of this misconception and be able to distinguish these from true groups. He will emphasize that true groups proceed differently: each member takes a responsibility related to the goal and in accordance with his capability, and the group disbands when the project or undertaking is completed.

A fifth negative possibility that confronts the group counselor is the lack of recognition of need for evaluation of the process in order to improve group functioning. There is commonly an unexamined assumption that improvement is a function of frequency of occurrence and therefore needs no special attention. The group counselor may need to initiate the idea of evaluation and be prepared to work with groups in their efforts to carry it out. In so doing he should be willing to accept the fact that cooperative planning and decision making can be impregnated with selfish concerns. He can be aware that human freedom improperly used may cause certain ambiguities. He will then be careful that evaluations remain open and acceptable to the developing perceptions of the members. Since evaluation implies change, he will do well to recall the basic elements in genuine change and their orderly interrelationship: "(1) the individual alters his perception of his world; (2) he modifies his valences and values, which include his attractions and aversions to groups and group members; and (3) he alters his disposition toward, and individual control over, his physical and social movements." [8]

He will help group members recognize improvements in functioning and be able to foresee the direction progress should take. As the usefulness of evaluation becomes apparent, he will be ready to aid in its inclusion as an integral part of group sessions.

Another need he will soon recognize is the necessity for development of membership and leadership skills. He will soon become aware that members function in groups with a stereotyped and limited range of roles. They perform in one or two ways in each group meeting regardless of the demands of the situation. In the evaluation he will assist through example and discussion in the development of skill and insight in diagnosing the role requirements in each stage of progress in the group. Benne and Sheats emphasize that "each group which is attempting to improve the quality of its functioning as a group must be helped to diagnose its role requirements and must attempt to train members to fill the required roles effectively." [9] He will of course remember that the individual roles of members and of leaders must be congruent with their personality structure or life style. Of course no members would be expected to function in all types of roles.

## PERSONHOOD OF THE COUNSELOR

The counselor's values, convictions, and attitudes have a pervasive influence on students, teachers, administrators, and parents. What he is, as a person, penetrates every group setting and reverberates in all discussions.

It becomes clear whether his values are horizontal or reveal a depth dimension, that is, whether he himself lives chiefly by the practical, expedient, and utilitarian values or whether he is inclined toward the depth perspective and shares with Albert Einstein the ideals of goodness, truth, and beauty.[10] Is he convinced that adjustment and

[8] Kurt Lewin and Paul Grabbe, "Conduct, Knowledge, and Acceptance of New Values," *The Journal of Social Issues,* vol. 1, pp. 56–64, 1945.
[9] Kenneth Benne and Paul Sheats, "Functional Roles of Group Members," *The Journal of Social Issues,* vol. 4, pp. 42–47, 1948.
[10] Albert Einstein, *The World as I See It,* Philosophical Library, Inc., New York, 1949, p. 2.

self-actualization are proper goals, or does he look beyond these and recognize that self-actualization must be in the service of a higher goal? Does he largely embrace the suggestions of Skinner that "we can choose to utilize our scientific knowledge to make men necessarily happy, well-behaved and productive. . . ."[11] or those of Viktor Frankl, who believes that man is not at his best when driven by drives but rather when pulled by meaning? Frankl is convinced that "only to the extent that man fulfills a meaning in the world, does he fulfill himself. Conversely if he sets out to actualize himself rather than fulfill a meaning, self-actualization would immediately lose its justification." [12]

Has he become able to see a member as a person who struggles for meaning and whose behavior makes sense from the member's frame of reference? Or are others persons or merely objects to be adjusted? Members respond more positively to those who believe in the unconditional worth of man, and such a group counselor is known to them, because his attitudes permeate his relationship with others in the group.

It is hoped that he does not assume that his values and convictions are ideal and stable, but rather that he makes regular assessment in order to keep his sense of direction and become increasingly more facilitative in his interpersonal relationships. In his discussion of our moral convictions Pusey emphasizes that "it is only as they are raised from obscurantism by examination and discussion and debate that they rightly and safely become operative in human affairs." [13]

He is a catalyst not only in terms of his being as a person but also in terms of the goals he supports and toward which he tends. He will perceive himself as an educator joining forces with his colleagues. He will emphasize the best in counseling and demonstrate its integral relationship to the best in education.

When one surveys the best in education, there are foci in an interrelated concept of goals, the development of the individual in relation to his own becoming, in relation to his contribution as a

---

[11] Angelo V. Boy and Gerald J. Pine, *Client-centered Counseling in the Secondary School,* Houghton Mifflin Company, Boston, 1963, p. 192.
[12] Viktor E. Frankl, "Beyond Self-actualization and Self-expression," *Journal of Existential Psychiatry,* vol. 1, p. 99, 1960.
[13] Nathan M. Pusey, *The Age of the Scholar: Observations on Education in a Troubled Decade,* Harvard University Press, Cambridge, Mass., 1963, p. 58.

citizen, and in relation to eternal values which give meaning and support to the other two. Indication of this breadth and concern regarding educational goals comes from many sources. A committee called by the United States Commissioner of Education in 1962 to consider educational problems concluded: "We see our fundamental goal as a world civilization and an educational system which in all ways support human dignity for all races, castes and classes; self-realization; and the fullest vocational, civic and social cooperation and service." [14] A statement by Pusey has a slightly different focus. He writes concerning American education: "Its major purpose is to train people who are able to think for themselves, exercise judgment and act upon that judgment, and deeply care." [15] Another point of view directs attention to what education should do for the individual student. "He should be helped to develop an internal security that makes him willing to take advantage of his freedom and to take risks." [16]

These goal statements from various sources are in agreement with the best in counseling. They place emphasis on key motivational concepts such as human dignity for all, service to humanity, internal security, development of good judgment, and the quality of deeply caring. The counselor's attitude and performance will demonstrate the congruence in purpose which is inherent in both education and counseling.

The counselor is also a catalyst in his operational approach. His work and experiences beckon him to broaden his perspective regarding the nature of man. He is engaged in discerning and in helping others to discern the sustaining meanings of life. Only peripherally is he involved in strictly academic and curricular responsibilities. On the other hand only peripherally are the teachers and community educators (parents and church, camp, club, and neighborhood leaders) involved in interpersonal relationships for counseling purposes.

Each group, teacher, community leader, and counselor needs the others to remain in realistic focus concerning the possibilities of

[14] Theodore Brameld, "World Civilization: The Galvanizing Purpose of Public Education," *Phi Delta Kappan,* vol. 44, p. 58, 1962.
[15] Pusey, *op. cit.,* p. 15.
[16] *Education U.S.A.,* published by the National School Public Relations Associations of the National Education Association, weekly report, Apr. 5, 1962.

group process. Since the majority of counselors were formerly teachers, they could be expected to be more cognizant of the need for communication, mutual assistance, and understanding. The counselor is in the unique position of being a catalyst to usher in more mutually beneficial and highly cooperative relationships. Although counselors, teachers, parents, and administrators may not at times recognize it, they are marching to the same drumbeat for the same purposes and toward the same goal.

## SCOPE OF HIS SERVICE

The group counselor believes in group process. The scope of his service is as broad as his recognition of need for group experience. It is as narrow as his time and energy for meeting primary demands. Although his first responsibility rests with activities in the school, he also participates in the community where his skill and understanding can be most useful: in church, club, camp, and neighborhood groups. In fact the breadth of his opportunity is such that he must consider to which groups he can make the most useful and necessary contribution. This means that frequently he works with potential leaders who in turn are going to organize and lead small groups. He is aware that working with groups dissimilar to those in his school setting broadens his perspective, helping him to understand those with whom he spends the major part of his time.

In trying to define the scope of his service in the school he asks himself what groups presently in operation could be improved by a discussion of problems in depth. Are these groups too large for meaningful exploration of defenses in relation to their functioning in their work and in the group? Could a small group interested in pursuing apparent problems be useful? In what areas of school relationships is there a need for informal discussion in a permissive, confidential atmosphere?

Looking at the school situation with the guidance committee he might ask, With which groups—children, teachers, administrators, or parents—should I concentrate my efforts? It may be just as important to try to assist teachers, parents, and administrators as it is to work directly with groups of children.

The following kinds of opportunities may present themselves:
The guidance director has been working with a group of parents

helping them to understand orientation and testing procedures. He reports that some of them are quite apprehensive and a few are mildly disturbed regarding the methods and practices used. Should the counselor join him and eventually become responsible for helping these parents to explore and understand these feelings?

A teacher reports that a number of his students feel defeated for various reasons in their academic work, especially in English and math. Should the counselor discuss this with the teacher and then invite others to clarify what they think may be the causes of this attitude and what if anything might be done to modify it?

The guidance director and the counselor recognize that meetings of the guidance committee lack enthusiasm. There is a hesitancy to become involved and perhaps some hidden schemes. Should the counselor assume responsibility for leading in an evaluation of the "here and now" and make himself available to discuss what they feel are deterrents to their progress?

The guidance director confers with the committee about the reports he receives from counselees regarding disputes with parents concerning their social activities. Should he and the counselor set up a panel of parents and students to discuss both the parents' and adolescents' viewpoints? Should such a discussion be followed up by the counselor's working with students in relation to the outcomes?

He also must weigh other considerations: What portion of his time should he spend with small groups organized voluntarily to discuss their concerns about life? How frequently should he have groups composed of those whom the teachers conclude could benefit from a small-group experience? How frequently should he and the guidance committee consult to make plans regarding those who may need either individual or group counseling or both? How much time should he devote to small groups of teachers in helping them understand and appreciate the usefulness of group process in the total educational effort?

The decisions regarding the areas to emphasize in group counseling will vary from time to time and from school to school. As some needs diminish, others will increase or new ones appear. The decision should be made in consultation with other guidance and counseling personnel and with the guidance committee.

Such decisions vary in difficulty from school to school. When the number of guidance personnel employed does not keep pace with increasing enrollments, less can be accomplished. As decisions regarding the wise use of time and facilities become more difficult, the guidance committee becomes more important. The counselor who is alone in the school will work closely with this committee in order to choose priorities wisely. He will avoid if possible becoming too broadly or too deeply involved in a specialty which was not emphasized in his preparation.

## ORIENTATION TO GROUP COUNSELING

The effectiveness of the group-counseling effort depends to an important degree on the knowledge of and respect for it by administrators, faculty, and students. Each of the other colleagues in the guidance and counseling area of the school supports him, and he in turn supports them. To be able to do this means that each educates the other as to his goals and practices. However, interfaculty support is not enough. What he does professionally and why he does it should be known and understood.

The group counselor then will carefully formulate the necessary key information. He will use all appropriate opportunities. He will participate in the general orientation program; he will speak to community groups, to parents' groups, and to classroom groups. He will work with the guidance committee.

## FORMING THE GROUP

The group counselor works with groups for various purposes. These groups form themselves or are organized for different reasons. Some small groups are composed of persons who informally discover they have a concern on which they would like help. Some are referred to the counselor by teachers or administrators because of one or more kinds of difficulties in their school life.

Some groups may have some homogeneous aspects. It may be that they have similar behavior difficulties or academic inadequacies. They may come from the same community stratum or the same age group, or have similar achievement records. Some groups are more heterogeneous with reference to problems, or age, or socioeconomic status, or race, or other distinguishing characteristics.

Much of the time the counselor has little opportunity to work with what he considers would be an ideal group. However, each perhaps reflects upon those conditions under which such a group would come together and who would compose it. He has guiding principles he would use if and when conditions were or could be so changed as to make it possible.

The conclusions he reaches regarding a rationale for the formation of groups is directly related to what he believes about the manner in which behavioral change takes place. If he believes that genuine change takes place when people are free not to change, then he will favor the formation of groups on a voluntary basis. If not, he gives preference to various means of forming small groups for some goal which he perceives could be attained through group counseling.

Each school is at some point along the continuum from the practice of encouraging voluntary groups to come for help to that of forming groups almost exclusively through some form of referral. In schools where it is customary for groups to form and seek help voluntarily, the counselor assumes that the members are interested and capable and will use group process as a means of personal development. The voluntary group is perceived by some to be genuine, since it is composed of individuals who have made their own decision to join.[17]

Voluntary groups form for various reasons. It may be that over the years this method of seeking help individually or in small groups has become the norm. Or a number of persons have experienced a mild or severe disturbing situation affecting their academic or social expectations and feel the need to discuss it.

Some counselors believe so firmly in students' voluntarily seeking help individually or in small groups that they take steps to modify existing practice. One such method used is to tell the students referred when they come to them that they have fulfilled the request and that whether or not they participate in counseling is their decision.

Such counselors believe that this practice will provide the students with opportunity to assume responsibility. Other counselors hesitate to rely on this method. They believe that students who need help will not take the initiative and that other mehods must be

[17] George F. Kneller, *Existentialism and Education,* Philosophical Library, Inc., New York, 1964, p. 36.

used. They set up small groups as they perceive them to be necessary. They also assume responsibility for involving students in discussions, analysis, and planning. These procedures may be more in accordance with the beliefs of their teaching colleagues, many of whom place emphasis on extrinsic motivations and association theories of learning. The perception of group counseling and the attitude toward it vary greatly in these contrasting situations.

The second issue of homogeneous versus heterogeneous groups is also controversial. Differences revolve around such concerns as the degree of homogeneity present even in groups in which care was exercised to make the group homogeneous; which kind of group generates the better psychological climate for understanding and resolving problems; and at what level, if at all, the members of a group have a common problem.

The effort expended in trying to form homogeneous groups on the basis of useful criteria may lead to the assumption that there is greater homogeneity than actually exists. Is it not possible that the uniqueness of individuals and the various differences in a so-called homogeneous group lend themselves to what appears commendable in homogeneous grouping? In fact the more a counselor does succeed in having homogeneous groups, the more risks he may be incurring. Members say: "We're not doing as well as we might, for each one knows what the other is going to say before he says it." They may also heighten the wall of defenses. Freeman and Sweet warn that "members of groups uniform with respect to personality tend to reinforce each other's defenses." [18]

Those who form heterogeneous groups entertain a different perspective. They assume that the wide differences in members' viewpoints do not limit the degree of groupness and interaction attainable. Instead they believe that the diversity increases the number of useful ideas, the breadth of understanding, and the possibility of enrichment.

Actually the diversity may exist only at certain levels of interaction. This becomes apparent since the deeper the members go psychologically, the closer they become, even though their referents may be quite dissimilar. For instance, such a group could be expected

---

[18] H. B. Freeman and Blanche S. Sweet, "Some Specific Features of Group Psychotherapy and Their Implications for Selection of Patients," *International Journal of Group Psychotherapy,* vol. 4, p. 357, 1954.

to have a wide variety of ideas regarding alienation and depersonalization. But when they go deeper and ask the results, they face the awesome state of loneliness. At that depth they are very much one regardless of their diversity. Loneliness in some form is for all an experienced fact.

Heterogeneity may appear not to be conducive to groupness and a climate of trust and responsibility, but this is only at a superficial, descriptive level and not at the level which is considered group counseling. In fact the presentation of data from several foci may be fruitful in the examination of the meaning of the data to their lives. It may impel them to look at their motives and their feelings from new perspectives, using different models of productive imagination.

The problem of what rationale to use in the formation of groups remains undecided. Experience indicates that each kind of group has its successes and failures. It is quite possible that we are asking the wrong questions and using the wrong criteria. One question we could ask is, Who is in the better position to decide, the person about to join a group or the counselor? Some counselors may wish to rely on the process of natural selection. They know that persons at every age associate with those toward whom they intuitively feel a natural bond.

It is conceivable that those who feel threatened may feel more comfortable with those who have similar feelings. They may wish to join a group which has some degree of homogeneity with reference to their perceptions of the forthcoming experience.

It is equally possible that those who feel adequate and interested in new experiences may wish to join a group in which there is great variety, since they enjoy the various viewpoints expressed. These persons may, when given a choice, elect to join a group whose members vary in background and experiences.

A second general method of procedure provides an added alternative: instead of a decision with reference to the membership, decisions could be made with reference to the leadership. It is important not only that members be able to help one another but also that the method of leadership be helpful to the members. Persons planning to join a group could be helped by an explanation of the method of leadership and what is expected of the members. This would enable them to join the group which they perceived would be most helpful to them. A person may decide to join a group which is permissive and accepting of the member regardless of his performance. Such a group climate, he may conclude, would help him to examine his problems in depth and to relate usefully to other members. Others may decide to join a group wherein interpretation, suggestions, and personal confrontation among members would provide the setting in which they would be motivated to examine their problems and to relate in the discussion of them.

Criteria are needed to guide the formation of groups. Such criteria should be psychologically based and addressed to the question of which kind of group provides the greatest possibility for the development of this prospective member. To be sufficiently comprehensive the criteria may need to include size of the group, purposes of the group, method of leadership, and the person's feelings in relation to these considerations. Whether a group is homogeneous or heterogeneous may be a minor consideration in comparison with other influential group conditions.

A third consideration in the forming of groups is the uncertainty regarding how well one age group may communicate with another much older or younger than itself. This is in part the result of applying to organic groups a point of view which may have some validity only in aggregate groups and among those who are already to some degree alienated from themselves and from one another. The degree to which communication can take place among those of widely different age groups is a function of the meaningfulness to all, the activity in which they are engaged and the genuineness of the respect one has for another as persons. The nature of the activity which is conducive to meaningful relationships can vary widely. Some leaders use drawing, drama, woodwork, or games, depending on the interest of the members. Some prefer to have a group-counseling session following the activity; others, informally during the activity. Group counselors who are successful in bridging the age difference have a high regard for the capabilities of each age grouping and high expectancy for the success of the undertaking.

Not only can persons of various ages relate successfully in a small group, but also it is possible for those from diverse racial backgrounds to do so. The author has known this to be the case in small groups composed of Polynesians, Japanese, Chinese, Japanese Americans, Chinese Americans, Negroes, and Caucasians. Small groups of this composition who accept one another as persons and are interested in the process, in self-understanding, and in understanding of others can become well-integrated groups with a sense of responsibility for one another's welfare. In fact the difference in reaction, attitude, and verbal fluency can be conducive to an increased interest in one another. Some Caucasian members of such a group said, "I believe we shouldn't talk so much, since some of the others do not verbalize so quickly or easily and they need to be heard." The keen listening and quiet, flickering expressions are silent reminders to many Caucasians of the other dimensions for meaning and understanding. Counselors working with interracial groups need to have realistic expectancies and to be able to recognize what are the signs of progress, however small and slow they may be in development.

Such a situation also highlights what is present to some degree in every group. Each group has both common and diverse elements and components. In this case there was considerable racial diversity, but equally significant in the process was the strong commonality expressed in a deep and growing desire to understand and be understood.

The group counselor also confronts the problem of the number of times most beneficial for a group to meet. This is a difficult decision, since each group varies in some important ways from every other. For example, a group of adolescents who have little or no experience in groups cannot be expected to develop a working relationship as quickly as the members of a group who are experienced in group process. Skills of listening and responding and the concentration these require need development before optimum functioning can be expected.

Group counselors in the school setting generally find it necessary to set a termination date in advance because of other responsibilities. The termination date can be made flexible to allow for a few more or less meetings. Then the exact time can be determined cooperatively in relation to the need and progress which has been made. The understanding that there is a termination date not too far distant not only provides a sense of structure and security but also increases the motivation to use the time well in accordance with group purposes.

## INNER–CITY EXPERIENCE

The group counselor employed in an inner-city school is in a special situation. Some of his considerations resemble those of the counselor in a suburban school; some are distinctly different. His problem is to discern between the similarities and the differences. The similarities are those related to the principles of behavioral change, the significance of congruence, and the need to perceive others as persons and to be perceived as a person by the other members of the group.

The differences revolve around the level of impulse control, forms of expressions, and quality of interdependent experiences. The suburban child or adolescent may rely more on his rational analysis and less on emotional discernment, or the "wisdom of the organism." The inner-city child may go deeper with his feelings and may grasp insights not recognized by the suburban youngster. A group counselor who had a heterogeneous group of eight children in the sixth grade in a middle-class urban school also counseled with a heterogeneous group of eight in an urban inner-city school. Using a tape recorder each group recorded questions which were responded to by the other group. One response was to the question "What is your first wish?"

A boy in the first group (middle-class urban) said he would like to be a professional basketball player but he was too short. A boy in the second group (inner city) taped the response for him. "I think if you work hard enough you could become a good basketball player, but if I were you I would give my first choice to something more important."

The inner-city youngster has had less experience in discovering alternatives in a conflict situation. He also has less facility in presenting an alternative to his peers. An inner-city group of eight seventh graders faced the situation in which one of their peers not in the group had marred a wall project on which the group had worked. The ideas they developed as a means of handling the situation all suggested some form of physical punishment. The same situation was presented to a middle-class group of eight seventh graders in the same urban center but not in the inner city. They suggested the following ideas:

"Find out first if he really meant to do it or if it was an accident."

"Maybe he was getting back at them for something one of them had done, so bring them all together and talk it over."

"Ask him to put it back in shape; maybe if he is really sorry, some of those who worked on it might help him."

"Ask him to get a group to help him and repair the damage by a certain time."

"Bring the group together and get their ideas of what to do, not just to punish him but something else."

Whereas the inner-city youth had difficulty in thinking in terms other than force, punishment, and conflict, the children of middle-class parents apparently did not experience the frustration and conflictual feelings and, as well, could think of other possibilities.

The inner-city youngsters are quite hesitant to try something new, especially when this is proposed by an authority figure, teacher or counselor. In part their perception of all those who are part of the "system" may inhibit them. Two group counselors each with a group of seven in the sixth grade came together with their groups to play some games requiring physical action. A bowling pin was placed midway between the two lines of players. After the players on each side were numbered, a number was called by the leader, and the one on each side having this number dashed forward to try to get the pin before his counterpart. Even after demonstration by the adults there was a long delay and hesitation before any were willing to participate in the game.

### Ego Functioning

The counselor will study the ego functioning of the child, adolescent, or adult in the inner city. Ego is defined as "that part of the personality which is charged with keeping us in touch with reality and with helping us to regulate our impulse expression so that it is within the bounds which such a reality dictates." [19] If the decision presents a choice between right and wrong, there is further complication because of the relationship between conscience and ego and between both of these and the impulses.

[19] Fritz Redl and David Wineman, *The Aggressive Child,* The Free Press of Glencoe, Inc., New York, 1957, p. 258.

In general their ego functioning is so different as to pose real difficulties for the counselor. Because of environmental influences in the home and community they have more frustrated and destructive emotions than suburban children. It appears in some to have become part of their primary or basic striving and is furthered by their frequent failure in task challenges. The result of this is their inability to face up to fear, anxiety, or insecurity without breakdown, generally in the form of disorganized aggression. As illustrated by their slowness to participate in a new game they appear unable to see the inherent implications of fun, and some may escape into impulsive behavior of various kinds. They do this instead of investigating new opportunities to learn other ways of gratification, which suburban children would generally do.

The counselor may also expect more variation in group performance from meeting to meeting. They do not store up enough of a memory image concerning a good experience to carry them through when they feel bored and unsettled. Thus their behavior yields to impulsive drives, and what they want, they want right now.

As well, they are apparently quite deficient in the use of both productive and reactive imagination. They are unable to use productive imagination to understand how their negative passivity and disruptive impulsive behavior provokes and annoys peers or authority figures, often to their own detriment. In some group protocol Boy and Pine quote one of the members as saying, "I'm willing to admit that I fool around, that it isn't always the teacher's fault I fool around, but I know when I'm going too far." [20] Such a comment would be unusual for the member of an inner-city group. Also their reactive imagination is deficient. If they are asked what happened a few minutes after it took place, they are apparently unable to look at it. Instead they blame something or someone else for the outcomes.

Surprisingly the explanation of their functioning on the basis of an underdeveloped ego is too simple. Their behavior is strange and paradoxical, since they display an ingenuity and vigilance in the use of their psychic energies. This ability regretfully is at the service of a wrong master. The youngster who is unable to cope with his impulses suddenly and with amazing efficiency defends his impulse gratification at all costs. Instead of the ego's using productive imagination in

[20] Boy and Pine, *op. cit.,* p. 241.

synthesizing desires, reality demands, and social values, it goes to the support of impulsiveness.

Depending upon the degree of inner control, the ego lends itself to impulse behavior in the following ways: [21]

1. The battle with the members' own inner choice (conscience). It is not that they so much lack the use of this inner potential but rather that impulse freedom is perceived as so necessary that they become skillful in finding reasons for acting against conscience.

2. The use of rationalization to maintain freedom for impulse expression. They become clever diagnosticians in recognizing others like themselves and in self-diagnosis for the purpose of self-exploitation; for example, "What else could I do? There was no way out."

3. The ego in direct defense against change. If the counselor unwisely makes a direct attack on their rationalizations, they will withdraw, block, and become apparently determined to make the counselor do something to give them more justification for noncooperation and possibly hate.

4. The ego moving downstage to make sure the defense against change really operates. To do this the person develops skills in handling those who represent the "system," those who would change them into "nice" kids or "good" citizens.

It is difficult to believe that the same children and adolescents who appear so blind in their social perceptions are very much aware of the attitudes and feelings of the counselor, but only in certain respects. They seem unable to tell when the counselor is fair and reasonable and when he cares. Especially is this the case in their less intense moments.

The counselor, then, faces different and greater difficulties when working with impulse-ridden persons culturally deprived and frequently described as *inner-city*. Unless he is able to establish and maintain certain conditions in his group counseling, much of his effort will be ineffectual. These minimum conditions are rapport, adequacy of communication, and protection of the experience from hyperaggressive and destructive behavior.

[21] Redl and Wineman, *op. cit.,* pp. 260–268.

## COMMUNITY SERVICE

The group counselor will be interested in using his professional knowledge and skills in the service of community organizations. One of his best means of understanding community values and mores is to participate informally in community groups. However, he will need to exercise insight and control in order to render the service which he is best prepared to give and to do so efficiently.

He needs to be able to understand the purposes of the group he is asked to assist from their standpoint. Coffey illustrates the disastrous results when the counselor misinterprets the goals of the group he has agreed to help. He provides three different and helpful illustrations. One of these follows:

> A staff interested in becoming more acquainted with group procedures along group dynamic lines requested assistance from a skilled leader. After four or five sessions frustrations and anxiety had reached a saturation point and they requested that the sessions be terminated. The leader had seen the group almost entirely as a therapy group and had assumed a completely non-directive role. His function, as he saw it, was to deal exclusively with individual dynamics in relation to group process. The need for any cognitive structure (that is, content and direction) was not apparent to him.[22]

He will work closely with the guidance director who is assisting those interested in educational groups. By close cooperation they can share their felt responsibility to the community, each making his special contribution. In their participation in informal adolescent groups they grow in understanding of their mores and special language of communication. They will in this manner also be viewed as an interested adult and not so strongly identified with "the system." Especially is this important in the inner city or similar community.

When other commitments permit it, the counselor will work with small groups of potential leaders, anticipating group leadership in church, camp, and other settings. By relating himself in his professional capacity to community groups he gains greater breadth of understanding of the problems he and members confront in trying to move from aggregate to organic group functioning and in becoming open and genuine in their interpersonal relationships.

[22] Coffey, *op. cit.*, p. 67.

## RESEARCH AND RENEWAL

Not every group counselor engages in formal research, but most engage in informal research; that is, each will scrutinize his practices, the degree of congruence between what he believes and does, and the outcomes as he perceives them. He will informally evaluate the means which he uses to understand better the individual members and group change.

Other group counselors, because of their interests and specialized preparation, will engage in formal research. They will do research on those problems which seem most urgent in terms of more valid information to guide their work. They will of course become acquainted with the published research in order to benefit both from the weaknesses and strengths in design.

The counselor should plan wisely and use time for renewal. He will cherish these opportunities for the purpose of reading, thinking, and planning. He will honor the adage that you light your candle at another man's hearth and will come to realize that insights come where disciplines cross. He will recognize that it is not enough to read and think within the confines of his own specialization of guidance and counseling. He will plan to study in other closely related disciplines and those farther removed such as philosophy, religion, music, and art. He will come to know that a problem in his work concerning which he has read and thought may take on clarity and understanding while he is reading in a discipline far removed from the problem. Something which he is reading may focus in his consciousness the key idea he needed to relate the parts of his problem and point the way to one form of solution.

He discovers that another means of renewal is through participation in recreation or engagement in his favorite form of art. Perhaps the most significant and most difficult to plan and use wisely is the setting aside of the pressing concerns of life and the entering into quiet, disciplined meditation. This could be a time when he looks deeply into the meaning of his work, his interpersonal relationships, and life itself. The depth dimension so necessary to him in working with others must be cultivated if it is to stand him in good stead in the heat of the working day.

Much of what he experiences does not help him to know what "significance may be found in his own existence, the succeeding generations of this kind and the vivid events of his inner life." [23] Tillich insists that "no one can experience depth without stopping and becoming aware of himself. Only if he has moments in which he does not care about what comes next can he experience the meaning of this moment here and now, and ask himself about the meaning of life." [24] Unless he engages in this search for meaning, he may assume that the high school student is interested only in those goals that provide security and status. He may not recognize a deeper hunger in the counselee for fear of acknowledging emptiness within himself.

[23] John S. Gardner, *Self-renewal: The Individual and the Innovative Society,* Harper & Row, Publishers, Incorporated, New York, 1964, p. 102.
[24] Paul Tillich, "The Lost Dimension in Religion," in *Adventures of the Mind,* Vintage Books, Inc., New York, 1960, p. 56.

# 16

## RESEARCH AND EVALUATION

The group counselor is engaged in three ongoing research activities: In the first place, he studies published research to become informed of the trends, to note various research designs, and as a means of stimulating his productive imagination in regard to possible studies with his own groups. Second, he plans formal and informal research cooperatively with the members of the group to provide information and assist understanding. In the third place, he and the members endeavor to use the results to improve their knowledge and functioning in the several areas of group process.

He is quite aware that his efforts are based on the assumption that a lawful cause-and-effect order exists in this complex and subtle realm of group counseling. He knows that research commences with hunches, which he and the members respect, and continues to the development of hypotheses for testing. He encourages the members and is ready himself to give full rein to creative ideas.

It is recognized that subtle variables cannot all be accounted for and that some will continue to challenge any form of empirical measurement. Nevertheless research is considered a means of reducing the probability of useless or harmful assumptions and procedures which limit the possibilities of constructive accomplishments. Until more evidence can be brought to bear directly on the troublesome problems, questions will be formulated and conclusions drawn only on the basis of experience and common sense. Through cooperative planning with the members of the group understanding can be greatly increased, useful research can be developed, and the results can become operative in the theory and practice of group counseling.

## CONSIDERATIONS

The counselor beginning research will find a useful reference in Mahler,[1] who lists weaknesses in group counseling research and elaborates on each. In the list are the following: ". . . lack of proper control groups; use of immediate, rather than long-term, criterion measures; use of too short a series of group meetings to justify an expectation of change; lack of experience and competence among group counselors."

In planning the counselor considers the theoretical basis of his contemplated research. His research design should be congruent with the assumptions and methods he uses. He should examine his hunches carefully, since not every one can be expected to be useful or worth the necessary time and effort which research demands.

He will select the research direction he wishes to follow. To do so he gives attention to such matters as these: Is the problem of sufficient importance that the outcomes could have significant results? Are the necessary conditions for conducting the research those which are ongoing and integral to the prsent group functioning? Is it reasonable to expect that the degree of member involvement will assure the validity of the outcomes? Can it be expected

[1] Clarence A. Mahler, *Group Counseling in the Schools,* Houghton Mifflin Company, Boston, 1969, chap. 9.

that the feedback will be relevant and capable of being provided in a manner directly useful to the groups? To what degree can one account for the important variables in order to have general acceptance for the validity of the outcomes? To what degree is it reasonable to anticipate that the outcomes could be used in future group functioning?

Current research in group counseling is inadequate in terms of its quality and usefulness to the practicing counselor, but it is hoped that the counselor can benefit by avoiding the pitfalls of those who have preceded him. He will not give his time to inconsequential investigations at the risk of limiting his efforts in group counseling. He will carefully choose the problems and engage in a study only after he has perceived as well as possible how it will affect his total service effort.

As he considers the possibility of research, he may wish to familiarize himself with some of the concerns of his predecessors. Such information as that developed by a seminar on group counseling authorized by the Cooperative Research Branch of the U.S. Office of Education in 1964 will be valuable. The members of the seminar concluded that research was needed in areas of definition, techniques, selection, design, and evaluation. Following his familiarity with research studies he will proceed to review the problems in his own group-counseling experience for which he would like more certitude than his observation and the use of informal techniques provide. From his list of problems he will select several and finally one which he considers holds the most promise of providing insights which he can use.

In choosing a problem he may wish to confer with other colleagues in the guidance and counseling area. A cooperative approach could lead to more insights, a sharing of responsibilities, more interest, and more use of results. If the school's guidance committee is also informed and the idea discussed with them, it could be a broadening experience for all and increase faculty interest in the use of group process for both educational and counseling purposes.

## PROBLEMS

In a discussion of research problems in counseling Patterson concludes that "an adequate criterion against which to evaluate counseling is probably the major one in research." [2] One of the chief reasons for this dilemma is the present lack of agreement regarding goals to be achieved. The goals are diverse and range from a quiet, well-run school, group members' satisfaction, good grades, graduation, and increase in the number of graduates going on to college to reduction in underachievement and in dropouts, selection of vocational objectives, and placement and stability in a job. Many of these objectives are limited and are in accord with Weinberg's viewpoint that the "criteria themselves by which the success of counseling is determined are generated out of the values of the institution." [3]

Not only are they institution-oriented, but also they are specific and limited, and some are questionable. The concept of adjustment should be questioned, and certainly many of these limited objectives apply only to a minority of students. Although questionable, such goals may have been used because they are specific and lend themselves to easy observation and measurement.

Necessary as enumerative and descriptive studies may be in the initial stages, progress should go beyond these. Research should also be increasingly undertaken for the purpose of understanding the conditions of behavioral change, of studying the means of gaining insight into one's problems and of making realistic decisions. Such kinds of analytic research are criticized as vague and intangible. It is hoped that they may be viewed as a challenge. The development of such techniques as the self and self-ideal Q sort [4] brings this more within the realm of possibility.

Research needs to be examined against the background of a comprehensive and more idealistic goal. Wolfe [5] provides the clue in emphasizing that everyone should be assisted in reaching the highest level he can in the area in which he has the greatest talent and interest. The degree to which analytic research in depth is undertaken will indicate the values which predominate and which influence the meaning attached to behavior and to research itself.

[2] Cecil H. Patterson, *The Counselor in the School: Selected Readings,* McGraw-Hill Book Company, New York, 1967, p. 409.
[3] Carl Weinberg, *Social Foundations of Educational Guidance,* The Free Press, New York, 1969, p. 179.
[4] M. S. Sheldon and A. C. Sorenson, "On the Use of the Q-technique in Educational Evaluation and Research," *Journal of Experimental Education,* vol. 10, pp. 143–151, 1960.
[5] L. D. Wolfe, "Diversity of Talent," *American Psychologist,* vol. 15, pp. 535–545, 1960.

Nevertheless it is only with difficulty that the counselor disentangles himself from enumerative and descriptive research and focuses upon meanings and cause-and-effect relationships. When he does, he must clearly explain and accurately define what it is he attempts to measure. This he formulates in a criterion of merit leading to a testable hypothesis. Before describing his hypothesis regarding therapeutic personality change Rogers states his definition in these words: "I mean that change in the personality structure, and in the behavior of the individual, which clinicians would agree implies greater integration, less internal conflict, more energy utilized for effective living. I mean a change in behaviors away from those generally regarded as immature and toward those regarded as mature, responsible and socialized." [6]

The counselor who studies the interrelationships in personality change must disengage himself from studies that support the ongoing usefulness of group counseling and devote himself to studying, refining, and defining the criterion to serve as the basis of his undertaking. The development of such criteria is a difficult task. Ideal subjects do not exist. As Good explains it, man is an interactive dynamic force who changes while being observed and even seems to influence the "objective" experimenter engaged in observing.[7]

The applicability of the results depends upon the validity of the sample. Great care must be taken to ensure that the students in the sample are representative of those for whom the counselor desires to use the results. Unless this is done, the application of the results to students other than those in the sample is a questionable procedure. Heterogeneous groups may provide a better sample upon which to draw conclusions concerning those outside the sample group.

Another important consideration is that of involvement. Unless members are involved, the results may be unreliable. Members can be expected to become involved when they share in planning the research objectives, voluntarily participate, remain anonymous, and receive feedback in a form which they can use. These conditions in their entirety are seldom met.

It is not unusual for research to be planned, conducted, and

[6] Carl R. Rogers, "The Therapeutic Relationship: Recent Theory and Research," *Australian Journal of Psychology,* vol. 17, pp. 95–108, 1965.
[7] Carter V. Good, *Essentials of Educational Research*, Appleton-Century-Crofts, New York, 1966, p. 254.

evaluated by someone outside the group and often outside the school. Such a person generally has his own purposes, which do not include the objective of change in the group and the school. The group members are unintelligent concerning the research. They participate because they have been asked to do so and may remain apathetic or even hostile toward the undertaking.

Sometimes this is permitted because the methodology of the research desired is not within the competency of those in the school. They are able to plan the goals, formulate hypotheses, and set up criteria but unable to initiate, execute, and evaluate. In such instances they should ask the aid of specialists in research methodology. It is important that these specialists assist only in a cooperative capacity. It is suggested that they "will advise in the investigation itself, supervise the statistical analysis, and feed back the results" [8] to the initiators and planners of the research.

In general the necessity of involving the participators in the research is passed over too lightly. This results in superficial involvement, which means that the data secured are not representative of the interests, desires, and problems of the participators. Both conscious and unconscious distortion are almost sure to result. When this is the case, the results may be quite misleading. The research may be worse than a waste of effort unless the members feel personally involved and interested in knowing the results for themselves in relation to their self-becoming and the group development.

In the study of the group in the local situation anonymity is of signal importance. Regardless of the high degree of group cohesiveness it frees the members to be unhesitatingly open and honest, a necessity for valid outcomes. Planning with the group to establish and maintain anonymity can be an important learning experience.

## METHODS OF RESEARCH IN SMALL GROUPS

Methods have evolved from the refinement of observational techniques. For over a decade there has developed a growing knowledge of variables which bias and distort the observations themselves. Investigations have proceeded along two fronts: those concerned with

[8] Donald T. Campbell and Julian C. Stanley, "Experimental Designs for Research in Teaching," in N. L. Gage (ed.), *Handbook of Research on Teaching,* Rand McNally & Company, Chicago, 1963, chap. 5.

the location and study of their effect on group-member interaction and those which explore their effect on administrative and leadership relationships within an established hierarchy. With reference to the first front, investigations have been concerned with the social structure and interaction within classroom groups, and in relation to the second, with administrative and leadership relationships within the intimate data of intragroup relationships.

Within the same period new methods for the study of groups have evolved. These methods are designed to study the current relationships within the group. Those chosen for presentation may generally be described as various forms of action research. Although each is a slightly different method, all have the same basic assumption.

Action research differs from fundamental research in significant ways. Some of the major emphases are the following: (1) It commences from an urgent need with the intention of applying results and improvement of practice in the actual setting. (2) It is planned by the members and counselor with or without the aid of research specialists. (3) There is a developmental design with the hypothesis and method subject to modification during the course of the action program. (4) Its usefulness is in terms of the extent to which methods and findings make possible improvement in practice in a particular situation.[9]

### Critical-incident Technique

One of these methods is the *critical-incident technique.* Good defines it as "a set of procedures for collecting direct observations of human behavior in such a way as to facilitate their potential usefulness in solving practical problems and in developing broad psychological principles, with emphasis on observed incidents possessing special significance, and meeting systematically defined criteria."[10] Flanagan[11] lists five steps in the critical-incident procedures. In abbreviated form they are as follows: (1) determining the general aim of the activity in the form of a brief statement, (2) de-

[9] Stephen M. Corey, *Action Research to Improve School Practices,* Bureau of Publications, Teachers College, Columbia University, New York, 1953, p. 161.
[10] Good, *op. cit.,* p. 258.
[11] John C. Flanagan, "The Critical Incident Technique," *Psychological Bulletin,* vol. 51, pp. 327–358, 1954.

veloping plans and specifications for collecting factual incidents, (3) collecting data reporting the incident in an interview or as written by the observer, (4) analyzing data in an effective and practical summary, and (5) interpreting and reporting a statement of the requirements of the activity.

This method is considered to have values difficult to obtain by any other technique, such as that (1) it places categories of human behavior on an empirical basis; (2) it provides a realistic base for a variety of evaluation techniques, although the incidents do not of themselves constitute a measurement instrument; and (3) incidents serve as a source of the raw material out of which evaluation items are constructed.[12]

ILLUSTRATION   The third meeting the group discussed the topic of involvement. Among other things they explored its meaning, the kinds of involvement, why some involve themselves more than others. They concluded that the matter of involvement was so important that they should develop some method of studying it.

They decided to record on tape several sessions and to analyze the critical incidents. They realized that it would be necessary to have criteria as a basis for analysis and for the purpose of comparison of one incident with another. Several had heard of the critical-incident method of analysis and volunteered to bring back information to the group.

Following a brief presentation at the next meeting of the purpose and method of the critical-incident technique they planned their approach. They discussed what would be necessary in order that an incident qualify for study. For what purpose or purposes would an analysis and study of the incident be made? What were reasonable expectations of its value for self-understanding and group functioning? They found this method of self-study particularly useful when they discussed matters on which there were conflicting ideas.

### Problem-Discussion-Action Method

A second form of action research which proved useful might be described as the *problem-discussion-action method.*

[12] Lewis B. Mayhew, "The Critical Incident Technique in Educational Evaluation," *Journal of Educational Research,* vol. 49, pp. 591–598, 1956.

ILLUSTRATION  Since there were eighteen enrolled in the group, the members concluded that they could get acquainted more quickly and commence meaningful relationships if they spent part of the time in three small groups. They planned that after a few meetings they would discuss together their progress. They therefore spent part of the meeting time each evening in small groups and the remainder together as a total group.

At first they thought it was a good plan, but after three meetings they had serious doubts. They found that their attitudes and ideas were too similar. Their discussions were not challenging, and they lacked the creative inputs of those with different perspectives. They felt that they would like to keep the idea of small groups but that they needed to change the membership.

They concluded that members with different points of view on important matters would improve their functioning and decided to use the results of an attitude inventory for the purpose of reformulating the groups. After they examined several, they chose the Dogmatism Scale Form E.[13] They remained anonymous by each one's using a self-chosen number and were placed in groups with as much variance in scores as possible. Their discussion of the results of using this kind of action research indicated great improvement and general satisfaction with the functioning of their small groups.

### Content Analysis

A third method which has grown in its usefulness is that of *content analysis*. It commenced in the 1940s with frequency counts of similar topics and word usages in textbooks for the purpose of identification and improvement. It has been developed in theory and practice to include analysis of cause-and-effect relationships and meanings. Berelson [14] in his survey found that it dealt with the body of meanings through symbols (verbal, musical, pictorial, plastic, and gestural) which makes up communication itself.

Its usefulness for analyses of group-counseling protocol took on increased importance with the improvement of sound recording.

[13] For the underlying theory and description of the scale and its standards see Milton Rokeach, *The Open and Closed Mind*, Basic Books, New York, 1960.
[14] Bernard Berelson, *Content Analysis in Communication Research*, The Free Press, Glencoe, Ill., 1952, p. 220.

Studies of counseling sessions were divided into three classes: those concerned with methodology, primarily for the purpose of developing measures; descriptive studies of cases; and theoretical studies of cause-and-effect relationships.[15]

This method is based on the analysis, with a specific purpose in mind, of those records which have been collected or are already in existence. The group counselor and the members plan the goals of such an undertaking, the kinds of records to keep, ways of improving their validity such as an immediate recording and anonymity, criteria, and methods of analysis. By planning with the members the research takes on meaning, and involvement is greatly increased.

ILLUSTRATION One group expressed an interest in trying to ascertain the degree of change in their personal attitudes and feelings from meeting to meeting. They decided to use self-reports. These were written under a self-chosen number immediately at the close of the meeting. Each described his feelings in relation to the interaction in the session. The counselor also wrote a self-report. The members' self-reports were studied by the counselor. He found these useful in helping him to gain insight into the dynamics of the process and of the goals and difficulties of each member. He compared his perceptions of his attitudes and functioning with those of the members.

After several sessions the counselor returned the self-reports. Each member analyzed his own and drew conclusions, planned goals, and concentrated on them during the remaining sessions. They discussed these after five sessions and again at the end of ten sessions. They felt this was an interesting and useful method of self-study.

EXPERIMENTAL EVALUATION TECHNIQUES

Each counselor and group develops and uses evaluation methods intrinsic in the situation. One group planned the following: At the conclusion of the discussion the observer in the group passed a 4- by 6-inch card to each member (Form 1 at the end of the chapter). He asked each to respond to questions regarding his perception of

[15] Frank Auld, Jr., and Edward J. Murray, "Content-analysis Studies of Psychotherapy," *Psychological Bulletin,* vol. 52, pp. 377–395, 1955.

the process and what improvement he planned for himself. The anonymously completed responses were passed to the observer, who relayed the information to the group.

Another group planned to do a self-study using a rating scale which each completed at the end of the session under a self-chosen number. They cooperatively developed the ideas for the scale (Form 2 at the end of the chapter), and one small group developed the descriptive items. The observer or another member collated these and informed the group of areas in which it was perceived that they were making progress and of those in which more attention was needed. These were given to the group counselor, who used them to gain insight regarding the members' self-perceptions of their progress.

After discussion it is customary for groups to choose self-reports as a further means of self-study. These are completed under a self-chosen number immediately following the session. They are returned under their code number for analysis and summary as often as requested, generally at every fifth meeting. In the self-report each writes a running record of his feelings in relation to the interaction which took place and of his perceptions of the group process. One group developed Form 3 (see the end of the chapter), which is used by most groups as a tool in studying their progress.

This form has proved instructive to the counselor, whom it helps to perceive better the interaction and process development from the member's framework. Members also report it to be quite helpful in understanding their participation in the group in setting goals.

In discussions of involvement, of group process in general, or of the results in working through "here and now" problems, members raised the question "Where are we in the process now? We have changed, but how far along are we?"

This led to a discussion of the nature of the steps or degrees of progress experienced. They planned to locate and study what had been written on the progressive steps in group process. The group counselor made several outlines available. After examination of these it was decided at the next session to use Form 4 (see the end of the chapter). On this form each checked the stage of progress for himself and for the group and wrote explanations of his choices.

Form 4 was used at every second meeting for the purpose of discussion and clarification regarding the levels at which they performed individually and as a group. The ratings were made under a chosen number and given to the counselor to enrich his thinking and understanding of the progress of the group.

The trainees realized early that the more information they have at each session regarding their performance in a member or leadership role, the greater the possibility of improvement. Recognizing this they developed two rating scales, one related to the performance of the leader and a second related to that of the members (Forms 5 and 6, respectively). These were done anonymously and completed immediately at the end of the session. Those on leadership were given to the leader of the session. He made a report to the group based on these and his own observations of his functioning. The observer for the session collated the members' scales and reported significant agreements or differences to the group.

In the study of the group and its evaluation the counselor will also search for published studies of the dynamics of the process. These will stimulate his own thinking about possible methods to use with his group. They may cause him to develop a method quite dissimilar from the ones studied. In any case he will be careful to plan directly with and for the group in progress. Illustrative of the studies which could lead to creative planning are *The Group Studies Itself*,[16] *The Behavior of Leaders*,[17] *Evaluating the Performance of Individuals as Members of Small Groups*,[18] and *Improving Your Leadership in Discussion Groups*.[19]

In general the results of informal research will be used to understand group process further and to improve the ongoing functioning of the group. Especially is this the case for groups of trainees. The results of formal research will probe relationships which will provide new insights into the dynamics of groups which conceivably could influence theory and practice.

In order for results to possess acceptable validity and have the widest range of influence the research should be planned with the trainees. By sharing in the planning members become intelligent,

[16] Alice Miel, "A Group Studies Itself," *Teachers College Record,* vol. 49, pp. 33–43, 1947.
[17] Andrew W. Halpin, "The Behavior of Leaders," *Educational Leadership,* vol. 14, pp. 172–176, 1956.
[18] Launor F. Carter, "Evaluating the Performance of Individuals as Members of Small Groups," *Personnel Psychology,* vol. 7, pp. 477–484, 1954.
[19] Thomas Gordon, "Improving Your Leadership in Discussion Groups," *Adult Leadership,* vol. pp. 13–14, 1953.

cooperative, and involved. Participants should know in advance the possible ways in which the results could benefit them individually and as a group.

Under no circumstances should the trainees be used to satisfy the whims of some research-minded person regardless of his interest and capability. This does not, of course, prohibit the use of specialists in research methodology but emphasizes that the research should originate with the counselor and his group, with the support of other school personnel. To assume that members are *ipso facto* subjects for a research study is to treat them as objects and to violate the purpose of group process. As well, the research findings may be highly questionable. Good warns that "in too many instances experimenters have published data in spite of such poor rapport with the classroom setting that their findings were misleading." [20]

The counselor should recognize that he is prone to place too much confidence in research results. He should strive to keep conclusions tentative and be ready to accept new findings. In fact he will engage as often as possible in some replication of studies, especially those in the area which he perceives as most necessary and in which results would be most useful. He should avoid the easy tendency to make direct application of outside research to his own efforts. He should keep before him the fact that conditions are likely to be so dissimilar as to make transfer of methods and conclusions unwise.

He will resist the temptation to apply to group behavior the results of studies based upon nonpersonal data. He will recognize that human personality is complex and the conditions of human interaction too involved to uncritically assume the validity of outcomes based upon research using animals and nonhuman conditions.

The members of the group should be involved in the planning, execution, and implementation of research results. They should assist in the evaluation of their usefulness and in plans for further research. The guidance committee should also share in the planning of research and use of results. This not only increases interest but places research within the broad perspective of a school function. In this manner the intelligent progression of research from the enumerative to the descriptive and to meaning will become understood and appreciated.

[20]Good, *op. cit.*

The counselor as a member and leader of the group should plan with the members to investigate his own practices to provide bases for understanding his theoretical approach and the usefulness of his methods.

## NEEDED RESEARCH

Each counselor should decide on needed research in terms of his own and the group's functioning. Also he should recognize the need for research concerned with the general problems that confront all counselors. Following is a list which focuses on some current research problems:

1. What criteria should guide trainees in the selection of their training experiences? Although it is established that counselors of contrasting orientations are able to assist counselees, it is not known why some counselees are helped by one method and not by another. It is a logical conclusion that no method in group counseling will be suitable for everyone either for counseling or for training purposes. Research could establish tentative criteria to enable each trainee to choose the method most congruent with his personality.

2. Why are some group counselors who use the same methods as their colleagues significantly more effective than they? One reason may be that their beliefs and actions are congruent. A study needs to be made to assess the differences in leadership and outcomes between those who are congruent and those who perform as they do for pragmatic considerations.

3. With the recognition that some people are generally one-dimensional in their approach to life while others are generally two-dimensional, or depth-oriented, it may be assumed that their counseling needs will differ. While the latter may engage in self-examination as a matter of course, the former may need specific encouragement to do so in a compelling psychological climate.

Research oriented toward the development of an objective means of determining whether an individual is chiefly one- or two-dimensional in his life approach would be extremely useful. This should be followed by further research on characteristics of the group experience suited to each kind of individual.

4. Since the value of group counseling is in large measure de-

pendent upon one's ability to listen, studies should be conducted to explore what is involved in the kind of listening necessary in group counseling. Further studies should attempt to elucidate the problems experienced in trying to become this kind of listener.

5. Both the group leader and the members should develop the ability to summarize ideas presented in the discussion. Since the vast majority experience great difficulty in doing this, research should be directed toward ascertaining possible reasons why this difficulty is of such magnitude. Such research could first explore the nature of the current attempts and then clarify the problems experienced. From this kind of research could emerge suggestions for improvement which in turn could be researched to determine their usefulness.

### With Inner-city Groups

Since the experiences and characteristics of the culturally deprived inner-city children, youth, and adults differ so widely from the general population, attention should be given to the development of research relevant to their special needs. If results are to be useful, practical hypotheses must arise from the experiences of group counselors and others who work with inner-city groups. Broadly described such research could clarify the perceptions of this group and the possible reasons for their particular reactions to emotionally laden situations.

Research goals must be oriented toward securing information which could be expected to help counselors, teachers, and others to work intelligently toward certain outcomes. These outcomes are improvement in impulse control; development of memory image, that is, of reactive and productive imagination abilities; reduction of need for aggression; and ability to perceive and examine alternatives.

Obviously these are very difficult research goals and present a challenge to methodologists. Group counselors will need much ingenuity in planning and in using various informal research means to test hypotheses related to one or more of these goals.

### Conclusions

The value of research is directly related to its relevance to problems for which more information and understanding are needed.

On the other hand findings must be expressed in terms which make them useful and capable of being applied. Those who use research focused on these goals must distinguish among its several purposes and design what is most useful in gaining the ends desired. Too often it is conducted at an enumerative and/or descriptive level when other research concerned with causal relationships is required. More attention should be directed toward understanding and meaning and the demands these make for creative approaches.

The group counselor will resist yielding to the demand for research to support present institutional practices. He will reserve the major portion of his time for, and devote his best effort to, the formulation of hunches, hypotheses, and research designs (with assistance if necessary) concerned with those problems which will further his understanding of group process and interpersonal relationships.

**Form 1** (Sides 1 and 2 of 4- by 6-inch card)

---

1. What was done which helped the group process?

2. What was least helpful to the group process?

---

```
┌─────────────────────────────────────────────────────────────────┐
│  1. What did you do to assist in the process?                     │
│                                                                   │
│                                                                   │
│                                                                   │
│  2. What do you plan to do to improve in the next session?        │
│                                                                   │
│                                                                   │
│                                                                   │
│                                                                   │
│                                                                   │
│                                                                   │
│                                                                   │
└─────────────────────────────────────────────────────────────────┘
```

**Form 2**

Self-evaluation Scale

Date _____                              No. _____

Circle the number in each category which agrees most with your conclusion regarding yourself.

1. Listening:

| I only partially hear the idea and not the person and what it means to him. | I hear the idea and to some degree understand the person and what the idea means to him. |

| 1 | 2 | 3 | 4 | 5 | 6 | 7 |

2. Sense of belonging:

| I feel strange and uneasy. | I feel comfortable and at ease. |

| 1 | 2 | 3 | 4 | 5 | 6 | 7 |

3. Acceptance of others:

| I do not feel friendly toward some members or interested in them. | | | | I feel kindly disposed toward, and interested in, the other members. | | |
|---|---|---|---|---|---|---|
| 1 | 2 | 3 | 4 | 5 | 6 | 7 |

4. Concentration:

| I have difficulty in following the strands of thought. | | | | I follow the strands of thought with only slight difficulty. | | |
|---|---|---|---|---|---|---|
| 1 | 2 | 3 | 4 | 5 | 6 | 7 |

5. Participation:

| I participate nonverbally only. | | | | I participate nonverbally and often verbally. | | |
|---|---|---|---|---|---|---|
| 1 | 2 | 3 | 4 | 5 | 6 | 7 |

6. Silence:

| I am uncomfortable and do not think well. | | | | I am able to use a silence to think on the subject. | | |
|---|---|---|---|---|---|---|
| 1 | 2 | 3 | 4 | 5 | 6 | 7 |

7. Creative differences:

| Differences of ideas make me uneasy. | | | | Differences of ideas are interesting to me. | | |
|---|---|---|---|---|---|---|
| 1 | 2 | 3 | 4 | 5 | 6 | 7 |

8. Sense of responsibility:

| I feel little responsibility for the discussion or for helping others. | | | | I feel responsible in relation to content, process, and member welfare. | | |
|---|---|---|---|---|---|---|
| 1 | 2 | 3 | 4 | 5 | 6 | 7 |

**Form 3**

Guide to Study and Evaluation of Self-reports

Many students have found the following guide useful in studying their self-reports in order to understand their progress over the weeks of the course. The headings used are not arranged to indicate an order in which change may have taken place or to suggest that all these changes may have taken place. Other changes may have occurred, and for these it may be useful to supply your own headings.

If after you have read your self-reports these headings appear to have some usefulness, try to appraise the degree using a five-point rating scale, that is, a scale of 1 to 5, 5 indicating the greatest degree and 1 the least. Also briefly describe or quote from the self-reports to support your rating.

1. *A movement from self-centeredness to care for others*
   Rating
   Supportive description or quotes

2. *A movement from doubt about self to trust of self*
   Rating
   Supportive description or quotes

3. *A movement from secrecy to sharing*
   Rating
   Supportive description or quotes

4. *A movement from unfreedom to freedom*
   Rating
   Supportive description or quotes

5. *A movement from irresponsibility to a sense of responsibility*
   Rating
   Supportive description or quotes

6. *A movement from mistrust to trust*
   Rating
   Supportive description or quotes

7. *A movement from the need to receive help to a concern for giving help*
   Rating
   Supportive description or quotes


**Form 4**

No. _____

Group-process Stages

Place a check mark after the number under *Personal* and *Group* to indicate the present stage in group process for you personally and for the group as a whole.

|  | *Personal* | *Group* |
|---|---|---|
| 1. Establishment |  |  |
| 2. Checking one another |  |  |
| 3. Checking the leader |  |  |
| 4. Giving rights to others |  |  |
| 5. Socialization |  |  |
| 6. Questioning what we are doing |  |  |
| 7. Questioning whether we can trust one another, what we shall try to accomplish |  |  |
| 8. Experimentation, trying out, commitment to one another |  |  |
| 9. Responsibility for one another |  |  |
| 10. Creative relationship |  |  |

**Form 5**

Leader-evaluation scale

Circle the number in each category which agrees most with your conclusion regarding leader performance.

1. The leader is responsible.
   Shows little responsibility for the discussion or in helping the members.

   Is responsible in relation to content process and member welfare.

   | 1 | 2 | 3 | 4 | 5 | 6 | 7 |

2. The leader provides resources.
   Provides little information or personal sharing.

   Provides helpful information as needed and shares his feeling concerning it.

   | 1 | 2 | 3 | 4 | 5 | 6 | 7 |

3. The leader provides strategies.
   Does not provide as needed clarifying, summarizing, and other functions.

   Provides the necessary processes as needed for optimum functioning.

   | 1 | 2 | 3 | 4 | 5 | 6 | 7 |

4. The leader communicates.
   Treats each member more as an object, does not share his ideas.

   Considers each member a person and is honest, open, and real.

   | 1 | 2 | 3 | 4 | 5 | 6 | 7 |

5. The leader listens.

| Hears the idea but not the person and what it means to him. | | | | Hears the idea and tries to understand the person and what the idea means to him. | | |
|:---:|:---:|:---:|:---:|:---:|:---:|:---:|
| 1 | 2 | 3 | 4 | 5 | 6 | 7 |

6. The leader trusts.

| Tries to assure outcomes, has a low level of expectancy, does not extend freedom. | | | | Has a high level of expectancy, is permissive, and extends freedom in relation to acceptance of responsibility. | | |
|:---:|:---:|:---:|:---:|:---:|:---:|:---:|
| 1 | 2 | 3 | 4 | 5 | 6 | 7 |

7. The leader encourages and conducts evaluation.

| Provides no encouragement or opportunity for evaluation. | | | | Provides opportunity; initiates, encourages, and assists members in evaluation. | | |
|:---:|:---:|:---:|:---:|:---:|:---:|:---:|
| 1 | 2 | 3 | 4 | 5 | 6 | 7 |

**Form 6**

No. _____

Self-evaluation

Check the number on the rating scale that corresponds to your evaluation of yourself in each of the following categories. For example, if you feel that your responsible participation was lacking, check 1; if you feel that it was present, check 7; if you feel it was somewhere in between, check an appropriate number on the scale.

| *A.* Responsible participation: I served my own needs. I watched from outside the group. I was "grinding my own ax." | 1 2 3 4 5 6 7 | *A.* Responsible participation: I was sensitive to the needs of our group. |
|:---|:---:|:---|

*B.* Leadership:
I did not cooperate. I felt little responsibility.

1 2 3 4 5 6 7

*B.* Leadership:
I cooperated and was responsible to myself and the group.

*C.* Communication of ideas:
I did not listen. I did not understand. Ideas were ignored.

1 2 3 4 5 6 7

*C.* Communication of ideas:
I listened and understood the others' ideas.

*D.* Communication of feelings:
I did not listen and did not understand feelings.

1 2 3 4 5 6 7

*D.* Communication of feelings:
I listened and understood, and recognized feelings.

*E.* Authenticity:
I was wearing a mask. I was being phony and acting a part. I was hiding my real self.

1 2 3 4 5 6 7

*E.* Authenticity:
I was revealing my honest self. I was engaged in authentic self-revelation.

*F.* Acceptance of persons:
I criticized, rejected, or ignored.

1 2 3 4 5 6 7

*F.* Acceptance of persons:
Accepting persons was an active part of my give-and-take. I recognized and respected the uniqueness of each person

*G.* Freedom of persons:
I did not feel free to express my individuality.

1 2 3 4 5 6 7

*G.* Freedom of persons:
I felt free to express my individuality. I respected others as persons.

*H.* Climate of relation-
ship:
I did not feel comfort-
able. I was uneasy
and felt threatened.

1 2 3 4 5 6 7

*H.* Climate of relation-
ship:
I felt mutual trust in
which evidence of love
for one another was
apparent. The atmos-
phere was friendly
and relaxed.

*I.* Productivity:
I was just coasting
along.

1 2 3 4 5 6 7

*I.* Productivity:
I was digging hard
and earnestly at work
on a task. I created
and achieved some-
thing.

# INDEX

Hutchison, John, 183
Huxley, Julian, 182

*I and Thou* (Buber), 184
*Ideas* (Husserl), 153
Imagination, 17–18
  productive, 18
  reproductive, 17–18
"Implications of Short-term Memory
  for a General Theory of Mem-
  ory" (Melton), 203
"Improving Your Leadership in Dis-
  cussion Groups" (Gordon), 296
Independence, 92, 113–114
Individual competition, 44–45
Individual counseling compared to
  group counseling, 69–71
*Individual and His Religion, The*
  (Allport), 152
"Individuality: The Meaning and Con-
  tent of Individuality in Contem-
  porary America" (Murray), 14
Individualizing preparation, 217–218
"Influence of Dogmatism on the
  Training of Counselors"
  (Kemp), 17, 217
*Inner World of Choice, The* (Wickes),
  48, 175
*Intangibles in Counseling* (Kemp),
  50, 192, 236
Interdependence, 113–114
*International Journal of Group Psy-
  chotherapy*, 190, 274
Interpretation, 198–200
Interview group therapy, 68
Intrinsic attitude, 51
Intrinsic motivation, 16, 124
"Intrinsic Motivation and Its Role in
  Psychological Development"
  (Hunt), 16
Involvement, 14–15, 189–193, 289
  theoretical differences in, 124–125

James, William, 52
Jaspers, Karl, 55, 184
Jennings, H. H., 162
Joiners, 46
*Journal of Abnormal and Social Psy-
  chology*, 14, 84

*Journal of Consulting Psychology*,
  199
*Journal of Counseling Psychology*,
  17, 101, 188, 217, 235, 263
*Journal of Educational Psychology*,
  162
*Journal of Educational Research*, 292
*Journal of Existential Psychiatry*,
  268
*Journal of Experimental Education*,
  288
*Journal of Humanistic Psychology*,
  14, 131
*Journal of International Group Psy-
  chotherapy*, 192
*Journal of the National Association
  of Woman Deans and Counselors*, 26
*Journal of Research and Develop-
  ment in Education*, 146
*Journal of Social Issues, The*,
  14, 26, 27, 83, 172, 263,
  267
*Journal of Verbal Learning and Ver-
  bal Behavior*, 203, 204
Jung, Carl G., 17, 42

Kant, Immanuel, 18
Kemp, C. Gratton, 17, 18, 44, 50,
  160, 164, 188, 192, 215, 217,
  235, 236, 263
Keppel. G., 204
Kierkegaard, Sören, 178, 182, 229
*Kierkegaard Anthology, A* (Bretall),
  229
Kneller, George F., 273
Knowledge, 97, 216, 238
  of process, 264–267
  self-, 46
*Knowledge, Morality and Destiny*
  (Huxley), 182
Knowles, Malcolm S., 27
Kornhauser, A., 83
Kroner, Richard, 17
Krumboltz, John D., 84
Kubie, Lawrence S., 7, 46, 176

Langer, Susanne, 56
Lazarus, L. A., 84

Potential, development of, 148–154
Pragmatism, 51–53
*Pragmatism and American Culture* (James), 52
*Prisoner for God* (Bonhoeffer), 191
"Proactive Inhibition in Short-term Retention of Single Items" (Underwood and Keppel), 204
"Proactive Personality, The" (Bonner), 153
Problem-discussion-action method, 292–293
"Process of the Basic Encounter Group, The" (Rogers), 15–16, 116
Productive conflict, 176
Productive imagination, 18
Psyche group process, 28
"Psychiatrist Considers Curriculum Development, The" (Kubie), 46, 176
Psychoanalysis, 16
"Psychoanalysis, Topological Psychology, and Experimental Psychopathology" (Brown), 33
*Psychoanalytic Quarterly,* 33
Psychodrama, 68
*Psychological Bulletin,* 291, 294
*Psychological Review,* 200, 203, 204
*Psychological Types* (Jung), 17
"Psychology of the Act, The" (Peirce), 172
*Psychology of Rumor, The* (Allport and Postman), 213
Psychotherapy, 73
  group counseling and, 29
*Psychotherapy for Reciprocal Inhibition* (Wolpe), 84
Pusey, Nathan, 268, 269


Radio, 49
Rand, Benjamin, 38
Rank, Otto, 42
Reality testing, 65, 67, 69, 74
Reason, technical, 45–47
*Recreation and the Total Personality* (Slavson), 44
Redl, Fritz, 168, 279, 281
Reflection, 197–198

Reinforcement, verbal, 85–86
Religious experiences, 230–231
*Religious Function of the Imagination, The* (Kroner), 17
"Renewal in Societies and Man" (Gardner), 219
"Repetition and Paired Associate Learning" (Postman), 204
Repressive-inspirational group therapy, 67–68
Reproductive imagination, 17–18
Research, 283–294, 298–300
  methods of, 290–294
  in structure, 162–163
  three ongoing activities, 285
Research courses, 46
"Resistance to Change" (Noy), 190
Responsibility, 57, 168
  self-, 92
*Revolution in Counseling* (Krumboltz), 84
Reymert, Martin L., 192
Riesman, David, 131
Roberts, Richard, 257
Robert's Rules of Order, 265
Rock, I., 204
Rogers, Carl R., 14–16, 54, 78, 100–102, 116, 132, 289
Rokeach, Milton, 144, 187, 213–214, 242, 293
Role concept, counselor's, 262–264
"Role of Repetition in Associative Learning, The" (Rock), 204
Rosenbaum, Max, 191–192
Rugg, Harold, 41–43


Sartre, Jean Paul, 9, 12
*Saturday Review, The,* 265
Scheidlinger, S., 73
Schlesinger, Arthur, 42
*Science and Human Affairs* (Farson, ed.), 163, 262
Security needs, 189
Self:
  openness toward, 213–214
  theory of learning, 100–101